Managing at a Distance

The world of hybrid and remote management is a territory that has yet to be completely explored – this book provides some simple navigational aids to help managers and leaders to find their way.

Research indicates that over 56% of college graduates currently work either remotely or in a hybrid arrangement, while prior to the pandemic less than 5% of working hours were remote. How to manage remote and hybrid workers has rapidly become a significant challenge, and one that often requires new policies and organizational restructuring. The remote work handbooks available are tactical, which can be helpful for day-to-day decisions but not to tackle larger issues and initiatives. This book presents a fully formed, research-backed strategic framework: more than a vehicle to the future, it will help leaders to understand where they are now and what is happening around them to change the landscape, and to decide where they want to be.

Speaking to senior executives and team leaders, as well as business students, this book will become the preferred tool for the development and evaluation of remote and hybrid management policy and strategy across industries.

Tom Coughlan, DBA, is a tenured Associate Professor of Graduate Business at Mercy University, and an Adjunct Professor at Sacred Heart University, University of Bridgeport, Quinnipiac University, and the Manhattan Institute of Management.

David Fogarty, PhD, MBA, is a seasoned Fortune 100 Chief Data and Analytics Executive and an Adjunct Professor at Columbia University, Cornell University, New York University, and the City University of New York.

Gary Bernstein, MBA, CPA, is a retired IBM Vice President. He has been an Adjunct Professor for 35 years and was a full-time Assistant Professor for five years in the Graduate Business Program at Mercy University.

Lynda Wilson, PhD, is an Associate Dean at California State University, Dominguez Hills, in the College of Professional and Continuing Education.

Managing at a Distance

A Manager's Guide to the Challenges of
the Hybrid and Remote World

Tom Coughlan, David Fogarty,
Gary Bernstein and Lynda Wilson

Routledge
Taylor & Francis Group

NEW YORK AND LONDON

Designed cover image: © Getty

First published 2024
by Routledge
605 Third Avenue, New York, NY 10158

and by Routledge
4 Park Square, Milton Park, Abingdon, Oxon OX14 4RN

Routledge is an imprint of the Taylor & Francis Group, an informa business

© 2024 Tom Coughlan, David Fogarty, Gary Bernstein, and Lynda Wilson

The right of Tom Coughlan, David Fogarty, Gary Bernstein, and Lynda Wilson to be identified as authors of this work has been asserted in accordance with sections 77 and 78 of the Copyright, Designs and Patents Act 1988.

ISBN: 9781032646640 (hbk)
ISBN: 9781032646626 (pbk)
ISBN: 9781032646657 (ebk)

DOI: 10.4324/9781032646657

Typeset in Times New Roman
by Taylor & Francis Books

Contents

Illustrations

Figure

Boxes

Managing at a Distance Team

Authors' Backgrounds

This book is the result of a collaboration between the co-authors, Tom Coughlan, David Fogarty, Gary Bernstein, and Lynda Wilson, each of whom has made a significant contribution to the book's content. Each chapter lists either the author or the co-authors who developed that chapter in the running head. Throughout the book the use of first-person pronouns refers to the author of that chapter. In Chapter 7, the only co-authored chapter in this volume, the first-person pronouns refer to Tom Coughlan.

Tom Coughlan, DBA

Tom Coughlan, DBA, is a tenured Associate Professor of Graduate Business at Mercy University, and an Adjunct Professor at Sacred Heart University, University of Bridgeport, Quinnipiac University, and the Manhattan Institute of Management. He is also an external Doctoral Evaluator for the University of Liverpool, UK. In the past he has held academic positions at several other institutions in both the US and in Europe.

Tom is on the editorial board of several peer-reviewed journals, and he has a rich portfolio of publications in the areas of management, innovation, marketing, and organizational structures; he has also held a contract writing position at Harvard Business Publishing.

Prior to becoming an academic, Tom spent over 25 years in industry as a marketing communications consultant. His work spanned both national and global projects for large technology companies, and his clients included a number of high-profile firms such as IBM, Cisco, and Oracle. In addition, he has both a personal and professional relationship with TRITEC Real Estate.

David Fogarty, PhD

David is currently the CEO and Principal of Global Decision Science Enterprises, a digital transformation and analytics consulting firm serving

Fortune 100 companies. He is also the founder of SEB Maxico AI, an AI startup firm focusing on developing patented AI solutions related to drones, pets, healthcare, and IoT.

David most recently worked for Cigna/Evernorth for 15 years as their Enterprise Marketing, Technology and Digital Analytics Leader. David also worked for 20 years at the General Electric Company and has held quantitative analysis leadership roles in the various business units of the company across several functions, including risk management and marketing both internationally and in the US.

David has over 10 US patents or patents pending on business analytics algorithms and is a certified Six Sigma Master Black Belt in Quality which is the highest qualification within the Six Sigma Quality methodology.

David is the recipient of the 2023 AI100 Innovators Award, which is a prestigious annual award that recognizes and celebrates the achievements of individuals and organizations that have made significant advancements in the field of analytics and AI in enterprises.

David also has nearly two decades of teaching experience having held various adjunct academic appointments at both the graduate and under-graduate level in statistics, international management, and quantitative analysis. The institutions where these appointments have been held include Columbia University in the City of New York, New York University, Cornell University, the University of Liverpool, Manhattanville College, the University of New Haven, SUNY Purchase College, Manhattan College, LIM College, Trident University, Chancellor University, Alliant University International, Northcentral University, University of Phoenix, and the Jack Welch Management Institute at Strayer University. David is also an Honorary Professor of Financial Economics at the Madras School of Economics in Chennai, India, and he has given guest lectures in Asia at East China Normal University, Ivey Business School in Hong Kong, and City University of Hong Kong. David has also taught business analytics courses at the esteemed GE Crotonville Management Development Institute in Crotonville, New York.

David is a best-selling author with over 50 published research papers in peer-reviewed academic journals, and he has published four books. His research interests include how to conduct analysis with missing data, the cultural meaning of data, integrating machine learning and AI algorithms into the statistical science framework, and many other topics related to quantitative analysis in business. He is currently working on a fifth book describing how to manage big data as an asset.

Gary Bernstein, MBA, CPA

Gary is a retired Assistant Professor at Mercy University and is now an active Adjunct Professor. He had previously retired from IBM

Corporation after 32 years and was a Vice President of Finance. He held a wide variety of finance, accounting and operations positions at IBM, with the last seven years of his career tasked with creating and leading Finance Centers of Excellence globally, as the leader of finance transformation globally as well. At the time developing the delivery of remote professional employee decision support centers was groundbreaking.

Gary has been active on several higher education advisory boards and is a Trustee at Mercy University.

Lynda Wilson, PhD

Lynda currently serves as the Associate Dean at California State University, Dominguez Hills, College of Continuing and Professional Education, which is located in the Los Angles South Bay area. Previously, Lynda held academic leadership positions at the University of California at Los Angeles and institutions of higher education in Louisiana, Florida, and Connecticut. Lynda earned a PhD from Louisiana State University in Baton Rouge, LA.

Prior to Lynda's 20-year career in higher education she served in human resource management positions in California and Louisiana and earned the SPHR certification.

In 2009, Lynda earned the Richard Swanson Research Award from the Academy of Human Resource Development. She has several peer-reviewed publications and conference presentations, and is an active member of the University Professional and Continuing Education Association.

Contributors

Our team has the rare ability to blend both the academic and practitioner perspectives. This blended, accomplished, and highly credible scholar-practitioner view leads to well-constructed, rich, actionable solutions that can deliver real results in the marketplace. It should also be noted that three of these authors (Fogarty, Wilson, and Coughlan) were early pioneers in online learning in higher education and developed many practices in remote learning which have been adopted into mainstream higher learning today. Finally, several team members have significant practitioner experience of leading large global teams with both remote and local employees at Fortune 100 companies.

Chapter 1

Setting the Stage

Setting the Stage

A Macro View of How the Remote World Developed

It's March 16, 2020. I step out of my office to find my daughter in-law uploading a playlist to the Amazon Echo in our living room. Inspired by some dark humor, the first song on her apocalyptic playlist, "It's the End of the World as We Know It (And I Feel Fine)" by R.E.M., begins to fill the room. A fitting anthem for the new era – or at least a new social and business reality. Like many families we had hunkered down early on. As soon as we began to realize how serious the COVID-19 crisis had become, my wife and I invited my son and daughter in-law to decamp from Brooklyn to our home in Connecticut. Fortunately, my son and daughter in-law were on family leave due to the birth of my new grandson, so fast action was not a problem. As for myself and my wife, the universities where I teach had gone completely online, while my wife works from home. So, going into an office, or to a public gathering place, was not necessary.

I was no stranger to working remotely; you might even say I was an early adopter. My first job out of college was as a field marketing rep for Atari, back in the early 1980s. Before becoming a full-time academic in the mid-2000s, I spent about 25 years in the technology industry – of which about 20 years were on the road in different sales, marketing, and management jobs – and as an entrepreneur. And when I did start teaching it was as an online instructor. Even though I have continued to teach online to this day, by 2006 my teaching portfolio had become weighted more to the traditional classroom. This, however, was a new world. I am now a tenured Associate Professor, and I teach at several other schools as an Adjunct Professor. But, by the second week of March 2020, all my teaching had moved online temporarily as the universities tried to deal with the pandemic.

I had started thinking about this book at least two years before the crisis, and over a year pre-crisis had contacted my writing partner David

DOI: 10.4324/9781032646657-1

Fogarty to get his thoughts on the idea. Our calendars were full, but we agreed that the whole field of remote management had some real issue for managers to be concerned about, and that these issues would only become more important over time. So, after roughing out the core concepts, we asked two colleagues – Gary Bernstein and Lynda Wilson – to help by writing a couple of chapters, and slowly began to piece together this book.

It was clear to us that we had entered a new world order. Geographically dispersed teams, global centers of excellence, freelance and contingent workers, and working from home (or WFH) ... simply put, the world of business has changed – and in some cases radically so. Many of the organizational structures, and the management principles used to develop our current processes, policies, and decisions, were built for a different age, with a different population, that had a different set of motivating factors. This has caused some progressive managers to reevaluate how they should be organizing their institutions and motivating their teams.

Over the past couple of decades companies and individuals have increasingly been finding that their ability to compete in the marketplace requires the development of broader networks of people, resources, skills, and capabilities than ever before. In addition, there seems to be a need to engage the people who embody these skills and capabilities in vastly different formats. We are moving away from simply hiring these people and are moving toward gig economies, partnerships, and loose organizational affiliations. The lines of where the organization begins and ends have become a little grayer or softer – which has confused and disoriented many traditional managers. Even when we do hire these people as employees, we are facing a new paradigm in management and leadership if we wish to maximize these relationships.

Working from Home

Complicating this further is the feeling that it seems harder to centralize these resources. There has been a tectonic shift in the number of people who find it desirable or necessary to work at home, or in a remote location – and this desire seems to increase with the level of skill and education of these employees. Prior to the COVID-19 crisis, a study by the US Bureau of Labor Statistics (2018) revealed that 46% of workers with advanced degrees worked from home regularly, whereas only 32% of those with a bachelor's degree, and only 12% of those with a high school degree did the same. Some 10 months into the pandemic, the reported level of remote work varied, but it is generally agreed that between 35% and 50% of the total working population had moved to remote work. Originally the shift was due to stay-at-home orders issued by state or local governments; however, many organizations used this opportunity to reassess their work from home or remote work policies. These policies allowed employees to reevaluate where they could live and still have a career. Almost immediately employees began an exodus from high-cost centers like New York and San Francisco to areas offering a lower cost of living and a better quality of life. One study showed that over 60% of employees would consider moving out of San Francisco if their employers allowed them to work from home permanently (Bindley, 2020).

By the middle of 2021, in addition to remote focused models, most white-collar organizations had announced their intention to develop some form of hybrid presence model. These models would look to develop organizational models whereby employees could work from home one or more days a week – many with the option of working remotely for multiple days per week or even the majority of the time with only occasional visits to an office for team meetings and management one-on-ones. Many employees have come to prefer the work from home model, or at least wish to have work from home as an option. Some employees have even begun to make future employment decisions based on their ability to partially or completely work remotely (Mims, 2021).

Employers are now considering allowing more remote/hybrid positions or assessing the need for positions to be collocated. This of course opens up new pools of potential talent – often at a lower cost. In addition, many employers are reevaluating the compensation packages both for existing employees who move away from high-cost centers, and for qualified remote talent, in an attempt to maximize the available talent.

Actionable Strategy

These facts alone may give managers pause and leave them wondering how to move forward. This book is all about actionable strategies that can help to address these and other issues we now face in an increasingly remote world. It looks to help managers to recognize the environmental factors business – technological and political – that are affecting the need for change. It also helps them to focus on defining the scope of the issues underlying the environment, and also enabling them to develop a rational plan to deal with the current issues – as well as being agile enough to position themselves to meet the challenges of an environment which has an ever-increasing rate of change.

Chess Master vs. Gardener

Many professionals in overly top-down management structures may find the pace of this new world order too frenetic, and that their organizations are adapting too slowly. It often becomes clear that the models of the past – especially centralized models – struggle with the new world order.

Managers might find it better to allow for broader tolerance of decisions being made close to the action and as low as possible in the organizational structure.

In his 2015 co-authored book *Team of Teams*, Gen. (retd.) Stanley McChrystal described having just such an experience when he first arrived to lead the US fight against Al Qaeda in Iraq. The environment was changing too quickly for the incumbent military governance structure to be as effective as he desired. This experience led him to a strategic paradigm shift. He moved from thinking of his leadership role as being a chess master and toward being a gardener.

Chess masters carefully move pieces around the board to gain advantage and outmaneuver the opponent – a single point of control attacking a single point of control. A gardener, on the other hand, prepares the ground and creates an environment where new things can grow and develop on their own – there is no single point of control. McChrystal allowed his troops, within specific parameters, to make many of their own decisions. Decisions were made quickly by those closest to the action, and the capacity to react effectively to a volatile environment was dramatically improved.

This concept is the very antithesis of micro-management. Also, the challenges to micro-management go beyond the pace of change, it also extends to the facilities to accomplish it. It is far easier to micromanage when you share the same physical space with your direct reports. Although many companies attempted to implement technology solutions to enable micro-management, as we will see later in the book, most failed to achieve their intended goals, whereas most trust-based models thrived.

The MAAD Framework

Managers today are faced with a structural crisis. Their organizational structures are at an inflection point. The structures they are using are not well suited to the changing environment and need reevaluation – and possibly dramatic change. In this change managers will need tools to help them to evaluate where they currently are and where they need to go. One such tool could be the MAAD (Managing at a Distance) framework.

The MAAD framework allows a manager to identify key factors in their environment and to assess how well these factors support or inhibit progress toward their organizational goals. Business outcomes are a function of the following:

- *Objectives/environment*: Do your objectives fit the current and future business environment? What is the environmental context?
- *People/talent*: Do you have the right mix of people and talent to do the task at hand, either within or accessible to the organization?

- *Culture/context*: Have you fostered a culture and provided the right context to enable your team to make the right decisions in the day-to-day tasks?
- *Autonomy/personal responsibility*: Are you leveraging your intellectual capital by allowing those closest to the issues to make the decisions? Are you providing them with the proper information and tools? And are they holding themselves responsible for the results?
- *Data/analytics*: Have you defined the proper key performance indicators? Can you see through the haze of the day-to-day to understand and better analyze where you are and where you should be going?
- *Proximity/information flow*: Proximity is a feeling not a geographic distance. Have you created that sense of closeness and enabled an information flow resulting in transparency?
- *Communication infrastructure*: Is the communication infrastructure robust enough to support your goals?
- *Organizational structure*: Is your organizational governance structure in line with the environment, your people, your goals, and your culture? Does it foster a team feeling and promote engagement?

Environmental Context

Business success is based on creating value for your customers in some fashion. However, what is valuable changes according to context. There are a number of environmental variables that affect the perception of value. Business schools spend a great deal of time building models like PESTEL (Political, Economic, Social, Technical, and Legal), or SWOT (Strengths, Weaknesses, Opportunities, Threats), to help guide the thinking of business professionals and give them the ability to begin to identify the critical issues and variables. Once we have a core understanding of the context of our environment, we have a far better chance of understanding what will be valuable – and to whom – and we can set objectives on what we wish to accomplish for your company, teams, customers, communities, ourselves, and families.

Given the scope of the task of creating context it is often helpful to break it down into macro and micro tasks. In this chapter we will begin by looking at some of the macro areas.

The Macro Environment

We could certainly write several books on the context of the current macro environment – this is the job of almost every economist and business journalist. However, for the sake of expectancy there are just a few factors we would like to explore in this chapter:

- technology and how changes in technology have affected our perceptions and actions;
- some of the critical demographic factors that will affect our organizations; and
- how our process changes and the changing rate of change.

Does Technology Change How and What We Think?

Most professionals have a sense that technology has had a significant impact on how we work and process information. On a day-to-day basis we might not recognize it. However, if we were to stop and reflect on the significance of the changes over the last four or five decades, the changes in technology, and business practices they support are breathtaking. My past career in technology gave me a front row seat from which I could see change as it happened. I enjoy sharing some of these changes with my students. Their reactions are often priceless. Today's undergraduates grew up with broadband at home so asking undergraduates about things prior to 2000 is often akin to asking questions about ancient Greece.

For example, early in my career I was a product manager for a floppy disk manufacturer. Just for fun, I will occasionally bring up a picture of these products in support of a class discussion. I have run into entire undergraduate classes who were not sure what these items were, and how they were used. Even my graduate students often have a limited perspective. With them I will swap out floppy disks for a slide rule. This is often done with a story of how my dad, who worked in real estate finance, had a slide rule he kept in a leather case. It was something he carried to work every day when I was a kid. I believe I was in middle school when my dad finally swapped out the slide rule for a calculator, and I was nearing the end of my college career when the calculator was replaced with two of the first 3,000 IBM PCs ever produced (one for the office and one for the home).

When I share with my students how much those PCs cost – and what you got for your money – most students nearly fall out of their chairs. The spec for the original IBM PC included an eight-bit processor that ran at about 4.77 MHz, with 16k of memory (that's right, not a gigabit or even a megabit, just 16 kilobits), and a text-only monitor. There was no hard disk – the PC came with two 160k floppy drives. Typically, you would have one floppy drive for the application, and one for data. Given the storage capacity – even with the simplest application often required you to flip floppies in and out as you loaded and unloaded different parts of an application. To allow enough workspace to run his spreadsheet application (VisiCalc), we upgraded my father's machines from 16k to 64k, and added a wide carriage dot matrix printer. So, his computers cost a little more than the standard PCs (but either way we are still talking about a pretty anemic machine). If I remember correctly my dad paid about $4,000 for each computer and printer combo (in 1981 dollars, equivalent to approximately $10,000 in 2023).

As anemic as these machines were, they were well worth the price. They changed the very nature of my father's day-to-day activities. In the era of slide rules and calculators he would do financial projections on large real estate projects, that could span decades, by using large sheets of paper lined with rows and columns to create cells – the kind old school accounts used for ledgers. I can remember him laying them out on the dining room table calculating and filling in each cell (where a row and column met) by hand. This was mind-numbing and grueling work. There was always a fear of making a calculation error – especially at the beginning of the project. And, of course, accounting for potential changes in a constant – like a change in the interest rate – meant hours or days of redundant work. So, in many cases it was impractical to account for all the what-ifs that entered the mind of an analyst or investor.

In the slide rule days, my dad was based in New York and managed a West Coast real estate portfolio for Metropolitan Life Insurance Company. When he leased commercial space, lease negotiations would take weeks. The original contracts were typed in New York and sent out by first class US mail (the kind with stamps and envelopes) to the West Coast client. The client would mark up the contract with any proposed changes, typically with a pen, and mail it back. Often it would take several rounds of mailing back and forth before a final contract was retyped and agreed to.

In the grand scheme of things, we are not so far removed from using first class mail. Over the past 20 years internet usage has increased from about 50% of adults to about 90% of adults. And internet use in the home has risen from about 1% to about 75% (Pew Research Center, 2019). The growth has been dramatic, and in many cases it has outstripped our ability to process these changes. This is particularly true of managers who may have developed their management processes a decade or more ago. Some may have joined the workforce when paper memos were the prevailing method of communication. They now find themselves in a world where the vast majority of companies are using internal social tools such as Slack, Yammer, Google Chat, Flock, or Microsoft Teams to handle most, if not all, of their internal communications (Leonardi & Neeley, 2017).

So, what does this mean? Our thinking, our analysis, and our ability to react are often functions of our environment. When there were no fax machines, or email servers, taking a week to turn around a small change in a contract seemed very reasonable. When you live in a world without cell phones, taking a couple of days to return a call because you are on the road seems perfectly acceptable. Clearly performance expectations have changed over time based on what has become possible due to changes in the business environment. We have hit another inflection point in the history of our organizations where what is possible and reasonable has seen a significant change. Some of this is due to technology, some is due to changing organizational structures and cultures, and some to our own absorptive capacity, but make no mistake – there have been changes and the rate of change will accelerate significantly as we move forward.

How Have We (Ourselves and Our Teams) Changed?

Education

Access to education changes what is possible for individuals, families, nations, and the world – *education changes everything*. Toffler was one of the first in the modern era to recognize this massive shift in the speed of change. Starting with *Future Shock* (1970) and continuing with several other bestsellers, he identified several critical factors that, given time, had changed the structure and pace of life, work, love, and the economy. Among the critical elements are education, communication, and transportation. The growth in education, and access to information and communications technology (ICT), is shaping the growth and availability of information – and has shaped how we process information into change. So, it follows that as we increase the level and accessibility of education and ICT we increase the level of innovation, shorten product life cycles, reduce the cost of innovation, increase the depth and breadth of product lines, and often narrow the target markets for future products. The pace of this change, and its organizational implications, are currently significant issues.

According to the US Census Bureau (2020) in 1940 about 19.6% of the adult population had earned a high school diploma as their highest degree, while just 4.6% had earned a bachelor's degree or higher. In contrast, in 2018 about 54% of the adult population had left school after earning a high school degree, and about 35% had a bachelor's degree or higher – an increase of approximately 760% in only a couple of generations. And the changes in other countries have been even more dramatic. In 1964 about 65% of Chinese adults had no education at all (Schrader & Cramer-Flood, 2012). However, by 2019 about 67% of Chinese adults between the age of 25 and 34 had entered tertiary education after leaving high school (trade schools, colleges, and universities) – which is 2% higher than the average for Organisation for Economic Co-operation and Development countries (OECD, 2019). In general, as we look at data on the level of educational attainment there is a clear upward growth trend, and the trend line is getting steeper.

Based on the works of Toffler, and many other researchers who have continued to explore these trends, it would seem there are some clear implications for managers. These trends are like snowballs heading downhill – they will pick up speed and volume as they go. This in turn will mean even greater change at a faster rate. More educated employees would also seem to lead to greater productivity and higher levels of expected autonomy. Therefore, there will be a need to reassess our own expectations of employee responsibilities, and the structure and style in which we manage. It is likely that we will see more autonomous or semi-autonomous teams, wider spans of control for managers, and more transparency within organizations.

Life Expectancy

It is no real news that people are living longer, that the birth rate is dropping in most developed countries, and that we are clustering in cities. What is important is the scope of the changes and their effect on our organizations.

According to the US Centers for Disease Control and Prevention (CDC, 2019) the average life expectancy for a US citizen in 1900 was 47.3 years, and if you made it to the age of 65 you were expected to live for about another 13.0 years. Between 2010 and 2020 the number of adults over 55 increased at a rate of about 27%, while the population under the age of 55 expanded at a rate of approximately 1.3% (Adamy & Adamy, 2021). By 2017 US citizens were expected to live to 78.7 years, and if they made it to the age of 65, they were expected to live another 19.4 years. And according to the US National Institutes of Health, those with higher levels of education are likely to live far longer than the national average (Hummer & Hernandez, 2013). Another significant factor in life expectancy is the level of education. There have been several studies that have concluded that lifestyles and behaviors promoting longevity improve with educational attainment (Kaplan et al., 2015; Sasson, 2016). Give the knowledge that there is a trend toward workers obtaining higher levels of education, and many are moving into less physically demanding jobs, i.e., jobs that might have less of an effect on morbidity, we can safely assume that most people will live into their mid-eighties. This means that they might live as much as 30 years past the traditional retirement age.

Similarly, if we compare the birth rate in most developed countries, we can see that it is dropping – and in many cases this drop is dramatic. In Japan, the government has predicted that the current population of about 126 million will decrease to approximately 50 million by 2115 (Statistics Bureau of Japan, 2020). In the US, the population growth rate contracted from about 1.7% in 1960 to about 0.7% in 2019 (World Bank, 2020).

It would seem increasingly clear that on several fronts the standard retirement age of between 60 and 65 is out of date. Individuals might have to consider issues such social connections, a desire to contribute, and possible financial need (outliving their savings). Many workers may not need or desire full-time work; however, it would seem reasonable that some part-time, seasonal, or on-demand contingent working relationships may be required. There are also the needs of organizations to consider. Many organizations will likely find it increasingly difficult to fulfill their staffing needs from a shrinking pool of candidates – and a demographic cluster of older candidates might provide the vast pools of skilled and experienced workers they need.

Dual Income Households

I grew up in the 1970s in a small town in southwestern Connecticut. Being a commutable distance to New York City, and not having a state income tax at the time, the area was flush with corporate headquarters, and executives looking to work in New York while living in a safe, lower tax, suburban community. But being mostly upper middle class, it was also the home to a number of "corporate gypsies" – executives who made their careers by moving wherever and whenever the company needed them as they climbed the corporate ladder. It seemed at the time to be an unquestioned reality of big company life. If you wanted to play in the big leagues you had to be willing to pay the price – which often meant moving to where the opportunities were.

It is fair to say that social expectations surrounding work have changed dramatically since the 1970s. However, historically in most of the world men have taken the head of the household role. This, of course, has had a number of workforce implications. One of these was the makeup of the working population. Well through the middle of the 20th century, the American dream included the man going off to work to support his family financially, while the woman stayed at home to care for the children and manage the domestic issues. This led to dramatic changes which could probably trace their origins back to women's suffrage and accelerated with the women's movement that began to take shape in the 1960s and 1970s. In the US the participation of women in the workforce rose from 32% in 1948 to approximately 57.9% in 2020. To put this in context, prior to the COVID-19 crisis the participation rate (the percentage of adults in the workforce) of all American adults was about 63% (US Bureau of Labor Statistics, 2020). Furthermore, if we look at couples, in 1967 approximately 43.6% of American households had both the husband and wife working. However, today approximately 70% of households are dual income, and even in households with children under the age of 18 of those 63% are dual income. More importantly, there are significant generational differences: only 47% of baby boomers, 73% of Gen X, and 78% of millennial couples are both holding down full-time careers. An associated trend is that 57% of workers today have some sort of flextime option available from their employer (US Bureau of Labor Statistics, 2019), and this is why 54% of workers say that they would leave their current jobs for one that offered flexible work options (Gallup, 2017).

Why has flextime become so important to the average worker? Some might wonder if this is simply an increasing feeling of entitlement developing in younger employees, which has been fostered by a growing number of helicopter parents over the past few decades. That may very well be a contributing factor. However, it seems fairly clear from the data that there are few fifties-style June Cleavers left – the stay-at-home mothers who dutifully handled all the issues on the domestic front, and who were willing to pack up and move at the drop of a hat when the their spouse's career required them to do so.

Today's working adults face a series of issues that their counterparts in the 1950s did not – at least not at the level they are facing them now. The modern reality is that both spouses are likely working, thus making domestic responsibilities such as childcare and elder care far more complicated to navigate. Such issues are much easier to manage with flextime. In addition, if a spouse is working, the domestic negotiations and logistics around moving to a new city become far more complicated. Therefore, it might be harder to source the available talent in order to have the same geographic presence.

Time Marches On – Toward a Remote World – at an Ever-Increasing Pace

The theme "time marches on" is certainly not a new one. In each era it is common for the older generation to lament the good old days, while most of the younger generation herald the coming of the new. Nothing has changed but the speed and the scope of change itself. In the history of economics, there have been brilliant figures such as Thomas Robert Malthus who believed that mankind's economic potential fluctuated within a limited range, and that economics were driven by some key limiting factors such as food production. In his classic "Essay on the Principle of Population" published in 1798 Malthus believed that populations could grow geometrically, but that food production could only grow linearly. This meant that if food production increased living conditions would improve and the population would grow, resulting in a drop in the amount of food available per capita. He also believed that wars, famine, disease, and other social phenomena would occur to bring the economic health and population back to stasis.

Before the industrial revolution, business environment changes were slow and often restricted, in Malthusian fashion, to a relatively narrow band. The moment that mankind discovered how to leverage key technologies (e.g., steam power) those former barriers were obliterated. The Malthusian models were no longer relevant. In the modern era, futurists such as Toffler shook the world with descriptions of how improvements in education and communications would reshape our models of what might be possible in the not too distant future. He predicted that the speed of change would increase dramatically, and that this trend toward more rapid change would accelerate over time. A little over a decade ago Richard Florida, in *The Great Reset* (2010), suggested that the speed of change is such that it is no longer possible to see changes developing slowly over time. Many of the important changes we are facing now are more of a reset than a progression of our world's economic, technological, and social structures.

It is also becoming clear that none of us are immune to these changes. Businesses and industries that were once titans and considered stable have disappeared sometimes almost overnight (e.g., Kodak, Blockbuster, Toys "R" Us, Boarders). There was a time when a company reached a certain size, and gained a certain level of market presence, it was nearly impossible to displace them; however, that is no longer true. In the mid-20th century if a company was large enough to make the S&P 500 or the Fortune 500 its tenure was likely 60 to 75 years. In the 21st century that tenure has shrunk to somewhere between 15 and 20 years – and it is dropping quickly (Brown, 2018; Knowles & Knowles, 2020).

More recently many managers had to reset their thinking relative to remote workers, or work from home, when the world was introduced to the COVID-19 pandemic. Many managers who up until that point had resisted such working relationships were introduced to a new reality – one in which remote or work from home structures have moved from being unnecessary, or an interesting curiosity, to a critical element of the organization. This was a wake-up call and a shock to the systems of many organizations. Globally we were forced for the first time to deal with a very different set of communications and work processes. The applications were foreign, the etiquette of the online world was foreign, and how you managed a team was foreign. For many this was akin to being thrown into the deep end of the pool for the first time. It immediately identified a number of inadequacies in organizational preparedness that had to be confronted in this new world order.

As managers survey the macro changes they will likely see a number of implications for their industries, supply chains, organizations, and careers. High on their list will likely be items such as diversity, work-life balance, the need for innovation, and even resilience in a crisis on both a macro and micro scale. Today, in addressing these needs, many organizations find themselves spanning multiple geographic locations, time zones, and industrial commons – disrupting the information sharing and cultural norms that have helped to get their organizations to this point. These new, or future, organizations will need to find ways to engage and manage workers who are no longer physically co-present. They will need to develop new ways to manage information flows and tap into a wider variety of resources from a broader set of physical locations.

To fully describe the changes that have already occurred, or that are likely to occur, would take more space than can be found in a single book. Therefore, our goal is to identify a few mega trends that might help you to reshape your thinking and identify some of the important trends or changes which specifically affect your organization.

The Process of Change

Even though change might be necessary many managers will find the process of change itself more difficult than initially imagined. In their book *Humanocracy* Gary Hamel and Michele Zanini (2020) point out that organizations find change far more difficult than do the people who work in them. But whether as an individual or an organization there are many issues around the idea of change itself that can be somewhat problematic. Not the least of these are our expectations about the pace of change, and the value that this change will bring us. We need to reset how we process change and our expectations of how these changes will play out on both a micro and macro scale.

Having spent my professional career in the technology industry, change to me seems like second nature. Sure, there are times when the uncertainty that often accompanies change leads to feelings of discomfort. However, as an eternal optimist, I generally look to the future with anticipation. Whether you err toward optimism or pessimism one of the coming challenges in this era will be balance.

According to that great philosopher Yogi Berra, "the future ain't what it used to be." It is fun to look back at predictions of the future made in the mid- to late 20th century about the 21st century. Of course, there are predictions of travel by jet packs, colonies on the moon, and then there are novels like George Orwell's *1984* (1949), or the Mad Max movies (the series began shooting in 1979) which are set in 2021. Of course, much of what was predicted never came to pass. Which might lead us to another Yogism: "it's tough to make predictions, especially about the future." So, even though many of the predictions made in the past were less than accurate this is not a reason not to try.

Dwight Eisenhower once said, "plans are worthless, but planning is everything." Or, to use another common military theme, "no battle plan survives first contact with the enemy – but planning is critical." These sayings seem almost oxymoronic. The point is you will never account for all possibilities and variables. However, if you take more of a Bayesian approach, make a plan based on what you know and constantly update it as new information presents itself, you will likely be far better off. As we look at the process of change, we can see several things that can affect our recognition and processing of that change.

Early adopters of emerging ICT over the past 50 years have often offered visions for what the future of work might look like. Looking back, it seems that in far too many cases they were caught up in the Gartner Hype Cycle (Gartner Group, n.d.). This model outlines how many professionals can get overly excited about the potential of new technologies – often imagining them to have far more capabilities than they do. This may result in aggressive plans that fall flat when expectations hit reality. Later, as technologies, and the understanding of their capabilities develop, more realistic projects are executed, which deliver significant (if not somewhat more modest) results.

In this fashion many organizations rolled out aggressive work from home programs as soon as ITC advances made it possible, and let employees live wherever they chose so long as there was an internet connection; however, reality soon came crashing in. Soon many became concerned that the quality of organizational culture was declining. This led to the now famous decisions of Yahoo in 2014, and later by other early adopters of work from home policies such as IBM, that dramatically curtailed their employees' ability to work remotely from their team. Often these policies effectively banned work from home. In the ensuing years there has been some progress in the technologies that support geographically diverse teams, and coupled with growing acceptance and experience we are now seeing remote working structures that are far more robust and effective than those put in place just a few years ago.

Due to the very nature of technology and the rate of change described above, the reality of how remote work and remote management of organizational culture will look in the future is still very unclear. What we can expect is that it will likely change from what we now know. Some of these changes will be based on technology, others will be based on our ability to absorb and understand its capabilities, and even how we can build relationships when the fidelity of the communications is different than being there in person. As with many other innovations practitioners began to realize that the issues experienced by Yahoo and IBM had to do more with the ability of those involved to internalize the changes than with the technology itself.

In March 2020 most companies were facing a new reality. In most of the developed world co-presence was not an option, and new ways of working and communicating were being forced on a number of companies and working professionals. In many cases the new tools could have been implemented earlier, but for many there seemed to be no compelling reason to do so. Over the years most professionals had gained some familiarity with simple video conferencing or video chat tools, e.g., Skype, FaceTime, Facebook Messenger, or Google Duo. However, most shied away from suggesting that they be used on a casual basis in a business environment. Instead, they used messaging tools with much lower fidelity in presenting a message. Familiar tools like telephones, email, or even texting were used. More often than not these were the lowest common denominator – at other times the lack of familiarity by the other party could cause an awkward encounter – or one could even argue that previous generations of these tools were sometime a little flaky. However, a major factor in the use of such tools, and just about every legacy technology, has been momentum.

When studying change in organizations it is often helpful to recall the now classic book by Thomas Kuhn entitled *The Structure of Scientific Revolution* (1996). According to Kuhn, "Scientists have a very hard time denouncing paradigms they have been working with for an extended period of time – even when evidence mounts against them. Rarely do scientists drop a theory unless they have a handy replacement" (p. 76). The problem with dropping the ideas that we are operating under is not unique to scientists. In most professions this has been demonstrated to be the case – especially as we increase the stakes.

This might explain why many business processes become calcified. Often a company's business models, processes, organizational structures, and communications practices are stuck in the past, and there seems to be no hope of changing them. Some of this might be attributed to comfort with the existing process or paradigm, it could simply be momentum, but in other cases it might come down to fear of the unknown. However, increasingly companies are facing situations where their existing organizations are out of sync with the reality they are facing. Yet many managers continue to demonstrate varying levels of cognitive dissonance. As Kuhn has described, even when they are faced with mounting evidence they refuse to accept that the current model is anything less than perfect – or even in need of some sort of update.

Why is there such denial of what might be obvious to an outsider? People become extremely risk adverse when they feel their job, or their career, is on the line. Or, as it was famously put by Upton Sinclair, "It is difficult to get a man to understand something when his salary depends on him not understanding it." In some cases, they are simply sticking their heads in the sand until the issues at hand go away on their own. Unfortunately, sometimes when they go away, they do so at a heavy price – even at the price of destroying the organization itself.

A term that often gets used by the modern military to describe a situation that is degrading the limits of a person's ability to cope is VUCA (volatile, uncertain, complex, and ambiguous). Often, as things begin to shift to VUCA, the default for many people is to "outsource their thinking to siloed experts and technologies that can help us optimize choices amidst a data deluge" (Schroeter et al., 2020). The problem with this approach is that at best the opinions of these experts, and expert systems, were formed while dealing with similar but different realities. As the statistician George Box famously quipped, "All models are wrong – but some are useful." Models are just that – models – they are not reality. They are simplifications that allow us to get some perspective on what is happening, and as we generalize these models to meet broader sets of situations, or environments experiencing rapid change, their viability to mirror reality decreases.

Toffler (1970) suggested that "there are discoverable limits to the amounts of change that the human organism can absorb, and that by endlessly accelerating change without first determining these limits, we may submit masses of men to demands they simply cannot tolerate" (p. 326). In some ways it would be interesting to wonder if Toffler may have fallen into a similar trap as Malthus, whereby neither accounted for how human beings might leverage their abilities through new and power-ful tools. It is important to remember that Toffler wrote his book at the very beginning of the computer age. As prescient as he was, it might have been hard for him to imagine the types of tools that are available to us today for making sense out of our data, never mind the kinds of tools we might have in the future.

In discussing Toffler's point of view, Grady Booch, in *After Shock* (Schroeter et al., 2020), posits that "except for regarding physics – there are no currently discoverable limits to the amount of change that a human can absorb" (p. 34). When developing our opinions, we start with what we frame as normal. As we are increasingly exposed to change our tolerance for change increases. In addition, the human race has devel-oped, at an increasing rate, tools which allow us to process the deluge of data we are facing; indeed, one only has to look at the analytics business to see this in action. Going one step further, a number of authors have discussed the coming of human machine partnerships whereby artificial intelligence (AI) is used in a supporting role to human decision-making.

In the late 2010s we saw that AI could be used successfully to augment human decision-making. Examples of this can be seen in freestyle chess where opponents were allowed to use AI chess applications to support their play and decision-making. Computers provided a series of options which the players could select based on the style and personality of their opponent. In these AI-assisted tournaments, lower level or mid-level chess players could potentially beat a grand master. Whether we are looking at chess moves or business decisions it is clear that fields like analytics are affecting how business decisions are now and increasingly will be made.

However, the rate of change has become a factor here as well. Moore's Law has reared its head. Over the course of 50 years Gordon Moore noticed that the technology in RAM chips was doubling in capacity while the price fell by about half every 18 to 24 months. Over time, people have begun to generalize this law to all technology, and it has mostly held true. When applying this to AI the effects of Moore's Law can be seen in the emergence of hyperlearning. In the past AI would typically need to be trained by humans in the rules of a game (or how a business process works), and how to make decisions. Hyperlearning systems can be given a minimal bit of information about the problem, and by running endless simulations it can learn on its own how to solve the problem or adapt to changes in the environment.

These systems have affected the viability of freestyle chess. In the case of chess hyperlearning systems have advanced so rapidly in their speed and ability that they have outclassed both human chess masters and human-machine duos. According to Philip Gerbert (2018), this would suggest that humans are becoming a redundant and unnecessary part of the equation, and going forward this trend will only get worse. However, not all researchers agree. Chess aside, Johnson and Vera (2019) suggest that AI is not an island and that the real power will be in teaming with humans. For the time being at least, machine and human intelligence are fundamentally different from one another.

Some may wonder why a discussion of AI is relevant here. It is relevant as an icon of change. If one takes a long look at AI today it is not a grand leap to see the potential for disruptive change if any of the current predictions or trends hold true. It would seem to have the potential to disrupt our world to the same degree or more than the internet has over the past few decades.

Moore, like Toffler, saw the potential for the rate of change to increase, so the models we have for dealing with this rate of change will have to change. We know from Malthus that we cannot domain our thinking and restrict it to the fundamental principles we have historically run our lives on. These principles are open to change as key variables that were once constant begin to change. Computers have dramatically increased the volume and flow of information in the past 50 years and this flow is likely to increase – which may lead to the formation of human-machine partnerships out of necessity for humans to be able to cope with the flow.

For those professionals who took a step back and who have been clinical about the management challenges which we will be facing in the future, the need for geographically diverse teams, or teams that cannot be co-present, has been on their radar for some time now. However, given the resistance to change in many organizations, most did not see something this radical happening quickly. However, that was before the outbreak of the COVID-19 pandemic, and stay-at-home orders which forced many organizations to choose between remote work or closure. But it probably would have happened even without the pandemic. Technological, demographic, economic, and social changes in recent decades have been pushing business to change their basic structures, as well as the rules of internal and external engagement. As we go forward, there will be no pat answers on how to handle these changes, but we can begin to develop new approaches and logical frameworks to process our current environments and attempt to position ourselves for the future.

Chapter 1 Takeaways

It will come as no surprise to anyone who has been paying even the slightest attention to world affairs over the past few decades that the pace of change is accelerating. The COVID-19 pandemic forced many trends that were already happening to move faster than they would have otherwise, but they were happening nonetheless. In a macro sense it is clear that we need to do the following:

- Our goals must be aligned with the environment around us and pivot when necessary.
- We need to evaluate the habits and affordances that our technology enables. The type of technology we use and how we implement it can and will affect how we think about the world and our place in it.
- We must reassess how we communicate, and if the technology we are currently using is adequate to deal with the challenges we now face, it will be increasingly necessary. Furthermore, changes in our method of communication will change what is both possible and probable.
- We need to look at our capacity to change our organizational culture, our business processes, and our infrastructure.
- We need to ask if we have fallen into the trap of using the least common denominator when working together, instead of assessing the environment for what is needed and implementing the necessary changes.
- We must recognize the changes in both the available global talent, our workforce, and ask ourselves whether we are willing to make the changes necessary to capitalize on both.

References

Adamy, P. O. & Adamy, J. (2021, January 20). Biden Will Lead an Older, Polarized and Financially Insecure Nation. *Wall Street Journal.* https://www.wsj.com/articles/biden-inherits-an-older-polarized-and-financially-insecure-nation-11611153710.

Berkeley Haas (2020, January 11). Supporting Dual Career Couples. Center for Equity, Gender & Leadership. https://haas.berkeley.edu/equity/industry/playbooks/supporting-dual-career-couples/.

Bindley, K. (2020, August 14). Remote Work Is Reshaping San Francisco, as Tech Workers Flee and Rents Fall. *Wall Street Journal.* https://www.wsj.com/articles/remote-work-is-reshaping-san-francisco-as-tech-workers-flee-and-rents-fall-11597413602.

Brown, B. (2018). *Dare to Lead: Brave Work. Tough Conversations. Whole Hearts* (1st ed.). Random House.

Centers for Disease Control and Prevention (CDC) (2019, October 30). *Health United States 2020–2021.* Health, United States—Data Finder. https://www.cdc.gov/nchs/hus/contents2018.htm.

Florida, R. (2010). *The Great Reset: How New Ways of Living and Working Drive Post-Crash Prosperity* (1st ed.). HarperCollins (e-book).

Gallup (2017). *State of the American Workplace.* https://www.gallup.com/workplace/238085/state-american-workplace-report-2017.aspx.

Gartner Group (n.d.). *Hype Cycle Research Methodology.* https://www.gartner.com/en/research/methodologies/gartner-hype-cycle.

Gerbert, P. (2018, May 16). AI and the "Augmentation" Fallacy. *MIT Sloan Management Review.* https://sloanreview.mit.edu/article/ai-and-the-augmentation-fallacy/.

Hamel, G., & Zanini, M. (2020). *Humanocracy: Creating Organizations as Amazing as the People Inside Them.* Harvard Business Review Press.

Hummer, R. A., & Hernandez, E. M. (2013). The Effect of Educational Attainment on Adult Mortality in the United States. *Population Bulletin,* 68(1), 1–16.

Johnson, M., & Vera, A. H. (2019). No AI Is an Island: The Case for Teaming Intelligence. *AI Magazine; La Canada,* 40(1), 16–28.

Kaplan, R. M., Howard, V. J., Safford, M. M., & Howard, G. (2015). Educational Attainment and Longevity: Results from the REGARDS US National Cohort Study of Blacks and Whites. *Annals of Epidemiology,* 25(5), 323–328. https://doi.org/10.1016/j.annepidem.2015.01.017.

Knowles, B. T. H. & Knowles, J. (2020, December 17). The Essence of Strategy is Now How to Change. *MIT Sloan Management Review.* https://sloanreview.mit.edu/article/the-essence-of-strategy-is-now-how-to-change/.

Kuhn, T. (1996). *The Structure of Scientific Revolution.* University of Chicago Press.

Leonardi, P., & Neeley, T. (2017). What Managers Need to Know About Social Tools: Avoid the Common Pitfalls So That Your Organization Can Collaborate, Learn, and Innovate. *Harvard Business Review,* 95(6), 118–126.

Malthus, T. (1798). *An Essay on the Principle of Population.* J. Johnson, in St. Paul's Church-Yard, 134.

McChrystal, G. S., Collins, T., Silverman, D., & Fussell, C. (2015). *Team of Teams: New Rules of Engagement for a Complex World.* Portfolio.

Mims, C. (2021, October 21). How Working From Home Could Change Where Innovation Happens. *Wall Street Journal.* https://www.wsj.com/articles/work-from-home-changed-where-innovation-happens-11634763139.

Organisation for Economic Co-operation and Development (OECD) (2019). *Education at a Glance.* OECD. http://www.oecd.org/education/education-at-a-glance/.

Pew Research Center (2019, June 12). *Demographics of Internet and Home Broadband Usage in the United States.* Pew Research Center: Internet, Science & Tech. https://www.pewresearch.org/internet/fact-sheet/internet-broadband/.

Sasson, I. (2016). Trends in Life Expectancy and Lifespan Variation by Educational Attainment: United States, 1990–2010. *Demography,* 53(2), 269–293. https://doi.org/10.1007/s13524-015-0453-7.

Schrader, A., & Cramer-Flood, E. (2012, June 4). Does China's Newly Educated Population Indicate a Changed Workforce Dynamic? *The Conference Board.* https://www.conference-board.org/blog/postdetail.cfm?post=704.

Schroeter, J., Kurzweil, R., Gilder, G., Rees, M., Gingrich, N., Kay, A., Brin, D., Bronson, P., & Westphal, D. (2020). *After Shock: The World's Foremost Futurists Reflect on 50 Years of Future Shock—and Look Ahead to the Next 50* (1st ed.). John August Media, LLC.

Statistics Bureau of Japan (2020). *Japan Statistical Yearbook 2020.* http://www.stat.go.jp/english/data/nenkan/69nenkan/zenbun/en69/top.html.

Toffler, A. (1970). *Future Shock*. Random House.

US Bureau of Labor Statistics (2018, July 30). Workers with Advanced Degrees More Likely to Work at Home. *The Economics Daily.* https://www.bls.gov/opub/ted/2018/workers-with-advanced-degrees-more-likely-to-work-at-home.htm.

US Bureau of Labor Statistics (2019). Job Flexibilities and Work Schedules Summary. *Economic News Release.* https://www.bls.gov/news.release/flex2.nr0.htm.

US Bureau of Labor Statistics (2020). *Bureau of Labor Statistics Data.* https://data.bls.gov/pdq/SurveyOutputServlet.

US Census Bureau (2020, March 11). *CPS Historical Time Series Visualizations.* https://www.census.gov/library/visualizations/time-series/demo/cps-historical-time-series.html.

World Bank (2020). *World Development Indicators.* http://datatopics.worldbank.org/world-development-indicators/.

Chapter 2

Elements of Success Within the Firm

The Microenvironment

Or the Elements of Success Within the Firm

In his book *Good Company*, Arthur Blank (2020), founder of Home Depot, and serial entrepreneur, emphasized the importance of factors within the company. I was struck by a story he told about playing golf with the CEO of a competitive big box retail chain sometime after he stepped down as Home Depot's CEO. The other CEO sheepishly admitted:

> I had my people visit hundreds of your stores – not just in North America but in South America as well. We copied everything you did – your merchandise, your design, your pricing, your signage. But what we couldn't copy was your service. As hard as we tried, we couldn't get our people to show up and serve customers like yours did.
>
> (2020, p. 43)

On hearing this story some might jump to the company culture, or management style, or human resource policies, or any of a hundred other factors as the reason that Home Depot was able to best this competitor. In some ways it is almost immaterial what the real reason is – there is a larger principle at play here. If this story illustrates anything it is that there are an endless number of possible factors for the difference, and understanding, managing, and executing in these microenvironments is critical to organizational success. In the next two chapters we will look at micro factors related to the firm itself and how many of these have changed with the move to remote work, and how they will continue to change.

This chapter does not intend to provide a complete or near-complete list of micro factors. Rather, it brings together a collection of factors that have a significant effect on the success of any firm, and are intended to serve as examples of the diverse characteristics that these factors can take on.

DOI: 10.4324/9781032646657-2

Organizational Responsibilities

It would be reasonable to suggest that organizations wishing to improve their odds need to take some responsibility and initiative in the process of doing so. They are responsible for building frameworks that encourage the process of success. Since each firm finds itself in a unique situation this infrastructure will be unique to each firm; however, there are some common challenges and themes to be discovered. The rise in hybrid/remote work environments is a significant change in how work gets done; therefore, organizations are responsible for evaluating what will be necessary to implement it properly.

Defining the Firm

Let us begin with the realization that organizational structures are at their core a social technology, and like any technology, over time, the environment in which they operate will force them to change in order to continue to be effective. If this is the case, then it would also seem logical that the very definition of what a firm is should evolve as well. In his seminal article, "The Nature of the Firm," Roger Coase (1937) asks the questions *what is a firm?*, and *why does it exist?* Being an early 20th-century economist, in his view the purpose of the firm is to promote the efficient use of resources, and to reduce transaction costs. It is typically more efficient to have key elements of the core business within the firm, where there is limited overhead need in terms of the marketing of services between different business disciplines, negotiating terms, and managing the transaction costs. There is some very clear logic here; however, since the introduction of Coase's concepts a number of economists, managers, and socialists have pointed out the limits of this early thinking.

A firm is both a social and legal entity that, if functioning well, has value well beyond the sum of its parts. Its reason for existing is to "produce the collective action necessary to serve all human needs" (Chassagnon, 2014, p. 197). Among its attributes are "identity, cohesion, culture, cooperation, and commitment," and therefore "the firm cannot be reduced to a simple function of purely private economic self-interest because the firm is also a social institution for the common good" (Chassagnon, 2014, p. 198). Members of the firm often transcend their own self-interest to promote the greater good for their team, department, organization, or even their customers. In a recent article by McKinsey and Company, the authors suggested that the real purpose of a firm is to create identity. That efficiency is created by being part of something and participating in a vision (Smet et al., 2021).

But where does the firm end and where do strategic partnerships begin? The efficiency advantage that Coase assumed may erode to the point of irrelevance in some situations due to automation. We can see examples in the modern two-sided markets, or platform business, such as Uber, Lyft, TaskRabbit, or Airbnb. These arrangements work where the deliverables are easily defined and measurable, but should the workers earning a living on these platforms be considered employees, or are they independent contractors? At the time of writing the jury is still out, and there are certainly legitimate points to be made on both sides of the argument here.

It is important to remember that at its core a firm is made up of people – no matter what the legal arrangement. In well-functioning firms there are most likely people who are looking for connections, the ability to make a contribution, and to be part of something larger than themselves. In addition, the environment we are living in has become far less stable than it was in the past; therefore, innovation and agility are becoming increasingly important. Having worked as a contractor or consultant for a number of large technology firms in the 1990s and early 2000s, I often worked on teams within my client firms that included multiple employment statuses (e.g., employees, contractors, consultants, contingency workers, temporary workers, strategic partners). In these situations, it was often difficult to know who held what status – or where the firm began and where it ended – and most of us didn't care. Even though the lines were gray and fuzzy, we all had a shared mission and goals, and we all felt like we were part of the same team.

As we work through this and later chapters, we will be exploring how the structure of a firm might promote greater efficiency, higher levels of engagement, and greater agility.

Engagement

For over 20 years Gallup has administered a national poll to measure employee engagement. As of July 22, 2020 – the most recent poll as of this writing – the percentage of employees who are *actively disengaged*, "those who have miserable work experiences and spread their unhappiness to their colleagues", sat around the historical average of 13%. Workers who were actively engaged sat at about 40%, up slightly from the historical average of about 37%. The remaining 47% were *not engaged* – "they are psychologically unattached to their work and company." These employees would quickly leave and may even be actively looking for other opportunities (Gallup, 2020).

It does not take a lot of management insight to understand that *disengaged* or *not engaged* employees will as a group typically underperform compared to *engaged* employees, and may even overtly work against the success of the organization. These underperforming groups are also unlikely to be innovative or agile, will likely only deliver the minimum effort necessary to stay employed while they scan the horizon for their next gig, and will typically focus only on their own short-term self-interest.

It would seem to make sense to shift the engagement ratio more in favor of the firm. Short of firing and replacing 60% of the firm's employees (13% *actively disengaged* and 47% *not engaged*), it would seem to be in the organization's best interest to see if it can get some of the disaffected employees to migrate to an *engaged* status – or at a minimum to shift from being *actively disengaged* to *not engaged*. This would seem obvious – but not necessarily easy. In a meta study published in the *Journal of Strategic Human Resource Management* in 2017, over 50 factors were identified as having a significant effect on employee engagement (Choudhury & Mohanty, 2019). However, Dan Pink (2009), in his book *Drive*, provides us with a much shorter list of key factors: autonomy, mastery, and purpose. Autonomy means allowing people to participate in the decision-making process and have some level of self-direction, while mastery involves providing them with an opportunity to develop their skills and abilities, and providing a purpose that employees can rally around.

No matter which list of key factors we use, it would seem to be clear that success does not happen in a vacuum. There are antecedents that have to be satisfied to lay the groundwork for success. There are environmental attributes that will allow the success factors to exist and thrive. Included in these attributes are vision, values, mission, transparency, and an information flow. The organization must provide context through a mission or vision of the future which creates clarity of purpose (Lai, 2017). Through the flow of information within the organization, employees need to understand how the business itself is operating, and what is already known about the customers, markets, and potential threats or opportunities. High levels of internal transparency, and access to information resources, are critical to allow the employees to see the implications of their decisions.

In a world of hybrid/remote work the fostering of engagement has become more difficult due to the reductions in the volume and fidelity of communications. Therefore, in order to foster the feeling of inclusion and commitment necessary for engagement to occur, managers often must be much more intentional on the volume, content, and quality of the communications that happen between both peers and management within the organization.

Communications/Serendipity Infrastructure

In developing this book, I had the chance to discuss the flow of ideas with several senior executives. Their insights have been extremely valuable in shaping my thinking on a few issues including serendipity. Serendipity is the unplanned good fortune that happens when people work together closely – or the accidental, unscripted, coincidental interactions that often happen when people are in close proximity with each other. Two executives who were particularly influential here were Sam Molinaro, former President of UBS Americas Holding, and Inna Kuznetsova, former CEO of 1010data – both of whom are dear friends.

In my conversations with both Sam and Inna they made it clear that this new post-COVID-19 world order could have a real effect on organizational culture and efficiency. They saw that the casual interactions that happen outside of the planned meetings or phone calls often build organizational culture and personal relationships. Sam described it as the "meeting before – and the meeting after the meeting." A lot of information changes hands while you are waiting for the meeting to start, as you hang out in the room a few minutes after the meeting, and as you walk down the hall to and from the meeting. You often exchange bits of relevant information that you might not get otherwise. These bits might be key pieces of information that spur a new idea, or innovation – or at a minimum help to deepen a relationship and build culture. These things do not happen as easily on a video conference call.

Both Inna and Sam were more concerned about new, or younger, employees. They saw these casual interactions as being highly instructive both professionally and culturally within an organization. In a conversation I had with Inna a few months prior to the outbreak of the COVID-19 pandemic, she used a cooking metaphor to describe the *work from home* or *remote work* situation. She said that "working from home is like spice, the right amount can create real flavor, but too much can ruin the dish." As it became clear that COVID-19 was going to affect our ability to be co-present for some time, I revisited this conversation with Inna. She had a firm understanding of the limitations around being in the same room, and even though we were only a few months into the pandemic, she was developing plans to reconfigure the structure of her company's offices to meet the new post-COVID-19 reality. However, even though it was clear that there would have to be some accommodations necessary for remote work, and that it would represent a significant part of her company's total man-hours, she was still planning to leverage co-present team meetings to help to drive culture. She also felt that a significant proportion of her workforce would regularly opt to come in to work in the company's offices.

Later in the book we will more fully develop the issues surrounding communication, information flow, and the management and leadership challenges they present.

Presence

It would also seem that the right amount of spice (work from home – or remote work) is highly contextual to the industry, the company, and the individuals involved. However, losing the ability to have unplanned exchanges completely would seem to be a real issue. But the danger here might be conflating physical presence to being necessary for these fortunate exchanges. In a later chapter we will discuss *virtual proximity* and *media richness* which might give us a better understanding of presence. Sam and Inna see presence as critical to serendipitous exchanges; however, it might be interesting to explore Sam and Inna's ideas on serendipity relative to those of Christian Busch at New York University. Busch suggests that serendipity is a skill that can be developed or fostered given the proper environment (Narayanan, 2020). For now, it might be enough to state that one of the models, or infrastructures, that will likely require change will be how we communicate and how we are taught to recognize opportunities. Our current information flows would seem not to be capturing all the information necessary for the highest levels of serendipity, but can we change that without requiring physical presence? In the next chapter we will explore the concepts of proximity and its role in information flow. However, for now let us just say that our understanding of being in the same place at the same time to exchange information is evolving and will continue to evolve.

Mindset

In her groundbreaking book *Mindset*, Carol Dweck (2006) of Stanford University discusses how our general mindset in approaching life has a major effect on our level of success. Dweck describes a two-ended spectrum with either a fixed mindset or a growth mindset. As an educator many of her examples are academically focused; however, it does not take much of an intellectual leap to see how these principles could be applied to a professional environment. According to Dweck, a fixed mindset sees IQ, talent, or ability as a fixed commodity, and a growth mindset sees them as things that can be developed and changed.

In a fixed mindset if you have the talent, you should not have to work hard – things should just come naturally. If you are working hard, it is because you do not have the talent. This of course is counter to the reality we see every day in sport – e.g., Ben Hogan, Tiger Woods, Michael Phelps, Herschel Walker – all of whom are known to have spent countless hours working to hone their talent. Her work suggests that it is important to take control of an experience and not let it define you. One example used in her book was of Jim Marshall of the Minnesota Vikings, who picked up a ball and ran the wrong way to score for the other team. Afterwards, instead of hanging his head in shame, he took control of the situation and used it to inspire himself to play some of the best football he ever had played (Dweck, 2006, pp. 33–34). "The growth mindset does allow people to love what they're doing – and to continue to love it in the face of difficulties" (p. 48).

Dweck suggests that a fixed mindset leads to a slow decline. People with a fixed mindset are looking to protect their self-image and their public image. They will shy away from challenges that might affect how they are perceived, whereas people with a growth mindset are often excited by challenges that they see stretching their ability. These people will experience a growth in skills and ability over time. Managers can affect the mindset of the culture through what they recognize publicly and what they reward. If we praise people for their talent we are promoting a fixed mindset, and if we praise people for their process and effort we are promoting a growth mindset.

One of my favorite "Dweckisms" is the author's use of *not yet.* She suggests that kids should receive grades of *not yet* instead of a failing grade. She points out that "test scores and measures of achievement tell you where a student is, but they don't tell you where a student could end up" (Dweck, 2006, p. 66). *Not yet* is not judgmental of the person's ability or character. It makes a statement about results. It leaves open the possibility of additional effort, which might lead to eventual success. It helps to promote what Angela Duckworth (2016) described as *grit.* Duckworth points out that success is not a fixed thing. Your probability of achieving success is affected by your willingness and ability to get back up when you are knocked down. Duckworth's premise is supported by a growing volume of academic work. One recent joint study between the University of Chicago and Maastricht University in the Netherlands suggested that IQ (a fixed factor) only accounted for between 1% and 2% of financial success. The bulk of such success was derived from self-discipline, perseverance, and diligence (Borghans et al., 2016). These are the growth mindset factors that our cultures need to promote.

The COVID-19 pandemic caused turmoil upsetting long-held beliefs and hampering or obliterating longstanding business practices. The concepts of grit, not yet, and a growth mindset may be very useful tools for managers and leaders looking to adjust. Dweck's work suggests that people can adapt and change if the environment around them is structured to allow it. Part of that structure is developing a growth mindset in managers, and a focus on where employees can develop into. This goes hand in hand with proper recognition of where employees are today, the process plan for improvement, and recognition for good process and progress in real time (or close to it).

Employee Responsibilities

For a number of reasons, which we touched on in Chapter 1 and which we will explore further later in the book, modern employees expect, and have been given, far more autonomy than they have had in past generations. This autonomy comes at a cost, and some of the responsibilities that were borne by the organization, or its managers, in the past have now been shifted to the employee.

Skills Development/Career Planning

In the past, when organizations assumed a more paternal role, employees looked to the organization for career planning. In the best of cases employees were groomed to climb through a series of positions within the organization during a career that often spanned decades. In such organizations managers would develop long-term plans, and human resources professionals would help in the development of those skills with the employees of the firm. Organizations such as GE, IBM, or Proctor & Gamble built legendary management training management programs for their high potential employees; however, these programs were often not only for the elite. Organizations regularly invested in short-term training and development programs for the rank and file to build specific skills and abilities.

I recently had a conversation with Dermott Whalen who, during his long career, held vice presidential roles in human resources at several large pharmaceutical companies including Baxter, Novartis, and Bristol Myers Squibb. Dermott told me that he has seen a shift in firms' willingness to make long-term investments in employees. The tenure of these employees is decreasing, and in weighing the cost of developing or hiring the skill, companies in recent years have looked to bring on new employees with the skill, rather than investing in building it.

This may prove to be short-sighted on the part of the organization; however, as an employee you might not have the time to wait for the trend to reverse itself. In such a world those employees who wish to get ahead will need to make investments in themselves. It falls on the employee to scan the horizon and anticipate where their industry is going and what skills might be in demand in the future – or worse, what skills and which employees will become redundant. In addition, this would seem detrimental to the organizational culture and levels of employee engagement – particularly in an environment of reduced proximity or information flow.

My conversations with Dermott took place at the beginning of the pandemic. What has changed since then is that we have experienced a prolonged period of full or near-full employment, and a growing trend of employees leaving jobs for greener pastures (known as the Great Resignation). The result of all of this is a reversal of the trend described in some cases. According to a study by McKinsey and Company (2022), many companies are looking to invest more in developing talent internally than they have in the recent past.

To complicate things further, the traditional corporate ladder is changing. In the past developing your career often meant climbing an ever-increasing series of managerial roles to the top of the corporate pyramid. Currently corporations are seeing broader spans of control, and flattening hierarchies, thereby reducing the opportunity to climb the traditional ladder. Other trends which seem to be taking hold include a growing need to take personal responsibility, an increase in the importance of agility, and promotion often does not equate to a managerial position. As they flatten and increase autonomy new types of roles will develop around specific skills and abilities which are more team- or project-based.

Self-Direction

The core thought here is autonomy – or the ability to make your own decisions – that comes with the responsibility to effectively use the privilege by actually taking on the responsibility of managing yourself – or to put it more succinctly self-direction. Make no mistake, this is a skill that requires learning and development. No one is born with this skill. Some have been lucky enough to have been placed in an environment that has encouraged its development, and have over time become very good at it; however, many have not. Just throwing these employees in at the deep end and telling them to sink or swim is not usually effective.

Even for employees who have experience it is often helpful to have frameworks or guidelines that identify the limits of their abilities, and develop a culture that helps them to sort out the type of decisions they can make, as well as the sort of conclusions that are within the range of acceptability.

Having been an entrepreneur, and coming from an entrepreneurial family, the idea of self-direction was always part of my life. So, as I entered the working world, I just assumed that this was a skill set that has been developed by most people. I was wrong, and in fairness there are some people (few) who are better off being watched.

When implementing self-direction in a team there are some principles that should be followed. The most important thing is that managers should create a list of company principles and values that should always be adhered to. An example of this would be the core principles at W.L. Gore, namely freedom, fairness, personal commitment, and waterline.

> *Freedom:* We believe in each other, and we will allow, help, and empower our fellow Associates to grow in knowledge, skill, and scope of responsibility.
> *Fairness:* Together, we are responsible for sustaining an engaging enterprise built on inclusiveness, striving to be fair with each other and everyone with whom we do business.
> *Commitment:* We make and keep our own commitments to demonstrate personal responsibility to each other, our teams, and our customers.

Waterline: We are all shareholders, and we will consult with the appropriate Associates before taking an action "below the waterline" that could cause serious damage to the long-term success or reputation of our enterprise.

(Gore, 2023)

In addition, team members may require coaching in areas such as:

1   *Vision development:* Creating a completing vision for the future that they themselves and their organization can move toward. This might include the ability to see opportunity where others see only chaos and confusion
2   *Planning and project management:* Developing plans, key performance indicators, and implementing tools and processes to make the vision a reality.
3   *Risk assessment and contingency planning:* Risk assessment involves not only assessing the risk, but understanding what is a good risk and what is reckless (which is often a fine line). It also involves having the discipline to protect the downside when and where it is reasonable to do so.

Network Development

One of the great values of a firm, or a personal network, is its ability to link ideas, skills, and talent to develop something greater than what any individual could produce on their own. Therefore, it is up to the firm to foster the development of personal networks; however, it is really the specific actions of individual employees that actually create and maintain these networks.

In developing these networks, it might be helpful to understand the principles that surround their development and maintenance, and what a good network looks like.

Robin Dunbar of Oxford University has developed a body of work around the limitations that human beings have in developing relationships. This is commonly known as the Dunbar number. The irony is that the Dunbar number is not one number, but rather a series of numbers relating to the ability of the human brain to process the transactions necessary to maintain specific levels of relationships. A simplified Dunbar number list might look like the following:

1   5 loved ones
2   15 good friends
3   50 friends
4   150 meaningful contacts
5   500 acquaintances
6   1,500 people you recognize

The important issue is not whether you agree with the specific number. In Dunbar's scientific studies he concludes that each level is more of a range based on individual abilities and proclivities. The greater issue is that there is a limit. This limit is based on the processing speed and capacity of the human brain. So, even if you are a superhuman you cannot have a meaningful relationship with your one thousand social media followers, or the five hundred direct reports (Ro, 2019). The simple fact is that each relationship requires a certain amount of cognitive effort. The deeper the relationship the greater the effort – so by this logic loved ones require more mental attention than do acquaintances. This is a zero-sum game if you invest in one person that leaves you with less mental capacity to handle additional relationships.

As organizations come under increasing pressure to flatten their organizational structure, they will face an increasing number of direct reports, and if those direct reports are hybrid/remote employees they will typically require a higher level of communication than they would if they were co-located. Because of the cognitive limitations of their managers, flatter organizations are under greater pressure to distribute decision-making to achieve a reasonable level of effectiveness. This means that managers will have to provide rules of engagement to employees, i.e., to provide them with a scope or range for their decision-making ability. And it will require employees to take more responsibility for the day-to-day decisions that fall within their remit, and to coordinate their actions with others in the organization who might be affected by them.

Employees will need to develop a broader view of what they do and who will be affected. They will also need to develop their own networks of resources that will both inform their decisions and help them to achieve both their organizational and personal career goals. This will in most cases require employees to develop their own professional networks both within and outside the firm.

The hybrid/remote organizational models have a direct effect on how employees form and maintain relationships. Later in the book we will discuss proximity and media richness, and how sharing a physical space often makes it easier to develop and maintain relationships. Also, whether the relationships are harder to maintain or not, it will require different skills and a different level of effort to do so.

Value Creation

There is a tendency for people to act as if the current market situation is a fixed market reality. However, nothing could be further from the truth. As we have already discussed the rate of change is accelerating. One problem is that employees are willing to accept that their smartphone and computer will change every year, but they act as if their industry, or their job, is somehow immune from such forces – or that their past investments in career development will carry them for life.

In the first business I founded after graduate school, I taught IT professionals how to pass certification exams. Novell was a hot corporate networking platform at the time, and Novell Certified Network Engineers (CNE) and Novell Certified Network Instructors (CNI) were paid a premium. I can still remember one young woman who contacted me at the time looking to take the classes necessary to become a CNI. When I asked why, she said once she got the certification she would be set for life. Not wanting to mislead her, I told her she had *maybe* a couple of years before the market would drive compensation down, and she would have to develop new skills to meet her income goals. She was beyond shocked and ended the call in a fit of cognitive dissonance, having told me that I had no idea what I was talking about. Of course, my assessment played out just as I told her it would.

Juliet Schor (2020), in her study of the gig economy entitled *After the Gig*, points out that the earnings of providers for Uber, Lyft, and TaskRabbit have dramatically decreased over time; however, this has not been the case with Airbnb. So why is Airbnb bucking the trend set by the other platforms? One explanation might come from traditional economic theory. There is low differentiation between the suppliers on Uber, Lyft, and TaskRabbit, and high differentiation on Airbnb. There are minor differences between the ride you receive between different ride sharing providers (Uber and Lyft); therefore, the differentiating factor is price – which will logically feel market pressure over time to decrease prices to the lowest possible level. On the other hand, each Airbnb property provides a unique experience. Of course, there is still some market pressure, but highly differentiated properties will command a premium.

Your skills or market position might provide you with economic rent (value above the cost of the inputs and a fair premium); however, these situations rarely last very long. If you are not differentiating, you might soon find that market progressively making your position less valuable and less relevant. However, the more invested we are in the status quo the less likely we are to recognize this. It might be worth taking the time to invest in some lateral thinking. Put yourself in the shoes of a competitor, a technology provider, a regulatory official, or anyone else who might potentially attack your market or your position (this might include the management of your own organization) and ask yourself how would you break the current model and what might you replace it with. If you take this exercise seriously you will likely find several ways in which your position could become irrelevant – and your next career move might become obvious.

Why this is so relevant in a remotely managed world has a lot to do with some of the other variables that have changed in the employment equation from both the perspective of the employee and the perspective of the manager. There is a long list of factors, and we might not have the time and space to address them all, but the list would include:

- The changing nature of the relationship between employees and managers;
- Autonomy;
- Less career development direction and training;
- The shortening of the shelf life of our skills and knowledge;
- The emergence of the Great Resignation;
- The need to develop one's own career plan and trajectory;
- The market value of skills and how they change over time.

Strategy

Endless hours go into strategy development – and rightly so. Without proper planning and strategy your probability of success is dramatically reduced. Or, as my father put it to me as a child, "Remember the seven "P's" – proper prior planning prevents piss poor performance." However, strategy is not a substitute for an inspired team. Having an inspired team that will go the extra mile to pick up the pieces and adapt is crucial – and team members will be able to pick up the pieces if they have planned well and understand all the variables they now need to reassemble. An inspired team is a function of a number of factors. Some of these factors are within the control of the managers and some are not. In this chapter we will explore some of the things that are under management's control.

If organizational leaders learned anything in 2020 it would be that many of the organizational structures and organizational cultures, which have served us well in the past, are now beginning to show their age and lose their effectiveness. Organizational structures and cultures should be thought of as social technologies and, as we saw in the last chapter, technologies have a life cycle. They move through a cycle of conception, development, introduction, growth, maturity, and decline. Often once they reach maturity, we begin to see a loss of efficacy – or a loss of relevance to the current environment. At this point managers need to begin to look for a replacement – structures that will better address the changes in the environment which have occurred since the design of the last organizational structure was implemented. Often this change comes in the shape of a significant reorganization (something we will address in Chapter 4). There seems to be two extremes in this process: tradition (incremental change from the current structure – usually championed by those invested in the status quo) and radical change (which to many is at a minimum uncomfortable – if not downright scary to all involved – and is typically championed by the under-served or those facing an uncomfortable reality). What is right for your organization will depend on your specific circumstances – there will be no one-size-fits-all model here. In addition, managers will need to look at changes as more of an ongoing process than a specific fix – due to the rate of change we have already discussed.

In Chapter 1, we outlined some of the issues that have disrupted the macro environment and facilitated a need for change. In the next two chapters, we will explore the antecedents or prerequisites for the changes we will need to make at the micro level to address the new environmental changes. Some of these changes will be on the organization itself, but others will fall squarely on the employees.

Values/Goals/OKRs to Reciprocal Responsibility

I can still remember a conversation I had with my grandparents when I was a young child. It was probably in the late 1960s or early 1970s. We were talking about how computers were beginning to change everything. I can remember them saying, "Tommy boy you should learn how to operate a punch card machine. Computers are the future. If you learn punch cards, you'll have a job for life!" For those readers who were born from the mid-1970s on, punch cards were a way to store computer data on a card stock paper. Of course, if that had been my career choice I would have been in a bad way. You might forgive my grandparents for their assumption. They didn't really understand computers, so not understanding that digital storage (hard disks and now solid-state storage) would certainly replace punch cards is understandable. This, however, might be a parable to help to illustrate the limits of our goal setting.

This is exactly the problem that is discussed by Theodore Levitt in his seminal article "Marketing Myopia." One of the things that Levitt points out in this article is that you have to understand what business you are in. The CEO of a railroad company might mistakenly believe that he is in the railroad business, but he is not – he is in the transportation business. Most people don't care very much how they get from place to place, so long as the selected method of transportation has some advantage over the alternatives.

Our goals should be set on the understanding that we should be creating value for the customer in whatever we choose to pursue. Value creation is dependent on the needs of the customer, not our needs, or the product we want to produce. Also, what constitutes value will likely change over time – often in ways we don't expect. Many people did not see the demise of the punch card in advance, nor did many early 20th-century railroad executives see the how their product (railroads) would be replaced by alternative methods of transportation.

Conventional business school teaching would suggest that organizations need values, which in combination with the needs of the market can lead to specific goals, which then can be put into action through the use of objectives and key results (OKRs). This process can be used by individuals, teams, departments, or even organizations. However, since 94% of Americans work on a team of some type at work, the focus here will be on teams, departments, and organizations. High-performing organizations need to find rallying points, where employees can become part of something bigger than themselves. These must be clearly defined, articulated, and supported by the actions of the organization's leadership. Collier (2018) points out that goals should help us to move beyond the self-interest, or even altruism, to a state of "belonging, obligation, and purposive action" (p. 48). Collier sees the foundation of successful companies to be a culture of reciprocal responsibility, whereby the employees feel a responsibility to care for the firm, and the firm for the employees. He uses as an antithetical example the Wall Street financial firms that contributed the global financial crisis in 2008/09. These firms had a primary stated purpose of making money – which employees took to mean to make money for themselves. This of course led to an agency problem – employees often made decisions that helped them to achieve their personal short-term goals, but which hurt the company and its customers in the long run. These broken cultures affected more than just the companies and employees – in this case they led to a global crisis. To ensure success for the company, community, and stakeholders (anyone affected by the firm's actions), values and goals should be strongly focused on developing this culture of supporting the community and its stakeholders over time.

Even though over 80% of firms have published their core values on their websites, there is significant overlap in the list from one company to another. For example, 65% of firms stated that *integrity* is a core value, including Wells Fargo, Volkswagen, and Barclay's, all of whom have suffered recent ethical scandals (Sull et al., 2020). So, it seems that for these stated values to be translated into a unique and effective culture, it takes more than just posting them on the company website. It takes demonstrated commitment to live the values. It takes goals that are instructive and can act as a guidepost when day-in and day-out decisions have to be made. And there need to be clear measures of progress that can be reviewed over time, while keeping the goals and the current environment in context. This is where OKRs come in.

OKRs have been attributed to Andy Grove, the former CEO of Intel. However, you would be hard pressed to find a person who has done more to have the concept broadly adopted than John Doerr of the US venture capital firm Kleiner Perkins. Doerr outlined the structure of OKRs and provided a number of examples of their success in his book *Measure What Matters* (Doerr & Page, 2018). What is wonderful about the OKR framework is both its simplicity and its effectiveness. However, like any business theory or framework (e.g., SWOT, PESTEL, Balanced Scorecard) there are good implementations and poor implementations – so this is not a magic bullet. But if it is properly used it can have a significant effect on the effectiveness of your success in reaching your organizational goals.

The OKR framework can be implemented as a single structure – let's say for the organization – or as a nested system with, for example, goals for organizations, departments, and individuals. In either case the structure is the same:

- *Objectives*: Long-range objectives that should inspire the participants to stretch. If they are not a little intimidating, you aren't doing them right. Examples might include President John F. Kennedy committing the US to go to the moon, or Google (an OKR user) as a start-up aspiring to be the largest search engine in the US.
- *Key results*: The milestones along the way that can be achieved in a specific period of time – typically the next quarter or the next year. Examples would include increase sales by 15%, or sign a contract with a major distributor in the northeast.
- *Initiatives*: The tactical activities and goals that will help you to meet your key results. Examples would include making 50 new prospects calls per week, or execute three new PPC marketing campaigns that result in 100 conversions each.

Unlike some earlier execution frameworks such as Management by Objectives (MBO) which were mostly between a manager and an employee, OKRs are public documents. This public affirmation of company, departmental, and personal drives culture. The OKRs and their completion status are shared with the entire team, the idea being that it allows for teammates to both support each other and see how their efforts are supporting larger goals. In addition, it provides the clarity necessary to allow for high levels of autonomous decision-making, alignment, and engagement.

Chapter 2 Takeaways

At the beginning of the chapter, we introduced the concept of social technology, and explained that an organizational structure is a technology to make the most of our organizational resources. This would, of course, include physical resources, intellectual capital, and most importantly human capital.

How we engage with our people will require foundational changes on the behalf of both the organization and the individual. There needs to be a willingness to change our culture, our reporting structures, and the level of freedom we give our team members. In giving more freedom we will need to be more transparent, and tolerant of failure.

We introduced the concept here that the firm is a network of individuals. The employment status of these individuals will likely be on a spectrum (one we will describe later in this book as a network) from direct employees, consultants, contractors, partners, suppliers, and others.

Our communications rules, habits, and protocols will need to change to accommodate the changes in information flow. To increase engagement, we will need strategies that look to foster reciprocal responsibility between the organization, employees, and key partners. And members of the firm will need to step up and take on more responsibility for their day-to-day actions, as well as their own career development.

References

Blank, A. M. (2020). *Good Company* (illustrated ed.). William Morrow.

Borghans, L., Golsteyn, B. H. H., Heckman, J. J., & Humphries, J. E. (2016). What Grades and Achievement Tests Measure. *Proceedings of the National Academy of Sciences*, 113(47), 13354–13359. https://doi.org/10.1073/pnas.1601135113.

Chassagnon, V. (2014). Toward a Social Ontology of the Firm: Reconstitution, Organizing Entity, Institution, Social Emergence and Power. *Journal of Business Ethics*, 124(2), 197–208. https://doi.org/10.1007/s10551-013-1849-1.

Choudhury, S., & Mohanty, M. K. (2019). Drivers of Employee Engagement: A Chronological Literature Review Excluding India. *Journal of Strategic Human Resource Management; New Delhi*, 8(1), 32–46.

Coase, R. H. (1937). The Nature of the Firm. *Economica*, 4(16), 386–405. https://doi.org/10.2307/2626876.

Collier, P. (2018). *The Future of Capitalism: Facing the New Anxieties* (1st ed.). Harper.

Doerr, J., & Page, L. (2018). *Measure What Matters: How Google, Bono, and the Gates Foundation Rock the World with OKRs* (illustrated ed.). Portfolio.

Duckworth, A. (2016). *Grit: The Power of Passion and Perseverance*. Collins.

Dweck, C. S. (2006). *Mindset: The New Psychology of Success*. Random House.

Gallup (2020, December 11). *7 Gallup Workplace Insights: What We Learned in 2020*. https://www.gallup.com/workplace/327518/gallup-workplace-insights-learned-2020.aspx.

Gore (2023). *Our Story*. https://www.gore.com/about/the-gore-story.

Hamel, G., & Zanini, M. (2020). *Humanocracy: Creating Organizations as Amazing as the People Inside Them*. Harvard Business Review Press.

Hsieh, T. (2010). *Delivering Happiness: A Path to Profits, Passion, and Purpose* (1st ed.). Business Plus.

Ibarra, H. (2018). *Satya Nadella at Microsoft: Instilling a Growth Mindset*. Harvard Business Publishing, 22.

Lai, L. (2017, June 27). Motivating Employees Is Not About Carrots or Sticks. *Harvard Business Review*. https://hbr.org/2017/06/motivating-employees-is-not-about-carrots-or-sticks.

McKinsey and Company (2022, February 25). *Look Inward, Not Outward*. https://www.mckinsey.com/featured-insights/coronavirus-leading-through-the-crisis/charting-the-path-to-the-next-normal/the-latest-word-in-industrial-efficiency.

Narayanan, S. (2020, September 16). Connecting the Dots in an Uncertain World. *Strategy+business*. https://www.strategy-business.com/article/Connecting-the-dots-in-an-uncertain-world?gko=6cec0.

PBS (2019, April 16). *David Brooks on Emerging From Loneliness to Find "Moral Renewal."* https://www.youtube.com/watch?v=SWqIn4JeLDo.

Pink, D. (2009). *Drive: The Surprising Truth About What Motivates Us*. Riverhead Books.

Ro, C. (2019, October 9). Dunbar's Number: Why We Can Only Maintain 150 Relationships. British Broadcasting Company. https://www.bbc.com/future/article/20191001-dunbars-number-why-we-can-only-maintain-150-relationships.

Schor, J. B. (2020). *After the Gig: How the Sharing Economy Got Hijacked and How to Win It Back* (1st ed.). University of California Press.

Smet, A. D., Gagnon, C., & Mygatt, E. (2021). *Organizing for the Future: Nine Keys to Becoming a Future-Ready Company*. McKinsey and Company, 14.

Sull, D., Turconi, S., & Sull, C. (2020, July 21). When It Comes to Culture, Does Your Company Walk the Talk? *MIT Sloan Management Review*. https://sloanreview.mit.edu/article/when-it-comes-to-culture-does-your-company-walk-the-talk/.

Chapter 3

Culture

Culture

I was out of school about 10 years and had developed a reasonably successful career in marketing communications within the technology industry. At the time I was working for a company that specialized in
technology road shows. When a large technology company wanted to
create a buzz around a new, or a relaunched product, we would create
events for both customers and prospective customers, in dozens of hotel
ballrooms in large cities around the globe. We would fill the ballroom
with between 200 and 500 people and do live demonstrations highlighting
how our patron's products were far superior to the current market solutions, and then we would help our patrons to track their investment in the
events (the level of resulting sales).

I led a team that would execute the work in the field, from design of the
content, to execution of the event, to follow-up with the attendees and the
customer. That meant that I spent two to three days a week on the road,
about 40 weeks a year. I was doing this while starting a family. My first
two children were born before my hectic travel schedule; however, I was
deep into the road warrior role when we were expecting our third child.
As my wife's due date approached, I told my boss (the firm's owner) that
due to my family commitments I would have to be close to home for a
period before and after the due date. This, of course, would be a fluid
period since babies come on their own schedule, and if there were any
complications I would have to be there for my wife and child.

My boss generally demonstrated a great deal of respect for the needs of
the individual employee, but my intentions were creating a problem for
him. Our largest client had been very pleased with my work on several
past projects and had specifically asked for me to handle a major
upcoming project – and the project required extensive travel from the US
to Europe. Attempting to find a way to make the deal work, my boss
offered to provide me with tickets to travel on Concord (a former super-
sonic jet that could fly from New York to Paris in about three hours). His

DOI: 10.4324/9781032646657-3

justification was that if the baby started to come, I could be home in time. When I rejected that idea, he had one of the other senior managers talk to me. This other manager had joined the firm after a multi-decade-long career with a very large, very traditional, technology company. In his world family commitments were subordinate to those of the firm. I can still remember the shocked and bewildered look on his face when I explained to him my rationale. I informed him that I had been there for the birth of my other two children, and I did not want this child to feel any less important to me. His retort was "but this is your job." My response was "that maybe so, but I can find another job – it's a whole lot harder and more painful to find another family."

So why this story? This story speaks to context and culture. The more traditional senior manager in my story had grown up in a very different time and place (context), and culture. The way he viewed the world and his responsibilities was very different to mine. However, so too was that of the boss, but he was attempting to bridge the gap in the changing context. Certainly, my story is not unique; stories like this happen all the time when there are changes in context or priorities – and they change all the time. So, if you are wondering how the story ends, yes, I did keep my job, and I was there for the birth of my daughter, and never doubted that I made the right decision for the context I found myself in.

What Is Culture?

In its broadest sense culture affects almost all our daily decisions – large and small. It affects the clothes we wear, what we eat, who we marry, the people we associate with, what we believe our available options are in most situations ... even our very process of thinking.

In his book *Thinking Fast Thinking Slow* Danila Kahneman (2011) divided thinking into two categories: System 1 and System 2. System 1 was based on rules of thumb – what Kahneman calls heuristics. Heuristics are used to make decisions quickly without a lot of thought, and this is how most of our day-to-day decisions are made. System 2 is mentally effortful and demanding thought, whereby we consciously go through all the options and carefully consider them without bias. Very few of our decisions are made this way because in most cases it is too time-consuming and effortful.

Kahneman is careful to point out that System 2 is cumbersome, often overkill, but sometimes necessary for the best results. In his book he suggests that many decisions can be made more efficiently with System 1 using heuristics. One example he used was a man dressing himself in a three-piece suit. If you were to use System 2 and consider all the options carefully (should you put the right sock on first or the shirt, or if you choose the right sock, what should go on next, the left sock or the pants?), mathematically the possible combinations of clothing expand geometrically with each item of clothing. It could literally take years to get dressed. So, it is often better to make rote decisions of little consequence in System 1.

Culture assists us in making these daily decisions. It helps us to understand which are acceptable options and which are not. Where culture is even more important is in the net effect of all these daily decisions in aggregate. If these daily decisions are focused in a particular direction, they can have a cumulative effect on the organizational effectiveness.

Every culture will have pluses, minuses, and limitations, and by their very nature cultures are only effective in a specific time, place, social, and business environment. Therefore, cultures need to evolve in order to stay relevant. This evolution is often driven by observation. I recently came across an interview that *New York Times* columnist David Brooks gave to PBS NewsHour. In it Brooks described cultural change as an event where "a small group of people find a better way to live and the rest of us copy them" (PBS NewsHour, 2019).

In *The Future of Capitalism*, Paul Collier (2018) points to culture as the defining attribute in building success within a group of people – be that a family, a firm, or a nation. Culture is an outgrowth of shared values, beliefs, shared practices or norms, and collective experiences. It is not formed by rhetoric – it is formed by context, action, and leadership. First, leaders need to communicate what the values of the organization are – but these have to be more than words. They also need to gain agreement from their team that these are the shared values of those expected to live by them. However, values often come across as platitudes unless there is action to back them up. Examples of this can be found in the value statements of companies such as Enron and Theranos which originally claimed that integrity and honesty were part of their core values, only to find themselves later at the center of a scandal of epic proportions. It is when a company or an individual stands up for their values – especially when it is inconvenient – that culture is formed.

Culture as a Process

Since culture is evolutionary it might make sense to attempt to build a process to direct the growth and evolution of the culture, because, if done well, as Peter Drucker (2001) famously quipped, "culture eats strategy for lunch." It can dictate to its members what to do when no one is watching. So, there seems to be general agreement that a strong culture is a really good thing to have. However, it is not something that is wholly codified, there is no cookbook of directions for building a winning culture; instead, it is more a lived experience that managers have to constantly monitor and modify as they go along. Culture is never done.

Drucker also took note of Thomas Jefferson's conclusion that "every generation needs a new revolution," that each generation faces a new crisis often because they have become disenchanted with the solutions of the past, and their appropriateness to solve the problems of the present. However, Drucker recognized that there is a problem with "root and branch" replacement of an existing culture. He saw cultural change as a step-by-step process noting that "changes should be pragmatic rather than dogmatic and modest rather than grandiose – that they promise to keep any society, economy, industry public service or business flexible and self-renewing" (2001, p. 323).

There are a number of reasons why culture is never done; among them are the ideas that the environment is never stable, and our understanding of the environment is incomplete. The great Catholic philosopher Saint Augustine suggested that both the future and the past are unknowable. The future has not happened, and the past is based on memories and incomplete information. Augustine wrote: "The present has, therefore, three dimensions … the present of past things, the present of present things, and the present of future things." Thus, with the present the only real thing the past is gone, and the future has not happened yet. However, he also recognized that our perceptions of the past and the future color our perception of the present. Therefore, we never really have a complete understanding of our past, present, or future – and all of these are affected by our personal bias.

It would seem clear that whatever we decide in terms of the development of our culture will be flawed. The best we can hope for is a solution that is close to correct so we can recognize the misalignment with our present situation and this gives us an opportunity to change it. If we are lucky, we can change it to something that is less wrong, and that we can continue the cycle of being less wrong, closer to the truth, and closer to being even more efficient and effective. All the while we are looking to the future to understand the effects our current decisions will have on our future selves.

Of course, all this requires a great deal of reflection. Ray Dalio (2017) of Bridgewater Associates (one of the world's most successful hedge funds) is an advocate of reflection. Dalio suggests that hedge funds have to be innovative in their thinking if they wish to achieve their goal of constantly outperforming the market. Bridgewater advocates that in order to achieve this you need a culture of extreme candor and transparency. Cultures such as these can lead to some very tough conversations which might leave a few team members feeling bruised and uncomfortable. Dalio's formula for his philosophy is Pain+Reflection = Progress. It is not the pain that moves us forward – it is our ability to clinically assess the situation that inflicted the pain and learn from it. From the outside looking in, this would seem to be valuable advice. On the other hand, it is often hard to be philosophical in the moment, because we are often too concerned with the immediate effect on our jobs, status, or salaries. Or as Upton Sinclair put it, "It is difficult to get a man to understand something when his salary depends upon him not understanding it." However, if we take time to catch our breath after the initial sting of failure, we might discover some valuable lessons from our experiences.

It would seem that the culture of an organization is driven by mission, vision, shared values, leadership, and a constant flow of confirming actions. As employees we need to believe in what the company stands for in both word and action. The leaders need to lead by example and make a concerted effort to engage employees in the mission, vision, and shared values. And the messages need to be regular and consistent.

Leadership is formed when others see your values in action and decide to follow you. So, culture requires the communication of values in action. In an office this often happens simply by sharing physical space. In a virtual world this is still possible, but it often requires much more intentional effort. It is often the result of the right communications infrastructure, training in both communication and leadership, and management practices structured to support a remote team. However, we will cover this in more detail in a later chapter.

Some managers might see soft skills conversations as a waste of time. They are of the belief that a business needs to less sentimental, and more driven by hard numbers. To them I would suggest a look at a study by Boston Consulting Group (BCG). According to BCG (2020), companies that focused on culture were five times more likely to have what they defined as breakthrough performance. Companies that ignored culture had breakthrough performance 17% of the time and companies that focused on culture achieved breakthrough 90% of the time. Furthermore, a study by McKinsey and Company suggests that companies with strong cultures produce three times higher total returns to shareholders (Smet et al., 2021).

The post-COVID-19 pandemic business world has created a number of changes in context. Our environment's attributes that many assumed were fixed have changed – sometimes dramatically – and will continue to evolve significantly. The appropriate culture for our firms will depend on the context in which we find ourselves.

Culture in Context

The factors that can affect company culture are practically endless, and the reality is that your company culture is nested within other broader cultures which include, but are not limited to, city culture, regional culture, national culture, class culture, industry culture, gender culture, ethnic culture – and recognizing this is extremely important. These factors are always at play, but become even more significant as the organization expands, potentially creating a more diverse population which can be affected by a broader set of factors.

Low Context versus High Context

Cultures, in particular national cultures, can be placed on a low to high context scale. In this case context refers to how the culture processes times and communications. Low context cultures tend to be more explicit in their communications and perception of time leaving little room for interpretation; one might say they are more literal in their communications and interpretation of time. High context cultures, on the other hand, are more implicit in their communications and tend to have a more fluid understanding of time. Participants are expected to read between the lines and have more shared experiences for communication to be highly effective.

One does not need to span tremendous distances to see significant changes in levels of context within local cultures. However, a lack of cultural awareness can often lead to unnecessary tension between people from different cultures. For example, Italy and Switzerland share a border but are very different in the level of context in their communication and their processing of time. The Swiss tend to be very low context, and the Italians not as much – particularly when it comes to time. A Swiss person would typically be very literal about the start time of an appointment and consider it rude to be even a few minutes late for an appointment, whereas an Italian person would typically have a little more fluid interpretation of time. Being a little late would not cause anyone to raise an eyebrow. These low and high context differences go beyond national culture. You might experience similar differences between groups. For example, you might find accountants or engineers tending to be more low context, whereas artists or some salespeople might be high context.

However, these changes go far beyond the measurement of time and the effectiveness of communication. In low context business cultures contracts are, more often than not, treated as literal agreements with little room for interpretation. They are the end of the negotiation, which is often not the case in a high context culture. In high context cultures a contract is taken much less literally and can be the beginning of the negotiation. An example of this can be found in the recent agreements between Foxconn (a Taiwanese electronics manufacturer – high context), and the state of Wisconsin (low context), to build a facility in the state. A contract between the state and Foxconn was agreed to in 2017, as of this writing in 2021, the deal has been renegotiated several times. Items from the type of facility to the scope and number of employees have changed several times, and it is currently unclear if a facility will actually be built. However,

believing that they had a contract the state has made significant investments based on what they believed was an agreement. This has led to
some political tension in the state and many believe that it affected the
reelection efforts of Governor Scott Walker who was instrumental in the
original deal between the state and Foxconn.

Parson's Five Relationship Orientations

In attempting to understand culture and context it might be helpful to
think of culture as a portfolio of relationships between people. As such it
would be helpful to understand the nature of those relationships and the
expectations of the participants. In the 1950s Talcot Parsons developed a
categorization system for relationships with five elements (Trompenaars,
1994, pp. 11–12):

Universalism versus particularism: "What is good and right can be defined
and always applies" (universalism), "depending on the circumstances" (particularism). An example of universalism might be found in those organizations which prescribe a step-by-step procedure on exactly how things should
be done and demand no variation, in a manner reminiscent of Fredric W.
Taylor's time and motion studies. Meanwhile, in particularism organizations
there may be general guidelines in place (or not); however, members are
allowed to make decisions based on the situation.

Individualism versus collectivism: Is it more about me (individualism) or
the group (collectivism)? Who is the primary concern of the decision-
maker? Is it themselves or are they more concerned with the organization
as a whole? Western cultures tend to be more about the individual, and
eastern cultures tend to be more about the group.

Neutral versus emotional: "Should the nature of our interactions be
objective and detached, or is expressing emotion acceptable?" (Trompenaars, 1994, p. 11). In Europe, many northern cultures tend to be neutral
or even stoic, whereas many southern cultures are more expressive when it
comes to emotions.

Specific versus diffuse: In a specific relationship the parties abide by the
contract and not much thought is given to personal contact beyond that.
In a diffuse relationship the contract elements are only part of the relationship – there is a personal element too. In a diffuse culture relationship
building and maintenance are an important element of business success.

Achievement versus ascription: Status is based on what you accomplished (achievement) rather than your social status or group affiliation
(ascription). So, in an achievement culture there will be questions about
what you have accomplished, whereas in an ascription culture it will be
about which school you attended, where you live, and who your family is.

In applying this framework to our own culture, we may consider where
our culture sits on the spectrum within each orientation in the past, where

we might have identified changes over time, or the trends that we see developing. This might help us to understand how our management style and initiatives will fare as our landscape changes.

Layers of Culture

A culture has several layers. There is an observable outer layer – the explicit culture – comprising "language, food, buildings, houses, monuments, agriculture, shrines, markets, fashions, and art. They are symbols of a deeper level of culture" (Trompenaars, 1994). The middle layer consists of norms and values. Norms lead to "this is how I normally should behave," while values lead to "this is how I aspire or desire to behave." The final layer is the core. If you come from a culture of abundance, your world view will be different from that of someone who comes from an environment where people struggle to survive. In history we often see this creating tension between generations, specifically when one generation may have lived through a particularly difficult period in history, only to have to watch future generations, who from their perspective, lack appreciation for their good fortune.

In addition to these layers, we find within a culture that there are several types of cultural layers. Any distinct group of people can develop a culture specific to that group. We could start at a national level of national culture. But within large nations there are regional cultures. For example, the northeastern US has a very different culture than the southeastern US. Even within regions you can find different cultures within subregions, states, counties, or cities. South Florida has a very different culture to that of Central Florida, and Central Florida to that of North Florida. Beyond national and regional cultures, there can be cultures within industries or professions, within organizations, within teams, or even within clubs, churches, or families.

Managers also have to understand that there can be times when these cultures come in conflict with each other. Therefore, constant monitoring and adjustments are necessary to keep a culture functioning effectively.

Mapping Cultural Differences

Beyond low and high context there are a number of other metrics that researchers have identified as contributing to our ability to document the differences between cultures. Although there are many who have done significant work in this process of mapping cultural differences, two researchers who stand out are Geert Hofstede, of Maastricht University in the Netherlands, and Erin Meyer, of the INSEAD Business School in Paris, France. Both have discovered significant measurable differences between national cultures that can be identified and mapped.

Hofstede's work identified six different dimensions of a culture that could be measured, and then mapped the cultures of over 50 different national cultures. Those attributes are:

- *Power distance*: This dimension measures the level of acceptance there is for special privilege based on rank, class differences, or hierarchy.
- *Individualism versus collectivism*: This dimension measures the tendency toward self-focus or focus on loyalty to the group
- *Masculinity versus femininity*: This is described by Hofstede as "The Masculinity side of this dimension represents a preference in society for achievement, heroism, assertiveness, and material rewards for success. Society at large is more competitive. Its opposite, Femininity, stands for a preference for cooperation, modesty, caring for the weak and quality of life. Society at large is more consensus-oriented" (Hofstede Insights, 2023).
- *Uncertainty avoidance*: The level of comfort the society has with ambiguity and the willingness to accept risk.

In a similar way Erin Meyer (2014) created a culture map that includes eight different parameters:

- *Communication*: Is the culture more low context (explicit) or high context (include implied content)?
- *Evaluating*: Is negative feedback given directly or indirectly?
- *Persuading*: Principles-first (deductive reasoning) versus application-first (inductive reasoning).
- *Leading*: Egalitarian (low power distance) versus hierarchical (high power distance).
- *Deciding*: Consensual versus top-down decision-making processes.
- *Trusting*: Task-based versus relationship-based.
- *Disagreeing*: Confrontational versus avoids confrontation.
- *Scheduling*: Linear-time versus flexible-time.

Both of these models are effective in helping managers to develop insight into their particular culture, and to the relative differences between cultures. We tend to think of our culture as normal, and any change from our culture to be abnormal. This holds true with all levels of culture national, regional, industry, organization, team, and family. What we see when comparing cultures on either the Hofstede or Myer metrics is that they have their own unique footprint – and the differences in cultures are often where tensions develop. It is also important to remember that we are all individuals, and even though we have cultural biases we do have our own personalities and have some level of free will in our decision-making processes.

It is also important to look at the relative differences within a culture. If there are significant levels of hierarchy within the culture, how people process the cultural expectations may be very different. In her book Meyer relates the story of the China's King Kong Rong (153 CE to 208 CE) who when asked as a four-year-old child which pear he wanted, a smaller one or a larger one, said that he wanted the smaller pear and that the larger pear should be given to his older brother. Kong Rong made this decision based on his relative position in the family. In traditional Chinese families it is common to refer to each other, not by name, but by family rank: older brother, younger brother, second sister, third brother, and so on. Thus, family rank is always apparent.

Culture Is a Living Thing

As an organization moves from meeting in an office every day to hybrid or remote work, there will likely be a significant change in the culture. What is expected, what is acceptable, will change. Culture is an autopoietic system, meaning it is a living system that develops and changes on its own – adapting to the environment and the inputs provided by the organization. Also, as a living thing, as the environment and other inputs change over time, so too will the culture – and not always in ways we might have planned or are even happy with. However, you can influence culture by proposing shared values, providing infrastructure, and reinforcing preferred behaviors, but you cannot dictate culture. In other words – you need to walk the talk – you cannot just dictate what you want your culture to be. Given the current business environment's tendency toward change, there must be a cultural bias to action, change, and a tolerance of *good failure.*

As mentioned in Chapter 1, Hamel and Zanini (2020) point out that typically people are much more open to change than organizations. Organizations gravitate toward stability and predictability; however, this requires a stable environment in which to operate. In environments of significant change, over time organizations that fail to adapt will often see a cultural entropy as their cultures become less relevant to the environment and less effective in generating the results they desire. Just as bad as not adapting is inattention to culture. If managers don't concisely attempt to direct culture, and make culture fit a significant part of the hiring process, the organization's culture will often take an unexpected turn for the worse. An example that comes to mind are the challenges faced by Tony Hsieh (2010), the venture capitalist and entrepreneur who made Zappos what it is today. Hsieh sold his first company (LinkExchange) because he hired too quickly and ended up with all the wrong people. He hated going to work at his own company and saw no way to fix it. You can't expect the right culture to just happen – it takes focused attention and effort.

As employees shift to some level of remote work, the need for increased levels of autonomy and responsibility are critical. As this happens there will be situations where the decisions will prove to be poor ones and these employees will encounter situations where they fail. This can be a test of the organization's culture. Strong cultures often delineate between good failures and bad failures. You might also ask what is a *good failure*? In many cultures failure is something to avoid at all costs, while in others it is seen as being part of the creative process – a reality that if handled well is part of the pathway to success. Innovation and progress are not linear or efficient. It is often a messy process and involves trial and error.

We typically don't have all the data necessary for a complete analysis of a situation before a decision needs to be made. We often don't even know all the critical factors necessary for our success. So, we can never completely insulate ourselves from failure. In addition, the more dynamic the market and the faster we move to keep up with it, the higher the probability of failure. However, if we fail while following a reasonable process, taking reasonable risks, protecting the downside, and positioning ourselves at a minimum to learn something. In such a case, a failure may not sting as much and might be valuable. Either way, the bias toward action and agility is becoming increasingly necessary.

Cultural Audit

As stated above cultures are living things that move, change, grow, and degrade over time. Therefore, any assessment of culture is historic and static. They can give you insight into either the way the company was or is at this moment, but they can't provide a definitive answer on where the culture will be at some point in the future. Because of this cultural audits are a practice that the company should undertake on a regular basis in order to stay on top of their cultural growth or decline.

According to Cameron and Quinn (2006), when assessing a culture there are several general areas of concern: dominate characteristics, organizational leadership style, management style, factors that hold the organization together (organizational glue), strategic focus, and the criteria for success. In the 1990s Denison attempted to assess culture on four criteria: mission, adaptability, involvement, and consistency (Denison et al., 2012). And others still have suggested that a cultural audit should look at how tasks are accomplished, how employees relate to each other, how new ideas are adopted and spread within the organization, how knowledge is captured and shared, how barriers are removed, the communications process, and the development of leaders (Hon, 2002).

It would seem that culture is one of those things that is extremely hard to define. However, many managers still feel that, as Supreme Court Justice Potter Stewart said of pornography in 1964, "I know it when I see it."

Because of all of this, and the fact that we are dealing with something that is in the collective minds of the member of our organization, the measurement of these criteria can be somewhat subjective, so the study methodology is a critical factor in the study's success.

Within larger organizations, this might be done by employee surveys, interviews (both employee and management), observations, and tracking of key digital activities. They are often undertaken by outside consulting firms, or highly trained members of the company's human resources team. Within smaller organizations the process could be done with the same tools as above, but it often relies on interviews and team meetings.

One might also consider having both the perspective of a team from across the organization, as well as outside professionals when assessing the results of the assessment, and the implications for the organization.

Remote Culture

Among the prevailing theories of culture is that to grow and maintain an organizational culture you need to be in the same physical location. You need to observe those around you to understand what the group sees as acceptable behavior, and what they do not. These observations also serve to reinforce the values and beliefs of those who are members of the culture and strengthen the ties between individuals. This is a powerful argument. This is how mankind has developed culture over millennia.

The problem is that the data that has been collected since the beginning of the COVID-19 pandemic appears if not to refute this dogma, at least to bring it into question. In January 2021 Gartner published a study of over 5,000 remote workers that indicated that organizational culture did not suffer during the pandemic. In fact, 76% said that it improved, 20% suggested that it got a little worse, and only 4% suggested that it got a lot worse (Gartner Group, 2021).

In 2022 MIT mirrored many of the same findings in a study it published. Although the study indicated marked differences between industries and generations, most workers felt that their organizational cultures improved once they had switched to remote work. Later in the book we will delve deeper into the theories around proximity, and both remote and hybrid work (MIT SMR Connections, 2022).

Additionally, this study showed that about half of all remote workers believed that camaraderie had improved, about 40% believed that it stayed the same, while just 9% believed that it had worsened. This was even true of the workers who had changed jobs during the pandemic. Even though they did not have relationships that were formed before their teams went remote, the majority felt that they were able to build strong relationships with their teams.

The MIT team was quick to point out that many companies had in the past allowed "stealth hybrid" work. Even though there was no formal hybrid work program in place, many employees were already working from home at least occasionally, if not regularly. Therefore, many firms have slowly been building competency in hybrid culture over time.

In a study published by Microsoft in March 2021, the company reviewed data collected from customers using Outlook and Teams to uncover some disturbing trends, namely that employees were working to the point of exhaustion, and that they were losing connections outside their immediate teams.

Much to the surprise of some traditional managers, without the distractions of the office employees were working harder, longer, and more productively. The unfortunate consequence of these new habits is that it has led some analysts to worry about employee burnout, and subsequently employee retention.

There are also concerns about the health of employee networks. According to the Microsoft data, the volume and regularity of our communications with our teams has been very healthy throughout the pandemic; however, there has been a significant drop in our connections with other employees outside of our teams. Of course, this brings with it a host of issues that have been discussed since Mark Granovetter introduced the concept of weak ties back in 1973. Granovetter suggested that our close friends and the people we work with closely represent "close ties." We know them well and share a common pool of information. However, we also have "weak ties" with people who are acquaintances but with whom we don't really socialize nor do we have a strong working relationship with them. Granovetter suggested that you are more likely to find a new job, or discover a new idea, based on information provided by weak ties. So, as employee networks lose richness, they may stay around longer, but they could very well suffer in productivity and innovation.

Another great fear is that employees are less likely to report having a best friend at work. Having personal relationships at work increases employee satisfaction, increases employees' connection to the firm, and decreases the likelihood of employees leaving the firm. This is not to say that it is impossible to develop such relationships; it does, however, often require a more deliberate process.

As with any human endeavor, there are few absolutes when it comes to culture. There are several firms that seem to be doing well or even thriving in the remote environment, while others struggle. Many that have been held up as exemplars have come from the technology industry: Automatic (developers of many web-based products including Word-Press), Adobe (developer of graphics and video editing software), and GitHub (builder of software development tools and platforms; it is owned by Microsoft).

As of March 2022 Automatic had over 1,930 employees, and GitHub over 2,500; both are proudly 100% remote, and both have been held up by pundits as company cultures to emulate. Both also focus on extreme flexibility in their culture – working where you want, how you want, and when you want. This creates the need for a very results-oriented culture, and one that is focused on autonomy and personal responsibility.

Adobe does still have offices; however, it has developed a digital-first culture. The company is focused on ensuring that remote workers are on an equal footing with employees who wish to work in an office. It recognizes that not all work is the same, nor are all workers. Therefore, it has focused on creating a flexible environment that will enable employees to work in the way they see best (Chen, 2021).

Drivers of Cultural Change

There are an endless number of factors that go into the development of organizational culture; however, a significant number fall under the categories of respect and ethics. This is followed by leadership and environment (often as a result of the aforementioned variables). All of this should be grounded in purpose.

Respect

According to studies published by the MIT Sloan School of Management, respect is possibly the single largest prediction of successful culture (Kotter et al., 2021). Respect takes many forms: respect for the individual (as I described in my opening story), respect for the customer, respect for partners, respect for government authorities. Talking about respect is one thing, but the real cultural changes happen when respect is demonstrated in action. Respect is demonstrated in how people are treated in day-to-day interactions. Respect can be demonstrated in the diversity of the people who are hired, and in who gets promoted. This diversity goes beyond the typical definition used in diversity, equity, and inclusion initiatives to include a true tolerance for differences in viewpoint and perspectives.

Psychological Safety

What often makes a team efficient may in fact make it less effective. People who share similar background, norms of behavior, attitudes, worldviews, values, and beliefs often find it easy to come to agreement on work priorities, goals, and speed of work. This, however, leads to a situation where assumptions are not challenged, broader perspectives are not included, and innovation and effectiveness suffers.

When employees feel respected, and included, it often leads to a feeling of psychological safety. This feeling of safety often results in higher productivity and innovation. Employees spend less time focused on non-productive activities and more on relationship building and productive work. They are also more likely to challenge the status quo and provide more innovative ideas and solutions.

Ethics

As with respect ethics drive culture when the ethical values are demonstrated in the actions that are taken by people at all levels of the organization. It is important to remember that simply making an aspirational statement about ethics or including it in the company's list of core values is not enough. Volkswagen and Wells Fargo both listed ethics and integrity as a core value, and both have undergone major ethical scandals in recent years.

Leadership

Leaders live the core values and drive engagement by embodying the culture they wish team members to emulate. They treat employees with respect for who they are, and for the contributions they have made and can make.

The source of cultural leadership is more often the organization's top leadership (the C-suite), which is often far more important than the frontline managers. They set the tone for what is acceptable and tolerated (Sull & Sull, 2021).

Purpose

In his book *Drive*, Dan Pink (2009) outlines that one of the major factors that gets employees excited and drives them to higher levels of success is a clear and inspirational purpose. They have to believe that they can change the world, if only in a small way. This again is a function of management and the vision that is provided and pursued within the organization.

Engagement

We have discussed the concept of engagement in depth in Chapter 2, so we have a theoretical framework for understanding its importance. It should be noted here that engagement is often fostered by the other factors listed in this section. In some ways it is an outcome as much as a driver itself.

Growth Mindset/Learning Environment

In Chapter 2 we also introduced the idea of a *growth mindset*. If we have developed this in our organizations, both within leadership and employees, we create a belief in the process of change and a willingness to take a risk or make an effort.

Recognition

Small acts of recognition can go a long way. They help to build a culture of respect, psychological safety, and ethics. One might even strive to make recognition a habit. It could be integrated into meetings where it is doled out by management or implemented as a peer-based program of acknowledgement. Either way it can be a powerful contributor by creating a way to reinforce the values and beliefs that an organization wishes to foster.

Cultural Strategies

It should be clear from this chapter that culture has many facets, is constantly shifting, and is very difficult to shape or drive. However, it is also a critical factor in long-term success, so even though it is hard companies need to be aware of its direction, effect on its effectiveness, and appropriateness for the situation it finds itself in.

A complete strategy guide would require more space and resources than we currently have allowed ourselves here; however, listed below are a few things managers might consider:

Connecting Culture to Outcomes

Assess the current culture and carefully consider the attributes you can measure and how they might be affecting your organizational effectiveness. What elements of your culture are helping, and what parts are hurting your desired outcomes?

Do Not Focus on Emulating "Great" Cultures

It might be effective to research what you consider great cultures in an attempt to understand why they are or were great. However, it is important to remember that culture is all about context. Cultures only work effectively in specific environments – and no two companies are the same – and if they are not, their cultures should not be the same.

Culture Is Led – It Does Not Happen by Edict

Don't be surprised if your team nods in agreement when you read out your value statement, only to violate those values at the very next opportunity. Stating the values is one thing, living the values, especially when it is hard, is another. In other words, your values need to be more than an aspiration. Your actions will speak louder than words, and your actions can lead to a change.

Encouraging Behavioral Change

We need to create what is known as a *burning platform* – specifically this means that we need to encourage immediate change. Our team must understand the current situation, connect their actions to results, and understand what the likely outcomes are of those actions – and what will likely happen if we don't change. Building this platform in the minds of the team is the job of team leadership. Leadership must also, with input from the team, provide an alternative vision, measure, and reward actions toward that vision, and provide a road map for the actions necessary to reach the vision (Hollister et al., 2021).

Chapter 3 Takeaways

Although it is difficult to measure culture, if you spend enough time with any group of people and observe how they make daily decisions and interact with each other, the group culture becomes obvious.

Those companies that focus resources and effort on culture, as a group, tend to significantly outperform the market. One of the reasons for this is that culture helps employees to understand the range of viable options and make the right decisions when they are not being closely monitored.

Culture is a living thing and should change and adapt over time to meet the needs of the organization and the needs of the environment. When beginning the process of creating an organizational culture leaders must develop a list of shared values that the group stands for and receive agreement and commitment from the group members. However, it is built not only on shared values, but also on tacit understandings, observed actions, and lived experiences. So, culture requires the regular communication of values in action, and in context. Most importantly, culture is more affected by actions than words – leaders must demonstrate the culture and their vision of what they want the culture to be through their actions.

Culture is nested in, but not limited to, city culture, regional culture, national culture, class culture, industry culture, gender culture, and ethnic culture. Leaders and managers need a high level of cultural awareness that will help them to navigate the effect of culture on management and leadership efforts.

To help managers to navigate these issues they should review maps of the national cultures involved, cultural drives, and develop a cultural audit to understand their current situation, and how that might affect their plans and ongoing initiatives.

References

Boston Consulting Group (2020, November 4). *How to Drive a Digital Transformation: Culture Is Key*. https://www.bcg.com/capabilities/digital-technology-data/digital-transformation/overview.

Bresman, H., & Edmondson, A. C. (2022). Research: To Excel, Diverse Teams Need Psychological Safety. *Harvard Business Review*, 9.

Cameron, K. S., & Quinn, R. E. (2006). *Diagnosing and Changing Organizational Culture: Based on the Competing Values Framework* (Rev. ed.). Jossey-Bass.

Chen, G. (2021, June 24). *The Future of Work at Adobe*. Adobe Blog. https://blog.adobe.com/en/publish/2021/06/24/future-of-work-adobe.

Collier, P. (2018). *The Future of Capitalism: Facing the New Anxieties* (1st ed.). Harper.

Dalio, R. (2017). *Principles: Life and Work* (1st ed.). Simon & Schuster.

Denison, D., Hooijberg, R., Lane, N., & Lief, C. (2012). *Leading Culture Change in Global Organizations: Aligning Culture and Strategy* (1st ed.). Jossey-Bass.

Drucker, P. F. (2001). *The Essential Drucker: In One Volume the Best of Sixty Years of Peter Drucker's Essential Writings on Management* (1st ed.). Harper Business.

Gartner Group (2021, January 7). *No, Hybrid Workforce Models Won't Dilute Your Culture*. https://www.gartner.com/smarterwithgartner/no-hybrid-workforce-models-wont-dilute-your-culture.

Granovetter, M. S. (1973). The Strength of Weak Ties. *American Journal of Sociology*, 78(6), 1360–1380.

Hamel, G., & Zanini, M. (2020). *Humanocracy: Creating Organizations as Amazing as the People Inside Them*. Harvard Business Review Press.

Hofstede Insights (2023). *Intercultural Management*. https://www.hofstede-insights.com/intercultural-management.

Hollister, R., Tecosky, K., Watkins, M., & Wolpert, C. (2021). Why Every Executive Should Be Focusing on Culture Change Now. *MIT Sloan Management Review*, 63(1), 1–6. http://rdas-proxy.mercy.edu:2048/login?url=https://www.proquest.com/scholarly-journals/why-every-executive-should-be-focusing-on-culture/docview/2573029251/se-2?accountid=12387.

Hon, C. M. (2002). *A Quantitative Analysis of Organizational Culture Perception in a Same Industry Merger* [PhD dissertation, Capella University]. https://www.proquest.com/abicomplete/docview/305485545/abstract/A13BDCB6D6444611PQ/2.

Hsieh, T. (2010). *Delivering Happiness: A Path to Profits, Passion, and Purpose* (1st ed.). Business Plus.

Kahneman, D. (2011). *Thinking, Fast and Slow*. Farrar, Straus and Giroux.

Kotter, J., Akhtar, V., & Gupta, G. (2021). Overcoming Obstacles to Successful Culture Change. *MIT Sloan Management Review*, 62(4), 1–3.

Meyer E. (2014). *The Culture Map: Breaking Through the Invisible Boundaries of Global Business*. PublicAffairs.

MIT SMR Connections (2022). *The New World of Work Is Transforming the Old Social Contracts*. Massachusetts Institute of Technology, 19.

PBS NewsHour (2019, April 16). *David Brooks on Emerging From Loneliness to Find "Moral Renewal."* https://www.youtube.com/watch?v=SWqIn4JeLDo.

Pink, D. (2009). *Drive: The Surprising Truth About What Motivates Us*. Riverhead Books.

Smet, A. D., Gagnon, C., & Mygatt, E. (2021). *Organizing for the Future: Nine Keys to Becoming a Future-Ready Company.* McKinsey and Company, 14.

Sull, D., & Sull, C. (2021). 10 Things Your Corporate Culture Needs to Get Right. *MIT Sloan Management Review.* https://sloanreview.mit.edu/article/10-things-your-corporate-culture-needs-to-get-right.

Trompenaars, F. (1994). *Riding the Waves of Culture: Understanding Diversity in Global Business.* Irwin Professional Pub.

Chapter 4

The Changing Organizational Structure

The Good Old Days

Just as we began to believe that the end of the COVID-19 pandemic was in sight, Peggy Noonan (2021) published an editorial in the *Wall Street Journal* titled "The Old New York Won't Come Back." As ominous as the title sounds the piece is less about gloom and doom and more about reevaluating our thinking. Noonan deftly points out that those who are looking to get back to the way things were before the outbreak of the pandemic will likely find themselves sorely disappointed, and it might be decades before we fully realize the significance of the changes we are experiencing. Work and the expectations of what is necessary to be successful at work have dramatically changed. So too have the expectations of our own levels of autonomy, personal responsibility, engagement, and work-life balance.

In preparing this chapter I came across a series of videos that were made by Tom Peters (2009) at the end of the Great Recession. Of course, Peters, who is known for his pithy one-liners had some gems buried in the transcripts. He reminds us that when faced with a crisis we should stand back and reflect on what the current reality is: "You try to forget about the 'good old days' – nostalgia is self-destructive"; and that you should "remind yourself that this is not just something to be 'gotten through'; it is the Final Exam of character." From Peters' point of view, we worked for decades to get our business and governance models right. It is hard to accept that within a blink of an eye they are no longer valid.

The Need for Change

Many of the ideas on how we should structure our organizations and our governance have a new set of criteria and metrics from which they need to be measured. One thing is for sure: many, if not most, of our organizations will need to make major adjustments, and these changes will likely be evolutionary. In other words, this will not be a one-and-done process

DOI: 10.4324/9781032646657-4

whereby we make significant changes, and that those changes are locked in place for a significant time. It is more likely that we will see a period of continuous evolution, a kaizen-like process, whereby we will make continuous small changes through trial and error, and in Bayesian fashion constantly reevaluate our situation, and our decisions, as information becomes available. As John Maynard Keynes suggested, when the facts change, we should change our minds.

So, this chapter will begin to provide frameworks from which to evaluate the effectiveness of our organizational structures, as well as paradigms that we can use to develop new organizational structures which are more in line with our current situations, objectives, and life preferences. Picking up on the advice of Peters, if we are totally honest with ourselves, we will find that the most popular models of organizational structure are broken, or at the very least ill-suited to the current environment. For decades there have been attempts by innovators to change these models and these attempts have been met with significant resistance. Many people continued to process the world with an inadequate paradigm for a number of reasons. Sometimes it has a lot to do with inertia; we are simply blind to the current level of ineffectiveness; it may have been fear of change and how relevant we would be under a new paradigm; and sometimes it is because the participants were invested in the incumbent ideas of how things should work and simply didn't want to let them go. Whatever the reason, organizational change typically proves itself a very hard thing to do.

Far too many organizations have failed to make the necessary changes over a significant period of time, and can trace their current organizational structure back decades, and sometimes even to the industrial revolution. Their current structures were developed in a time when the pace of information, change, and business itself, were much more stable and far slower than they are today; indeed, in a time when the workforce was far less educated, had fewer options, and was less mobile.

This is the environment in which Fredrick W. Taylor developed the concepts of *scientific management*. This model began by breaking down complex tasks to simple repeatable tasks that could be done by low skilled, poorly educated workers. Under Taylor's model there was a very distinct hierarchy. Workers did just that – they worked. They did not think. Thinking was reserved for a limited number of senior managers and carried out by a hierarchy of supervisors who reported back on the progress of the workers. Actual data collection on the process was fairly limited and data was only shared with the hierarchy of managers, many of whom lacked context for the data or the tacit knowledge to understand how best to evaluate it. Taylor's model works well when the tasks are clear, the environment is highly stable over a long period of time, and the organization can benefit from an economy of scale (Wren, 2004). The problem we face in most of our organizations today is that we do not meet the success criteria for a Tayloresque model. Our environments are at best fluid and at worst experience dramatic changes on a regular basis. Therefore, we should be shifting to organizational designs that are designed to operate in such environments, but the process of shifting often comes with its own challenges.

The Purpose of an Organizational Structure

Although it is tempting to assume that the purpose of the firm and the purpose for the structure are the same, they are two very different things. The firm's purpose is to guide the direction and strategy – where the structure is a strategy/set of tactics that help you to achieve the purpose. And given that environments and resources will change over time, it would seem reasonable that we should reevaluate our organizational structures over time to match the environment.

When evaluating our organizational structures, we should use a six-element framework to help to lead our evaluation:

- *Efficiency/effectiveness*: The structure should make efficient and effective use of our resources. Efficiency means that there is only a limited amount of wasted resources, and effectiveness means that the resources are helping to achieve the purpose.
- *Clarity*: There is a clear purpose for each employee. They understand what is expected of them and how their efforts will contribute to their team and organizational success.
- *Control*: The information necessary is captured, and the management and leadership can use that information to effectively manage and lead the organization in achieving their goals. Furthermore, it provides a mechanism to direct the resources to be more efficient.
- *Accountability*: It provides accountability for actions taken or not taken in pursuit of the organizational goals.
- *Incentives*: There are effective incentives for employees to participate, and those incentives produce the outcomes that the organization is looking for.
- *Cohesion*: There should be a gestalt effect (where the whole is greater than the sum of the parts) produced by the structure – one where there is an efficient flow of information, work, and output.

New Social Technology

As we do with manufacturing, transportation, or even personal productivity we can make use of technology or structure in order to improve our organizational effectiveness. In a very real sense, we need to introduce new *social technologies*, and/or new *social products*, into the market – technologies/products designed to deal with our current environment and to meet the new goals and challenges we face today. These technologies and products would be rules, recommended practices, and processes to help us collectively to be more effective.

When considering how to frame the associated models and rules, we might consider reviewing the successful models and rules for the introduction of other types of new products/new technologies that we have used in the past. One thing to keep in mind is that the first generation of a new products often underperforms the incumbent products. Once adopted, the pioneers of the new concept make a number of changes, through trial and error, and several new versions of the new technology or concept begin to appear on the market in short order. The successful versions take hold with innovators and early adopters, but these early adopters are often looking past the current capabilities of the products and toward a vision of what the future might hold when the paradigm is fully developed (Christensen, 1997; Moore & McKenna, 2006).

Things such as social norms, culture, and information technology have huge effects on the potential success of any new organizational model, or social technologies, and its ability to move beyond what early adopters originally experienced. There are patterns of adoption that can be predicted, and many of these predicted patterns can be useful when planning the introduction of a new system. In these models – such as the ones developed by Evert Rogers (2003) and Geoffrey Moore and Regis McKenna (2006) – outline how there is often a tipping point where a critical mass of users has adopted the product and an almost viral adoption cycle begins to drive its success. In the last couple of decades, we have begun to see a number of new organizational models being used by forward-thinking companies. However, the outbreak of the COVID-19 pandemic, and the consequential need to socially distance, has kicked this into overdrive.

Modern Organizational Structures

Below we will explore several organizational structures that have emerged in recent decades that in some way attempt to deal with the shortcomings of many older models of management and leadership. We will attempt to put models in context with the current environment. This is not intended in any way to be a complete taxonomy of modern organizational structures. It is only intended to provide a glimpse of some new and creative models that may help managers to develop a new perspective on the shortcomings of their own organizational model, as well as a glimpse of what is possible with some creative thought and concerted effort.

Lattice

Beginning in the late 1950s Gore & Associates developed an organizational structure that was highly team-focused and almost devoid of direct management authority. The company is based on a flat lattice organization in which teams are self-directed. Self-direction requires potential team leaders to begin by developing a list of projects they wish to work on, and then recruiting a team to help move the ideas forward. Even project funding and employee compensation are driven by teams that primarily consist of employees who choose to be on the teams (Harrington, 2003).

Since its inception some decades ago Gore has expanded into an organization of over 10,000 employees. Through flat lattice organizational structure, and its commitment to keep group sizes (groups are in this case a co-located collection of teams) to a maximum of 150 employees, it has been able to maintain a culture of innovation that is rare in organizations of its size and scope. Deutschman (2004b) contended that the atmosphere at Gore was collegial; there was an energy and excitement about projects; team members were encouraged to contribute; and there was a general conscientiousness that no one wanted to let the team down. Peer pressure and fear of letting the team down supplanted the role of traditional first-line management.

Key elements of this structure include the following:

- *There are no titles*: With rare exception, Gore employees are referred to as associates.
- *There are few and limited job descriptions*: For most employees, their job responsibilities are fluid, and change based on the needs of a project or the business.
- *Leaders emerge in practice.* At Gore you are considered a leader if you call a meeting and people show up. With limited exception leadership is not typically part of a formal role.
- *Team focused*: Employees join teams within the organization by choice and can be part of multiple teams at the same time.
- *Commitment is made by choice*: Employees make their commitments themselves. No other employee and make a commitment for them. Their word is considered their bond and the team often holds them responsible to deliver on their word.

In addition to the team culture, one of Gore's rules encourages all research associates to spend 10% of their time *dabbling with new ideas*. This rule has generated some of Gore's most successful products. The culture has also had a dramatic effect on the quality of the work environment. Gore was listed among the best places to work in the US, the

United Kingdom, Germany, Italy, and the European Union (Deutschman, 2004a). Clearly at some level the governance style translates well across national cultures. However, there may be concern going forward with regards to Gore's expansion into non-European cultures that do not have a history of open discussion, collaborative team debate, or peer leadership. The Gore approach of self-directed teams may be too much of a cultural shock to Asian cultures, such as China, which has a history of more authoritative governance styles.

Open

Jim Whitehurst (2015), the president of IBM and chair of the board of Red Hat, describes his philosophy of organization development and leadership in his book *The Open Organization: Igniting Passion and Performance.* Although some might argue there is not a unique theory within Whitehurst's book it does provide a number of clear examples of the implementation of progressive organizational theories.

Unlike Gore, Whitehurst does see the need for formal leadership positions in large organizations, albeit not in the traditional hierarchical sense. The leadership role is focused not on *command and control* but rather on building, supporting, and moderating a meritocracy. He believes that organizational success is enabled by high levels of employee engagement. Gallup polls suggest that employees in over 60% of organizations today are disengaged and unwilling to make any discretionary effort, and 24% are actively disengaged to the level to the point that they are spreading their disengagement to other employees (Crabtree, 2013). Therefore, even moderate buy-in by employees would lead to a significant competitive advantage.

Whitehurst suggests that you start with a mission. In his view a well-developed and supported mission inspires employees to higher levels of effort and lower levels of turnover. Moreover, if managed properly a well-developed and supported mission might inspire a community of supporters including customers, contributors, third party developers, and channel partners – the essence of the open source model.

Taking the mission, meritocracy, and community concepts a bit further, Whitehurst believes that employees need to have high levels of discretion within a decision framework. He sees them as members of a community that are driven by a cause – not by a transaction mindset – and for the community to work, and the decisions to be sound, there needs to be extreme levels of transparency, as well as high levels of involvement on key decisions by the community at large.

All significant decisions will be transparent and involve input from the community. Many of the day-to-day decisions will be made as close to the work as possible, by the teams who will live with the consequences. Also, as a general rule all those affected by a decision are consulted in the process of making the decision – often publicly. Employees are expected to be engaged with their work and to act as if they are business owners. Within these *open organizations* contribution will be more important than credentials, and your status within the organization will be dependent on the value that you create.

As with Gore, leaders are expected to emerge from the group naturally. They are expected to drive engagement through their actions and examples. If the leader is also a manager, they should spend their time "building, supporting, and moderating the meritocracy" (Whitehurst 2015), without stifling or micromanaging.

Accountability is a core value in open organizations. Both managers and employees are held responsible for their actions. However, the concept of accountability is not outside in – it is inside out. Individuals and teams are encouraged to make accountability part of their process. Part of this accountability process is debate. Debate and even dissension is encouraged. The goal of an open organization is to build a culture where members can have passionate disagreements on principles and still respect the individual. The intent is to carry out these debates in open forums that all community members can see and contribute to – regardless of their status or position within the firm. There is no social or cultural bias against the crossing of boundaries when challenging an idea.

Key elements of this structure would include:

- *Limited management*: There are few managers. These managers focus their time on providing leadership and frameworks for the decision-making process and on making important decisions only after public debate.
- *Meritocracy*: Status within the organization is built on the quality of your ideas and your contribution to the company mission.
- *Autonomy*: Individuals and groups within the organization are allowed to make decisions on how to do their job, but are held accountable for their outcomes – typically in a public forum
- *Core values are freedom, courage, commitment, accountability*: Employees have the freedom to act within a broad decision-making framework. They are encouraged to attempt to find innovative solutions to problems. They should make a personal commitment to their team and personal responsibilities. Furthermore, accountability should be shared by all those involved.

Teal

In one of the most popular articles published by Wharton in 2015, Frederic Laloux (2015) suggests that over the 100,000 years of mankind's anthropological history there has been a number of step changes in how organizations have developed. He has identified five distinct phases of this development. In addition, given the rising level of tension and disillusionment in modern organizations, he believes that we are due for another significant step change in the not-too-distant future. This belief is based on the concept that "human societies, like individuals, don't grow in a linear fashion, but in stages of increasing maturity, consciousness, and complexity" (p. 70).

Laloux defines a series of steps that organizational structures have taken over time. He correlates the scale for his steps to the infrared to ultraviolet light spectrum with red being the oldest structure and teal being the most modern. He recognizes that the amber organizations, the Tayloresque structures, which on his scale are incompatible with the high levels of engagement necessary for knowledge workers to effectively compete, and command and control practices have issues with efficacy as organizations attempt to scale. He suggests that we need to step beyond simple empowerment and egalitarianism. "Efforts to make everyone equal often lead to hidden power struggles, dominant actors who co-opt the system, and organizational gridlock" (p. 73)

Under Laloux's model the most evolved organizational structures are defined as teal. The more enlightened teal organizations have several things that make them distinct from their predecessors: self-management, wholeness, and evolutionary purpose.

Laloux is clear that self-management is not about consensus. It is about allowing people to have "authority within a domain, and the accountability to coordinate with others. Power and control are deeply embedded throughout the organizations, no longer tied to the specific positions of a few top leaders" (p. 74). Of course, this requires training for all involved to understand the frameworks with which these decisions should be made, and how to effectively coordinate their efforts across the organization.

Wholeness is about being authentic. The premise is that *total professionalism* is a facade built on self-censorship and one that inhibits engagement and innovation. With wholeness parts of the employee's *personal life* are exposed to the professional environment. Examples of wholeness include having daycare facilities in the office so that children can join their parents for lunch, or creating a dog-friendly office where one might find several personal pets attending a meeting.

Evolutionary purpose grows out of a mindset where the organization is viewed as a living entity that must adapt and change to meet the environmental needs – or die. Such a mindset encourages participants to move away from a *predict and control* mindset and toward a *sense and respond* approach. For example, companies with older organizational structures might develop a five-year strategy and a detailed one-year plan. However, companies under a teal structure would take more of a farmer's approach.

"A farmer must look far out when deciding which fruit trees to plant or crops to grow. But it makes no sense to plan for a precise date for the harvest" (pp.77–78). They need to sense and adjust their plans based on weather, other environmental variables, and the ability of the organization to adapt to those conditions.

The Helix Organization

The *helix organization* would in many ways seem to be the next generation of the *matrix organization*, only with less conflict between competing managers. As many readers probably remember, in a matrix organization employees typically have two managers – one for their discipline and one from their project or division. In many situations the employee has solid line reporting to one of these managers and dotted line reporting to the other. This model seems to work fine until the two managers have different priorities or provide conflicting directions.

In the case of the helix organization employees still have two managers; however, the responsibilities overlap far less than in the matrix model, and in theory should lead to far less conflict between managers. The two categories of managers under helix are the capabilities manager and the value creation manager:

Capabilities manager: Oversees the hiring, firing, and career development of employees, and does performance evaluation with input from value creation manger. In practice this is someone with deep discipline knowledge in fields such as marketing, engineering, or finance. Their goal is to develop the employees and build their capabilities in the discipline within the organization.
Value creation manager: Sets priorities, day-to-day oversight, and ensures the meeting of business objectives. In practice they fill the role of product manager, line of business manager, division leader, etc.
This structure still requires respect and cooperation between managers. Some priorities may in some way conflict, and there may be a problem with availability between the two; however, this goes a long way to reducing the conflict.

One positive attribute of this model for remote work is that it often creates two communities that the employee becomes part of: the discipline, and the project/line of business. This could broaden the scope of the employee's network, and lead to both greater professional development and innovation.

Team of Teams

McChrystal et al. (2015) outlined the changes to the US military structure in Iraq that were implemented while General McChrystal was heading the US operations there. Through engagements with Al Qaeda in Iraq, he realized that the insurgents had a much more effective structure for the type of conflict being waged in Iraq. Historically the US military has been exceptionally efficient in its operations; however, efficiency and effectiveness are very different. Systems and processes in Iraq had to be rethought in order to increase the level of flexibility and agility.

The hierarchical decision-making structures that are common in the military take time to function. In a highly fluid environment such as Iraq this means that the opportunities to successfully engage the enemy may have passed before approvals were gained. General McChrystal found that it was much more effective to provide information, decision-making frameworks, and specific authority to teams in the field. These teams were allowed and encouraged to make their own decisions. This dramatically increased the speed of decision-making and dramatically increased the effectiveness of the teams.

Information flow and communications became one of the most critical components of the war effort. Workspaces were redesigned to allow for far more collaboration. Large technology investments were made to tie together teams in the field, and support groups around the globe, allowing for ubiquitous sharing of information. All this allowed the level of information sharing to be ratcheted up to an uncomfortable level. Of course, the danger of this level of information sharing is that the information could fall into the wrong hands. However, this risk is often worth the dramatic increase in agility, innovation, and effectiveness.

A culture of transparency and sharing developed. There were still the remnants of a formal military hierarchy; however, the daily operations were accomplished by a highly effective network. At the core were small teams where communications were constant between the team members. In addition, each member assumed responsibility for being the contact point for other teams across the network that were sharing and coordinating efforts in real time. These contact points were often just informal relationships; however, at other times when there was a need to overcome cultural or organizational issues, formal liaisons were embedded for extended periods with other teams in order to build communication and relationship bridges.

The military has had a long history of strong leaders passing on detailed instructions to those under their command – leaving little room for interpretation. However, General McChrystal realized that given the complexity and speed of developments taking place in Iraq, it was far better to develop an environment where leadership and decision-making responsibility could deployed at all levels of his organization. He described it as the difference between being a chess master and a gardener. A chess master looks to position highly compliant pieces in such a way to strategically outthink and outmaneuver their opponent. However, chess pieces don't think, and the game breaks down when the opponent does not play by the same set of rules, whereas a gardener develops an environment in which things take root and grow on their own. In an organization the gardening approach grows smart autonomous assets that make their own moves without the need for the intervention of the chess master.

Therefore, critical elements of General McChrystal's organizational plan included:

- *Autonomy*: Teams were provided with strategy and intent for their operations, and a broad set of parameters to work within.
- *Leaderless teams*: Team members were expected to take the role of leader or follower when and where appropriate. It was expected that these roles would be informal and very fluid.
- *Transparency*: Information about the strategy, resources, and intentions of the organization, teams, and individuals should be communicated freely and often.
- *Values*: Shared values and a common purpose are critical to the success of teams.
- *Complicated versus complex*: The critical difference between complicated and complex problems is that through hard work complicated problems can be predicted. Complex problems are often unpredictable, so success is dependent on adaptability.

Network of Teams

Drawing parallels with the team of teams concept developed by General McChrystal, Smet et al. (2020) published an article for McKinsey and Company describing a *network of teams*. Like the *team of teams* this model was based on the concept of small two pizza teams (a reference to the famous quote by Jeff Bezos of Amazon, who set a rule that no team should be so large that could not feed the team with two pizzas), that operated with a high level of autonomy and actively communicated across the organization to develop a network.

There are a few subtle differences in McKinsey's approach:

- Under the McKinsey model there should be a specific leader, and this leader should communicate with high levels of transparency and authenticity.
- Leaders should actively solicit input from team members; however, he/she should be willing and able to make unpopular decisions for the good of the team and of the organization.

- Although it is implied in *team of teams*, the *network of teams* calls out the need for leaders, along with the goals and objectives, clearly communicate the *commander's intent*.
- The roster of teams is intended to be dynamic. Teams are formed, modified, and dissolved as the needs of the organization changes.
- There should be a bias toward innovation and the development of a learning organization. The intent is to create an organization where information flows freely from teams across the organization to help it to learn and innovate.
- Senior management should take the role of servant leaders enabling the clear functioning of the network.

Holacracy

Conceived by Brian Robertson in the early 2000s Holacracy dramatically increased it profile in 2014 when Tony Hsieh, CEO of Zappos, decided to implement the governance structure (Robertson, 2015). At the core of the structure is an organizational constitution which outlines key beliefs and rules under which the organization operates. In the strictest sense there are no managers. Individuals are self-directed but must keep their circles (or teams) informed of their intentions and actions. The hierarchy (for lack of a better term) is based on circles (or teams) and begins with the development of a general company circle. This general company circle, and every other circle, can have sub-circles. Each circle or sub-circle assumes responsibility for some task or work effort. Members of a circle have defined roles. These roles carry with them a series of responsibilities, decision-making authority within a specific domain, and the accountability for actions taken or not taken.

Individuals can, and often do, hold several different roles – and these roles can be in different circles. One of the key roles would be a link, or representative, to another circle. These links allow for information to flow between the circles. When functioning properly they help circles to coordinate their efforts. There is also a lead link, who acts as a facilitator within the circle and is responsible for the delegation of roles for that circle. However, the lead link is not a manager. Once the role is delegated they have no authority over the team member who has assumed that role, or how the role is executed.

Governance meetings are held in every circle and sub-circle to define the structure and operational rules for that circle and align those structures with the constitution. Issues that might be considered in a governance meeting would include:

- Defining the work of the circle;
- Creating sub-circles when necessary to assume some responsibility;

- Dissolving sub-circles that are no longer necessary;
- Developing the roles and the responsibilities of those roles;
- Defining what links are necessary and recruit a member to those roles;
- Processing tensions, or discontinuities, felt within the group.

In addition to governance meetings, there are tactical meetings within each group. Governance meetings are designed to make structural changes to the organization and deal in principles – not specific project issues. Tactical meetings are project meetings that help to organize the work and project-related issues. A key part of these meetings is to discuss issues or problems that the group or an individual has recognized. Under Holacracy issues and problems are defined as tensions. Examples of issues that might be dealt with in a tactical meeting include:

- Triage of tensions related to a specific project;
- Deciding next action on a project by a specific role;
- Tracking the progress of a project;
- Directing of attention or resources.

Both the governance and tactical meetings are scheduled on a regular basis, but the level of regularity is based on what the circle feels is necessary. It is common for circles to have meetings in shorter intervals in the beginning and to extend the intervals between meetings over time. In addition, what many people new to Holacracy find odd is the level of structure and rigor that is part of the typical governance or tactical meeting. It is highly reminiscent of Robert's Rules of Order. What is counterintuitive is that the structure creates efficiency and allows the participants to focus on the roles and the circles, rather than the personalities and people involved.

Decentralized Autonomous Organizations

A decentralized autonomous organization or DAO (pronounced dow) is a new and developing organizational structure based on blockchain using tokens and smart contracts. Members or owners of the DAO gain rights to make decisions based on the ownership of blockchain-based tokens issued by the DAO. These tokens can be purchased or earned through acts performed on behalf of the DAO.

In theory most of the day-to-day decisions should be based on a series of rules that are set out at an organization's founding, and where possible those rules should be encoded in smart contracts that execute automatically. Operating funds and profits are stored in the blockchain in the form of cryptocurrency.

These funds are to be distributed by the rules of the DAO, where possible by smart contracts, so fraud or misappropriation can be limited. As of this writing most DAOs are based on Ethereum, and this would be the currency that is used to operate the DAO.

Changes to the DAO can be proposed by its members (owners of the tokens) and voted on by the membership. Voting rights are tied to the amount of DAO tokens owned and are typically calculated by an automated system.

In practice DAOs can hire employees, some of whom will be full-time, and others will be gig or contract workers. However, these workers will likely be remote and have flexible time schedules. Many early participants in the DAO workforce split their time between several DAOs simultaneously.

As an early-stage technology and organizational structure there have been some issues as it has been rolled out. There have been issues of fraud and questionable ethics. Some DAOs (such as The DAO, one of the earliest pioneers in this space) have seen millions of dollars in Ethereum stolen from the DAOs by hackers. Other DAOs have been shut down by the Security and Exchange Commission for questionable or fraudulent practices.

Some may argue that these are the natural growing pains of a radically new idea, and as time goes on and technology matures many of these issues may be ironed out. However, it is also possible that DAOs may be a stepping stone to a yet to be developed distributed organizational structure. Either way, the core concepts of flexibility and distributed decision-making will be with us for some time.

Common Features of Modern Organizational Design

Although each of the modern organizational models presented here is very different, there are a few things that seem consistent across many of the newer organizational. Some factors that help to make these models highly effective are:

- Communication across all levels needs to be rapid and ubiquitous.
- Teams and organizations need to share information to the point that it is uncomfortable for traditional managers.
- Diversity of thought and perspective are key to the decision-making process.
- There need to be structures designed for rapid aggregation of ideas from a broad set of people and disciplines.
- New ideas should stand up to the scrutiny of a team.
- Agility and proper response time expectations are more important that the efficient use of resources, or the quality of the response, once both have passed a minimum hygiene level.

- Gardening creates engagement and trumps chess as a basic strategy of attack.

Managers in highly traditional organizations might find the ideas outlined above very uncomfortable. The structures are foreign and lack some of the privileges of rank that senior managers may have enjoyed in the past. However, as we move forward it would seem clear that these more open, flexible, and agile structures are harbingers of even more open, flexible, and agile structures to come.

Non-Traditional Roles

Many organizations today are beginning to reassess the traditional roles of employees, or even the need for employees. Roles within organizations are becoming more fluid, new types of roles are being created, and we are seeing a rise in the non-full-time labor. These non-full-time roles include part-time workers, contractors, contingent workers, consultants, strategic partners, and outsourced service providers. It is fair to say that we are seeing a shift in what it means to work for an organization, and what it means to be an employee.

As we saw in some of the models mentioned above, in many industries there has been a shift to project-based work, whereby a job becomes a series of roles that are completed as necessary by the worker. This worker may not be an employee and may not be geographically co-located with other team members.

In other cases, we begin to see what Claudio Fernández-Aráoz (2022) describes as *corporate nomads*. These are individuals who maintain full-time employment within an organization, but who increasingly find themselves devoting more and more time to part-time roles in geographically dispersed initiatives and projects within their employer's global network. In the context of the DAOs described above in future we may find workers splitting their time between several different organizations – be they DAOs, gig platforms, or traditional organizations.

Customizing Your Structure

If you read enough management theory you soon realize that there are no perfect structures, nor is there only one set of best practices that fit any situation. Business is all about context. What works for you today, with today's set of environmental variables may or may not work tomorrow, and what failed in the past may not be successful now. Day to day things change – and some days the changes are more significant than others. Therefore, your organizational design should be flexible and fluid enough to adapt to the current environment.

Our best bet would seem to be to broadly assess our environment. Look at the social, business, industrial, and environmental factors. Assess our metrics' validity and design new metrics to better indicate where we sit today. Then we should gather as much information as we can before designing a new organization built for our current context. This in no way is intended to suggest that we should forget our history. History provides context. It helps us to understand how we got to where we are and why. We need to look at our history and the history of other successful organizations and find a way to honestly assess what is working, what is not, and why. We might consider disassembling the structures of the past, with an eye to understanding why they were created the way they were and how effective they were both when they were created and today. By dissecting them into their core components, we can decide how to adapt, or whether we need a completely different structure for the future.

Applying the MAAD Framework

One tool that might help in guiding these efforts could be the MAAD (Managing at a Distance) framework introduced in Chapter 1. In applying the MAAD framework to our structures there are a few things that we need to be aware of:

Business Outcomes

The desired business outcomes of the past may no longer be relevant – or at least not exactly in the same way as they were in the past. Our outcomes should be value focused – not feature focused. We should be focused on the value of the outcome we create for our customers and ourselves – not the feature we used to create it.

For example, in Chapter 2 I shared a story about how as a child my grandparents told me to learn punch cards – not really understanding that they were a temporary solution to a long-term problem, and that the punch card would surely be replaced over time. We would develop better solutions for data storage.

So, what are the goals of our organization? In making these goals we should be outcome focused. There should be specific results that we are attempting to achieve. At the same time, those results should not be focused on the features of our current solution. The solutions we have used for years or decades might be closer to the punch cards of decades past than to the cloud storage of the present.

Objectives/Environment

The COVID-19 pandemic aside, our environment has been changing for decades, and the speed of that change has been accelerating. All COVID-

19 did was to push down the accelerator further. This acceleration has exposed issues that would eventually have surfaced when the trends reached a critical mass or stage of maturity.

This pace of change has left many organizations in a difficult position. Their organizational objectives may have fallen out of line with their environment. Objectives that made sense in the recent past are now at odds with their current reality.

So, what then are the factors that make up the environment, and how should we measure them? In Chapter 1 we started to outline the frameworks that managers have used in the past to begin an environmental assessment. The two most pervasive tools would be SWOT (Strengths, Weaknesses, Opportunities, Threats) and PESTEL (Political, Economic, Social, Technical, and Legal). However, even when used well (often a big assumption) they are only a starting point. These tools are often used primarily at the start of a qualitative analysis. The users state the issues that they uncover as bullet points on a slide.

When uncovering the truth of a business environment we should recognize some basic facts:

- The environment is analog not digital. It is a flow of factors that blend together to create a state that is in constant motion. It might be useful to imagine the state using the metaphor of a river fed by multiple tributaries. Heraclitus said, "No man ever steps into the same river twice – for it is not the same river and he is not the same man." The environment may look stable at times, but even when it looks stable there is always movement beneath the surface.
- Understand not only the state but the trends. As the great philosopher Wayne Gretzky said, "I skate to where the puck is going to be, not where it has been." Do not just build for today – build for where you will be in the future.
- There are more variables than we can account for. SWOT and PESTEL are a great start, but your analysis needs to go further. Understand that you will never identify all the variables that could possibly affect your business, nor will you ever have perfect data. The trick is to have enough to make a bet on where the environment is going.
- The pace of change is different for each element that affects our business. Since things change at different rates, unless we have a broad view, we might not recognize what has changed significantly, and what has not.
- Our environment and objectives should be reviewed regularly. Only through regular review of the environment and the objectives will we recognize our misalignment.

People/Talent

Some of the issues that our organizational structures will have to deal with have been listed in detail in the first few chapters. But in summary they could include:

- Changes in the nature of our workforce;
- The level of education;
- Dual income families;
- Decrease in the willingness to travel or commute;
- Multi-generational teams and workforce will become an increasing norm;
- Increase in the perceived need for greater flexibility in work schedules;
- Flexibility in where employees can live;
- Environmental factors that limit co-location.

All this leads to the reality that most of us will need to either accommodate or promote some level of remote work. There will be no hard and fast rules on the level of remote work – this will be context-dependent. The work being performed will be a significant factor here. Some work will require presence (e.g., driving a bus), other work will be highly portable (e.g., copy writing), but many jobs will involve a mixture of tasks, some of which may require presence while some will be portable.

Key skills and abilities will continue to change, probably at an increasing rate, and the demand will become industry- or context-specific. However, some themes will cross boundaries. Among those skills will be strong analytical skills in both quantitative and qualitative abilities.

Organizations will have to decide if they intend to build these skills through training and professional development, or whether they intend to purchase these skills in the market. This will be both an economic and cultural decision. There is no absolute right or wrong here; however, the implementation of these decisions could affect the morale of commitment the organization can expect from its employees.

In many cases, your specific environment's context will be critical in the success of your organization's strategy. However, according to a recent survey of business leaders, 94% of the respondents expected employees to pick up skills on the job, up from 65% in 2018 (Gratton, 2021). This has several implications for organizational design. First, if the expectation is that employees will pick up these skills, that should necessitate a robust training and development infrastructure, or at a minimum an ability for employees to observe team members, or to be mentored by more senior employees.

Creating an opportunity for employees to observe others or be mentored in a remote or hybrid work environment will most likely have to be more deliberate than in one where employees are co-present. It may require managers to set up scheduled one-on-ones for their direct reports, or to use tools such as video that allow employees to observe how others solve problems and to interact with each other.

Culture/Context

Culture happens in the decisions and interactions we share and observe each day within our teams, organizations, industries, and tribes. Limiting our interaction will likely affect the culture – how and to what level has yet to be seen. However, it would seem prudent to be conscious of this possibility, and to monitor the level of interaction.

Monitoring a culture is not easy – because changes are often subtle in the short term but can have devastating effects in the long term. In addition, it may be very context-dependent on the type of work, or team, within an organization. You will likely find that 100% remote work is fine for some teams but not for others. As a broad rule of thumb, it would seem that if teams can have some physical contact, even if that only takes place once a year, it will likely have a positive effect on team cohesion and morale.

When looking at culture it is important that culture is not owned by one person. It is a set of shared experiences and agreed upon norms. In order to maintain a culture, there needs to be communication on what those norms are, and a reinforcement in observed actions. Therefore, regular meetings have become important, both as one-on-ones with managers, as well as with team members. In addition, I would suggest that, where appropriate, you consider two additions to this strategy: team liaison, and work-from-pledge.

In *Team of Teams* General McChrystal outlined how he had implemented a team liaison structure. Each team member was responsible for maintaining an active relationship with another team whose method of working or coordination could benefit the team. This helps to create an information flow and a broader organizational culture. It also helps to break down the silos that often developed within an organization. This could even be extended to include the representatives of other teams sitting in on team meetings.

Another deliberate and highly visual way to influence a culture can be seen in the IBM Work From Home Pledge that was launched at the beginning of the COVID-19 pandemic. Started as a grassroots effort by some IBMers to reinforce the culture early in the pandemic, it spread all the way to chairman and CEO Arvind Krishna who posted his own work from home pledge on LinkedIn (https://www.linkedin.com/pulse/i-pledge-support-my-fellow-ibmers-working-from-home-during-krishna/). These pledges reinforce many of the values that IBM has espoused for decades such as respect for the individual, a bias toward innovation, and a willingness to set boundaries in order to support a more sustainable work-life balance. Importantly for the maintenance of a culture, it set clear expectations on what was, and was not, acceptable.

Autonomy/Personal Responsibility

There are several factors driving the need for greater autonomy: education, physical proximity, and the maximization of intellectual capital. Older organizational models were conceived and developed in eras where employees were less educated, co-located, and often doing far less intellectually taxing tasks. Today promoting engagement with employees, and accessing a total inventory of knowledge, skills, and abilities would seem to require some very basic changes in structure.

Organizations that are attempting to electronically track employee activity are missing the boat. The management and leadership paradigm should be more focused on results, and metrics of engagement, rather than promoting hours of frenetic activity. In addition, organizations should be looking to allow employees to develop a work schedule that can maximize their effectiveness. This might mean breaking down work hours into non-traditional schedules. These schedules might help employees to better accommodate personal commitments such as childcare, healthcare, or even naps that could improve their overall effectiveness. These schedules might require a little coordination between team members so that team meetings can still take place.

What would seem to be clear here is that the level of autonomy should in general increase from traditional levels; however, there should be some guidelines and limits. A number of studies have shown that providing too much choice can make the decision-making process overwhelming (McRobbie, 2021). In addition, providing a framework or guidelines often leads to higher levels of innovation.

Therefore, managers should provide a basic framework of what success looks like for both the individual and the team. Decision boundaries should be clear, but should promote personal decision-making, coordination, and engagement.

Data/Analytics

Later in the book we will cover the changes in the analytical environment. At this point, however, it should be clear that many of the key performance indicators (KPIs) that we have used to manage our teams in the past may no longer be all that effective. We will have to rethink what we are measuring and why we are measuring it for example the number of hours we are clocked in, the number of keystrokes we have made, or the speed in which we respond to a colleague may have very little effect on our effectiveness.

Proximity/Information Flow

It is pretty clear from our discussion in the last chapter that levels of proximity will be important on several fronts, including culture, team continuity, professional relationships, efficiency of communications, ability to recruit talent, engagement, and employee retention. The type and frequency of different types of proximity should be carefully considered and regularly reevaluated. For example, environments where employees are regularly, or permanently, not geographically co-present may be highly effective from some more senior employees, but devastating for many junior employees who are not yet invested in the organizational culture.

In order to maintain relationships, there should be a strategy for how to maintain the proper level of cumulative proximity. This level of proximity will vary based on the type of work being performed, the industry, the organization, willingness to take personal responsibility, and even the quality of the remote environment. Even for teams that are co-present it may make sense to have a media strategy on how to create a more effective information flow.

Policies for information flow might include how often managers will have one-on-one meetings with employees. How these meetings will occur, the structure of the meeting (e.g., personal check-in, project status, progress toward personal goals), and the media (e.g., over the phone, on video chat, in person) will depend on the relationship and environment.

There should also be a commitment to team communication, and the frequency and format of the meeting. The bias should be toward shorter meetings and asynchronous tools to provide background documentation. Mary Baker (2021) of Gartner suggests that often it might make sense to reduce the number of attendees at meetings, but to have a summary of the meeting posted either to a distribution list or to a team platform such as Slack or Teams.

Even with a bias toward remote working it will often be advantageous to have a live in-person meeting of the team, and between the employee and the manager. Given the richness of in-person meetings they can often shorten the time it takes for managers or teams to develop a strong, personal relationship. The maintenance of these relationships can then in many cases be moved to electronic media – either synchronous or asynchronous.

Communications Infrastructure

The effectiveness of your proximity schema will in many cases be heavily affected by the type of communication infrastructure your organization or team has in place, and how well they use it. Just having a team messaging platform in place does not mean that your team is leveraging it to meet your organizational goals. Therefore, it is not only necessary that you have an effective training on your communication infrastructure – there needs to be an effective communication and information culture. In his book *A World Without Email*, Cal Newport (2021) looks at both the positive and negative effects that electronic communications platforms can create. Newport suggests that far too often a frenetic hive-mind begins to develop, which reinforces the need to quickly respond to an ever-growing number of emails, chats, and text messages. This type of culture and these type of response expectations have had a negative effect on deep work (work that requires high levels of concentration and creativity).

Information should be there when the employee needs it, but should not be detracting from the workflow or levels of concentration necessary to do deep work. Therefore, the communication infrastructure should be focused on capturing information in an accessible format but should require as little effort in terms of maintenance and mental effort as possible. In addition, this should be supported by a culture where the expectations of response times are much more reasonable.

Gartner did a series of studies around what managers should expect as employees return to work. From this work a number of recommendations were made. It is clear that we need to hold fewer meetings but those that we do should be more meaningful, and our communications content should match the media (Baker, 2021). Often this means shifting more content to asynchronous platforms, and holding regular short meetings to coordinate efforts.

Organizational Structure

This is a key element of the framework. However, I don't wish to construct a redundant message here as this entire chapter has been about organizational structure. It might be enough to say that the context that every organization finds itself in is unique. As such we can look at the models presented with an eye toward adaptation and modification – pulling elements out of some of these models, understanding their value and purpose, and modifying them to meet our goals and context.

Chapter 4 Takeaways

Change is hard, but not changing will be harder in the long run.

When assessing our structure, we should ask six questions:

- Is our organization efficient and effective?
- Does it provide clarity of direction to employees?

- Is the proper information captured to allow for the control of the operations?
- Does it encourage and provide for accountability?
- Does it provide for the proper incentives?
- And does it allow for cohesion – where the whole is greater than the sum of the parts?

Organizational structures are social technologies that like any other technology are subject to a product life cycle – it will experience an introduction, growth, maturity, and decline.

Throughout history an almost endless number of organizational models have been introduced. These models have proven successful in specific contexts, during a specific time period, and given a certain environmental context; however, in order to stay relevant models must adapt to their environment as they change.

This is where the MAAD Framework can be helpful in evaluating your current environment, and how well you are adapting to the needs of that environment.

References

Alexander, A., Smet, A. D., Kleinman, S., & Mugayar-Baldocchi, M. (2020, April 8). *To Weather a Crisis, Build a Network of Teams.* McKinsey and Company. https://www.mckinsey.com/business-functions/people-and-organizational-performance/our-insights/to-weather-a-crisis-build-a-network-of-teams.

Baker, M. (2021, March 17). *You Can Create Employee Connections Without More Meetings.* Gartner Group. https://www.gartner.com/smarterwithgartner/you-can-create-employee-connections-without-more-meetings/.

Christensen, C. (1997). *The Innovator's Dilemma: When Technologies Cause Great Firms to Fail.* Harvard Business School Press.

Crabtree, S. (2013), October 8). Worldwide, 13% of Employees Are Engaged at Work. Gallup. http://www.gallup.com/poll/165269/worldwide-employees-engaged-work.aspx.

Deutschman, A. (2004a). A Call to Remember. *Fast Company*, 89, 18.

Deutschman, Alan. (2004b). The Fabric of Creativity. *Fast Company*, 89, 54–62.

Fernández-Aráoz, C. (2022, March 30). The Rise of the "Corporate Nomad." *Harvard Business Review.* https://hbr.org/2022/03/the-rise-of-the-corporate-nomad.

Gratton, L. (2021, March 8). An Emerging Landscape of Skills for All. *MIT Sloan Management Review.* https://sloanreview.mit.edu/article/an-emerging-landscape-of-skills-for-all/.

Harrington, A. (2003). Who's Afraid of a New Product? *Fortune*, 148(10), 189–192.

Laloux, F. (2015, July 6). The Future of Management Is Teal. *strategy+business.* http://www.strategy-business.com/article/00344?gko=10921.

McChrystal, G. S., Collins, T., Silverman, D., & Fussell, C. (2015). *Team of Teams: New Rules of Engagement for a Complex World.* Portfolio.

McRobbie, L. R. (2021, February 26). There Is Such a Thing as Too Much Freedom. *strategy+business*. https://www.strategy-business.com/blog/There-is-such-a-thing-as-too-much-freedom?gko=2ebf6.

Moore, G. A., & McKenna, R. (2006). *Crossing the Chasm: Marketing and Selling High-Tech Products to Mainstream Customers* (rev. ed.). HarperBusiness.

Newport, C. (2021). *A World Without Email: Reimagining Work in an Age of Communication Overload*. Portfolio.

Noonan, P. (2021, February 25). The Old New York Won't Come Back. *Wall Street Journal*. https://www.wsj.com/articles/the-old-new-york-wont-come-back-11614296201.

Peters, T. (2009), November 30). *Recession Thoughts: 44 Strategies*. https://www.youtube.com/watch?v=QCRdfnUSq1M.

Robertson, B. J. (2015). *Holacracy: The New Management System for a Rapidly Changing World*. Henry Holt and Co.

Rogers, E. M. (2003). *Diffusion of Innovations* (vol. 5). Free Press.

Smet, A. D., Kleinman, S., & Weerda, K. (2019, October 3). *The Helix Organization*. McKinsey and Company. https://www.mckinsey.com/business-functions/people-and-organizational-performance/our-insights/the-helix-organization.

Whitehurst, J. (2015). *The Open Organization: Igniting Passion and Performance*. Harvard Business Review Press.

Wren, D. A. (2004). *The History of Management Thought* (vol. 5). Wiley.

Chapter 5

The Death of Distance

The Death of Distance

At the beginning of this book, we introduced the concept of *the death of distance*. Many historians have pinned the start of this concept, in an electronic media context, to Samuel Morse; however, if we step back through history it was applied to even earlier technologies such as schooner ships, the printing press, or even signal fires. It seemed that any technology that extended our ability to communicate or travel was touted as having the ability to make distance disappear. The hyperbole in these cases has been lost on modernity. At the beginning of this century may authors published works with titles such as *The Death of Distance* (Cairncross & Cairncross, 2001) and *The World is Flat* (Friedman, 2005). These works posited that internet technologies made physical distance almost irrelevant. We don't have to delve very deep into these works to realize that much of the future utopia they predicted hasn't yet come to pass, and that distance is still a significant issue for modern managers.

Even though we can tap out a text, send an email, make a phone call, or join a video conference, part of the message is lost if we are not sharing the same physical location with the people we are communicating with. Just moving the location of a key person or resource by a few meters can dramatically drop the level of interaction and therefore the level of productivity and innovation an organization will produce (Allen, 2007). But the sharing of information is not just about physical distance – it is about a shared connection. To truly understand these connections, and in turn how productivity and innovation happens, it is important to understand the concepts of proximity, effective communication, information architecture, and some of the properties of the media used in intra-organizational communication.

Managers, entrepreneurs, researchers, and innovators of all types need to find new ways of leveraging both their existing resources and discovering new potential resources. Our business processes and products were designed and built to solve a specific problem in a specific

DOI: 10.4324/9781032646657-5

environment. We are facing the fact that those pre-pandemic processes or products may no longer be valid, or at least far less effective, given our current situation; therefore, we are facing the need to change. Innovation and productivity increases are often a function of recombining ideas and resources that often already exist or building on the ideas of others – who may exist both inside and outside your organization (Kelley, 2005). Unfortunately, given the pace of modern lifestyles, our ability to travel, and the required commitments of many of our potential collaborators, it is often difficult if not impossible to be in the same place at the same time. However, some level of proximity is necessary in order for ideas to flow and collide, and for serendipity to occur. Therefore, we need to develop a new virtual type of proximity that allows our collaborators to be aware of the new ideas or potential resources when and where they could be useful. This awareness could lead to the development of a feeling of presence and possibly engagement – an engagement which could very well result in productivity and innovation.

Although organizations have been experimenting with telecommuting since the 1970s, prior to the outbreak of the COVID-19 pandemic the vast majority of knowledge workers worked in close physical proximity to each other. Some of this was often due to a lack of effective information and communications technology (ICT) infrastructure, or other logistical issues, but it was just as often due simply to tradition and culture. This chapter will help to develop an understanding of the issues of proximity and will provide some simple and actionable recommendations:

- Identify different types of proximity and their roles;
- The effects of communication and media use on proximity;
- Outline key factors surrounding regional clusters and their effect on innovation;
- Dispel some of the misconceptions surrounding virtual proximity;
- Provide a foundation for a solid proximity strategy;
- Explore the role that synchronous and asynchronous work plays in proximity and the creation of presence;
- Review how presence could affect the process of recognition and promotion.

Proximity

A simple definition of proximity is the acknowledgment of the relative nearness of two objects. What might be the most important attribute of proximity is the concept of sharing space in order to facilitate that perception of nearness. The trick here might be how we define both distance and space. In some ways it is helpful to consider the Japanese concept of *ba*, i.e., "a shared space for emerging relationships" (Nonaka & Konno,

1998, p. 40). According to Nonaka and Konno, "knowledge is embedded in ba (in these shared spaces), where it is then acquired through one's own experience or reflection on the experience of others ... The concept of ba unifies the physical space, the virtual space, and the mental spaces" (pp. 40–41). Ba helps us to define proximity as having multiple attributes, but we have not yet defined what those attributes are and how they might be important.

Proximity to resources, and the clustering of resources by specific industries within a geographic region, has long been considered an important factor in the promotion of both the volume and the quality of productivity and innovation (Doloreux, 2004; Porter, 2001). The belief is that close geographic proximity to key resources would reduce friction and speed access to those resources and therefore increase productivity and innovation. Some researchers have gone so far as to suggest that tacit knowledge (that knowledge that can only be gained by experience) is an essential ingredient of productivity and innovation, and that tacit knowledge can only be transferred in close physical proximity. The true value of clustering emerges when proximity of both key resources and tacit knowledge fosters the spillover of knowledge within and across industries (Greunz, 2003; Knoben & Oerlemans, 2006).

The definition of proximity dramatically changed when Wilfred Beckerman (1956) introduced the term psychic distance. Beckerman's contention was that distance is not an absolute. The distance between two individuals is a function of the disparity of their cultures, not the physical distance between them. The concept of psychic distance has been expanded by a number of researchers, leading to the development of additional concepts such as:

- *Cultural proximity*: How similar the cultures of network participants are on a national level (Hofstede, 2023); Knoben & Oerlemans, 2006; Sousa & Bradley, 2006).
- *Cognitive distance*: The level of diversity in the skills, knowledge, and cognitive frame (Wuyts et al., 2005).
- *Organizational proximity*: The distance felt by members of the same large or multi-site organization (Knoben & Oerlemans, 2006).
- *Technology proximity*: The level of overlap between the firms' technology or patent portfolio.
- *Vision proximity*: The similarity in vision of what could be, and what is desirable (Cantц, 2010).
- *Virtual proximity*: The level of emotional closeness developed through the use of ICT (Coughlan, 2010).
- *Virtual distance*: A combination of physical distance, operational distance, and affinity distance that leads to a feeling of detachment (Sobel-Lojeski, 2015).

These descriptions of proximity are not mutually exclusive; it is often unclear where they begin and end, and there are gradient scales to each one. For example, even geographic proximity, one of the most straightforward of the proximity metrics, can be measured in either physical distance, or travel time, or effort necessary to span the distance. Some researchers have gone so far as to develop meta indexes that attempt to combine several of these elements into a single measure of proximity (Amin & Cohendet, 2005; Coughlan, 2010). So, defining how close you are to a resource can be more difficult than what originally might have been assumed.

Proximity and Communication

An organization results from the sum of the conversations and dialogue that occurs within its boundaries; therefore, the quantity, tone, and quality of those conversations are key elements in defining what our collective selves become (Zaffron & Unruh, 2018). The principles of proximity, culture, and cognition have a dramatic effect on the encoding, transmission, decoding, and processing of an idea from one individual to another. However, when understanding the strategy of communication, it is just as important to understand the *what and why* (i.e., the architecture) of the communication. Allen (2007) suggested that relationships within the organization affect the success of the communication, and that there are three types of communication, each of which is affected by its own proximity or relationship dynamics:

- Type 1: Simple communication required to coordinate group or team projects;
- Type 2: The sharing of codified knowledge;
- Type 3: The transfer of tacit knowledge, which is the most important type of knowledge for innovation and the one most affected by distance.

Allen's study also found that, unsurprisingly, people who work in close physical proximity to each other will typically communicate more often than those who do not. However, what was surprising is that, when this relationship is plotted on a curve, little to no drop in the level of communication can be seen beyond 50 meters. Allen posited that visual clues to a person's existence are important in prompting communication.

So, offices with open spaces or transparent dividers (i.e., glass or partial glass walls) foster a better flow of information than offices with solid walls or dividers that limit the view of team members, or other potential resources. Put another way, *out of sight out of mind* is an issue when attempting to foster new ideas. What is even more interesting is that you don't have to see the actual person to have a visual clue that reminds you of them. Seeing an icon that represents them on social media or a chat app is often enough to trigger a feeling of presence for a team member.

Media Richness

In order for teams to properly communicate key ideas their choice of communication media is often extremely important. Each media has inherent properties and limitations. As we increase the distance between team members, and reduce the time they are physically co-present, the importance of this choice increases. Media richness theory (Daft, 1984) posits that the performance of communication improves with the richness of the communication media. For example, phone conversations are richer than text messages, and video conferences are richer than phone calls. In addition, as the equivocality of the task increases, so too should the richness of the media used (Daft, 1984). In other words, if there is any chance that the receiver might misunderstand you increase the level of media richness used.

After decades of study it has been discovered that real communication often transcends the media (Dennis & Kinney, 1998): our successful use of media is often dependent on our familiarity with that media, and our familiarity with the recipient of the message. Another key finding is that the less natural we feel in using a media, the more cognitive resources we will need to expend (Dennis et al., 2008). However, with time and effort, our familiarity with a specific media improves and the cognitive effort declines (Dennis et al., 2008).

This concept of media familiarity is often driven home for many professionals when you ask them to remember what it was like to video chat with an elderly family member (typically a grandparent) for the first time. These interactions typically follow a script where grandma is in awe of this fancy new technology and is moving her head around and looking at the device rather than at the person sharing the conversation. She seems a bit uncomfortable – perhaps afraid of doing something wrong or breaking the device. Her mental processing powers have been captured by the device, and the content of the conversation often seems pretty anemic.

However, to a lesser extent these same issues plague professional conversations as well. Typically, this occurs after the introduction of a new technology that is dramatically different from the incumbent technology. The mental load of learning and mastering the new infrastructure often affects the quality of the resulting conversation.

Anatomy of Clusters

According to Porter (1998), "Clusters are geographic concentrations of interconnected companies and institutions in a particular field" (p. 77). Porter's work has often been cited as a seminal work in outlining the concepts of clusters, and why clusters provide a competitive advantage in efficiency and innovation. Porter points out that clusters often provide a company with access to employees, suppliers, specialized information, and key services that are difficult and more expensive to obtain outside the cluster. Some of these advantages are simply a factor of density. Logic dictates that there would be more potential resources to solve problems in an environment with greater density. However, the clusters that have historically worked best have clear industry foci and many interorganizational relationships allowing the advantages to become specialized to a specific industry or the needs of a particular type of customer (Porter, 1998).

Sandy Pentland (2014) of the MIT Media Lab has developed a series of concepts he calls *social physics*, which includes a set of rules on how information flows between individuals and organizations. Pentland points out that the flow of information between firms in the same industry is easier in clusters, as is the movement of individuals between firms who typically carry with them industry intelligence. This was also observed by Pisano and Shih (2009), who described the development in clusters of *industrial and engineering commons*. These *commons* are the clustering of *knowledge, skills, and abilities* that become part of the local environment, and accessible to the members of the environment through either the movement of people from one company to another, or simply the tacit movement of data through professional/social interaction.

What makes clusters work is the access to resources. So, logic dictates that increasing the available resources should increase the rate of innovation. One simple solution would be to increase the volume and density of local resources; however, for a number of reasons that is not always possible. This begs the question: can we supplement the advantages of geographic proximity with other forms of proximity? It would seem reasonable to assume that other forms of proximity, such as virtual proximity and cultural proximity, could provide an even greater competitive advantage. For example, in comparing California's Silicon Valley to Route 128 Corridor in Massachusetts, there is a cultural difference in how innovation has historically been handled. Although both regions are focused on the technology industry, Silicon Valley has been much more open to interorganizational relationships and sharing, resulting in a far more dramatic regional growth (Saxenian, 1994). Knoben (2008) demonstrated that it is not just about the density of firms or the size of the population; the success of innovation is dependent on the membership of the internal team as well as the connections and relationships developed outside the firm. The makeup of the regional economy has a strong influence on local success: "simply bringing firms together, for example by building science parks, is unlikely to effectively stimulate the innovativeness of firms and might even hamper it" (Knoben, 2008). The cluster of firms must have a culture and a resource profile that not only allows but also encourages them to interact with each other (Ben Letaifa & Rabeau, 2013). Virtual proximity might help to fill a gap in a team's talent profile with a person or firm that has a better cultural fit than a local resource.

Studies I have done in the New York metropolitan area have shown that firms that have a portfolio of interorganizational relationships, which include both local and non-local linkages, are typically more innovative (Coughlan, 2010). In addition, top performers have interorganizational relationship portfolios that are very broad in terms of the types of firms and industries included (Coughlan, 2010; Knoben, 2008). However, it is possible for a portfolio to be too broad. It is important that cognitive distance "be restricted for the sake of coordination" (Wuyts et al., 2005). Diversity in thought is critical in innovation, but in this case you can have too much of a good thing. If a plot were developed to show innovation initiative over a scale of novelty and understandability an inverse U-shaped curve would develop. Too little diversity limits the available intellectual capital and too much diversity makes it difficult for team members to cognitively process the available information. So, organizations should be looking for a balance.

A related topic here is the concept of *Centers of Excellence* (COE). The short description has historically described a team that was co-located, and focused on a key area of the business in a very structured way. A core premise was that the team benefited from both proximity and business process structure to complete specific tasks (e.g., accounts payable, accounts receivable, logistics) more effectively. One question worth asking is what kind of proximity is necessary for the positive effects needed by a COE.

With clusters and COEs the prevailing logic has always been that physical proximity was necessary to create a community and information flow that would facilitate growth and innovation. Recent history has led some to question if this is still true. It might be that the real effects are generated by information flow and a feeling of community fostered by some form of proximity.

Virtual Proximity

Robin Dunbar (1993, 2008) is an anthropologist and evolutionary psychologist and a specialist in primate behavior. He is particularly famous for a series of numbers known as the Dunbar numbers, which set limits on the typical number of relationships that can be maintained by a primate (humans are included in the definition of primate). It might seem strange to bring Dunbar into this discussion until you recognize that his core argument is that relationships create a cognitive load – and that load increases with the intensity of the relationship. Most importantly, when we recognize there is a load, we are forced into the realization that there is logically then a limit to the number of relationships that can be maintained.

Dunbar suggests that there is a hygiene level (or minimally acceptable level) of contact in order for the relationship to be maintained. If these levels are not met entropic forces take over and the relationship experiences some level of progressive atrophy. The relevance to virtual proximity is that there is a limit to the professional relationships we can maintain, and there is increasing evidence that ICT can assist in maintaining those relationships. It is possible to use technology as a relationship power tool. For example, one way to maintain a relationship is to share the occurrence of a significant life event, e.g., the birth of a child, acceptance into a university, the purchase of a new car, taking the trip of a lifetime. In the past sharing these events might require a face-to-face meeting, a letter, or a phone call – all of which require time at an individual level, and therefore present a problem of scaling as we increase the number of relationships we wish to maintain. However, today sharing significant events like these takes far less effort. Young professionals don't have to tell their friends about their life events – their friends see them on social media – and one post covers a significant number of their relationships in one shot.

Compared with the pre-digital world, a world of increasingly efficient ICT can help us to maintain relationships over significant distances and might even ease the effort needed to reach relationship hygiene, but there are limits to what we can expect. In addition, there are a number of misconceptions or misunderstandings of how or when virtual proximity should be leveraged – or even what it is.

Virtual proximity is about leveraging ICT to build and maintain relationships – the emphasis being on the relationship and not the technology. Simply having or using technology does not necessarily equate to an improvement in virtual proximity. Here it might be important to think about the factors that can nullify the advantages of media richness, such as familiarity with a specific media tool and how cognitive ease improves with use (Dennis & Kinney, 1998). Simply put, it takes far more cognitive effort to use a tool that we are not familiar with than one we use regularly. Once the use of a tool becomes familiar, and easy to use, we can free up cognitive resources to work on productivity and innovation. It is through the use of the technology and its integration into our work processes that we experience the advantages of virtual proximity. Although technology is not stagnant, we may struggle to keep up with the growth and change in these technologies and platforms. We face a dichotomy when it comes to virtual proximity – we want the latest technology, but we also want familiarity and efficacy. These are logically at odds with each other.

It is tempting to assume that virtual proximity is primarily used to engage resources or individuals that exist outside the local region, and that it is not required for local relationships. However, this assumption is false. There is significant evidence that physical distance can affect a team's success. This led many to believe that the lack of physical presence brought on by the COVID-19 pandemic would result in significant stagnation in team performance and productivity. However, for the most part, this did not happen. In many cases productivity increased. Through the use of virtual tools teams were able to maintain relationships.

Prior to the pandemic a number of studies, some going back to the 1970s, looked at how physical distance affected the likelihood of collaboration. Among the most famous is Thomas Allen's (2007) study which points out that the probability of using a resource drops for every meter of separation up to 50 meters. Thus, the notion of *nonlocal* starts at 50 meters. He also suggests that often we need visual clues to remind us that the resource is there. Increasing the number of visual clues or contacts should help to remind the network of the existence of a resource and increase the probability of it being integrated into the innovation process.

Just as the feeling of presence can be triggered by a number of factors – including visual – so is virtual proximity. Measuring virtual proximity requires the development of a matrix, which includes a variety of different electronic media, the level of use, the proficiency, and the impact of the use. In some way, it is similar to the concept of the Klout score. Between 2011 and 2018 Klout attempted to develop an index which measured the influence of a given user across social media. However, there is no claim that a virtual proximity measure is an absolute measure. It is intended to be a model for thinking, just as one would use the product lifecycle in marketing or Tuckman's stages of group development in management. As with these models, there are generalities that do apply. For example, a high degree of virtual proximity does generally result in higher levels of innovation and higher levels of disruptive or intersectional innovation (Coughlan, 2010).

Virtual proximity is similar to the notion of the mental processing of social presence on the internet, which has been described as

> the moment-by-moment awareness of the co-presence of another sentient being accompanied by a sense of engagement with the other ... as a global, moment-by-moment sense of the other, social presence is an outcome of cognitive stimulations (i.e., inferences) of the other's cognitive, emotional, and behavioral dispositions.
>
> (Ning Shen & Khalifa, 2008)

Whereas social presence emphasizes the real-time awareness of a resource's presence, virtual proximity emphasizes the ongoing awareness of a resource's existence. The key difference is that virtual proximity does not require engagement until the point it is integrated into innovation, productivity, or process. In a sense, virtual proximity is more an awareness of the resource and the ability to readily engage the resource.

Virtual proximity is also different from the other forms of proximity outlined earlier in this chapter. However, it can act as a catalyst to improve other types of proximity such as psychic distance, cultural proximity, cognitive distance, and organizational proximity – all of which are broader concepts and span both the virtual and terrestrial worlds.

Cumulative Proximity

Cumulative proximity is a theory I have been developing slowly over a number of years. The core of the theory is that the depth of our relationships is a result of our cumulative communications, and teams or individuals might require different levels of relationships to reach peak performance on a team task or project. However, as we learned with media richness theory, not all media nor all messages are equal. And as we learned with the Dunbar numbers, as we increase the depth of the relationship, we increase the efficiency of our communication; however, we also increase the level of effort necessary to maintain the relationship.

Emotional Weight and Engagement

Imagine that each message had an emotional element associated with it. The deeper the emotion connected to the message the greater the weight or higher the emotional score. For example, your colleague sends a note to remind you of a deadline you have well in hand would have little emotional weight. However, your daughter sends you a note that tells you that she has just been promoted – all because of the lessons that you taught her, and thanks you from the bottom of her heart for you setting her up for success in life – and this would be off the charts in terms of emotional weight. Your colleague's message might not deepen the relationship, but your daughter's might.

Adjacent to the concept of emotional weight is the concept of engagement. For decades relationship experts have extolled the virtue of *quality time*. The premise being it is not just the amount of time we spend together, but also the level of engagement that we feel when we are meeting. One effect of the shift to remote work during the pandemic was the increase in the number of meetings workers had to endure, while at the same time there was a decrease in the quality of those meetings and a concomitant disengagement from them (Subel et al., 2022). An example of this is the level of engagement required in a face-to-face team meeting versus one on Zoom with your camera off.

Media Richness

As we saw in media richness some media carry more of the message than others. Or put another way, some media have higher fidelity in reproducing the intended message. For example, it is possible that the recipient could read a text differently from the way you intended. Part of the reason this happens is because a text message does not convey the tone that a voice message carries, or the body language that might come from the same message given over video or in person. So, each media might carry a richness score that could affect how it might be used. In practice low richness media would be for messages with low equivocality (e.g., "meet me at the clock in Grand Central at 2:00 pm today"). Messages with high equivocality would need a media with a very high richness score (e.g., "what is your opinion on how we should execute the new media plans and how our customers might react?").

Relationship Hygiene

If different levels of relationships require different levels of cumulative contact within a specific period of time they are assisted by a certain level of shared emotion. In theory we could measure that contact by scoring the richness of the media, and the emotional weight of the messages delivered. For example, low richness media such as text messages could have a richness score of 1, whereas high richness in-person meetings could have a richness score of 100. Coordinating a shipment for a customer would have a low emotional score of 1, for example, while a message to announce the loss of a loved one could have an emotional score of 100.

In addition, we could set a hygiene level to be achieved in order to maintain the relationship – and we could even set a strategy to deepen a relationship. A business acquaintance would have a low hygiene score, whereas a work team member would have a higher hygiene score, and a best friend an even higher one.

There might be a strategy for reaching relationship hygiene. Do I text you 10 times a day or just meet with you once a week? Do I combine different media to reach the score more efficiently? Do I step up the richness of our conversations in order to develop a closer relationship?

When developing these strategies, it is important to remember that participants in a relationship are constantly fighting the effects of entropy. Without constant attention, and contact of some form, the relationships you have will slowly wither and die.

Relationship Efficiency

The closer or richer the relationship the more efficient the communication is likely to be. An example of this is the way your spouse can look at you across a room and communicate something to you in a glance that would have taken a full conversation with someone you know less well. One question would be how close and how efficient does a specific relationship need to be, given that closeness requires an investment of time and possibly of resources.

Network analysis

Our organizations are networks of individuals and groups. These networks can be described with the traditional formal organization chart that defines divisions, teams, and reporting structures within the organization. Alternatively, it can be described by other sets of attributes and connections between individuals and groups. The organizational charts that historically have been used provide very limited information about how the organization really functions, and the informal relationships that exist between people and groups.

The field of Organizational Network Analysis has been developed to discover those relationships, and to analyze how these relationships affect a number of factors, including:

- business culture;
- innovation levels;
- efficiency;
- level of effectiveness;
- the implementation changes;
- distribution of knowledge and information.

An important thing to remember in any type of network analysis is that it is about relationships. The framework we use to describe the network is nodes and connections. When attempting to develop an understanding of the network typically nodes are described either as individuals and their identifying attributes (e.g., name, role, training, affiliations, contribution to knowledge flow), or as groups that share an attribute (e.g., division, team, cohort). Then we look at the nature of the connection between the groups. For example, in these one-way or two-way connections, who typically initiates the contact, how often are these connections made, what is the nature and volume of the information or knowledge shared, and so on.

Information on the attributes of the nodes and the relationships can be collected either actively or passively. Active collection defines the type of data desired about the relationships, and the proper methodology in which to collect it. Typically, this is done with surveys of the network members. Passive collection involves the use of secondary data that already exists. In this case it is often existing communications data (e.g., email, chat, phone calls, swipe data).

Often the information is displayed in a network visualization or diagram. The purpose of these visualizations is to uncover and support an analysis of different aspects of the researcher's analysis of the relationships – on the understanding that this is an evolving system that changes constantly, adapting to the needs of the members and the environment.

When planning the appropriate presence model for an organization an ONA would be invaluable in confirming or disputing assumptions we have of how our organization works, and what specific model will help in achieving the organizational goals.

However, there are a number of challenges when developing our research methodology, starting with validity and reliability. The questions might include:

- What metrics should we use?
- What exactly do those metrics measure?
- How should they be collected?
- How will the participants feel about the measurement process?
- How might the metrics be misleading, or how might they be gamed by the players?

It is important that there should be high levels of transparency in the process. The intent, goal, methods, and results of the study should be clearly communicated to the participants. There should also be an effort to develop context for whatever data is collected, so that decisions are consistent with the best interests of both the employees and the business.

Environmental Factors Affecting Proximity Requirements

Demographic

As we discussed in Chapter 2 a number of demographic factors are exerting pressure on the existing co-location models that many organizations have traditionally held. These include:

- *Child/elder care*: Between both commuting and presence in the office some employees may develop conflicts with their child/elder care arrangements.
- *Dual income*: Similarly to child/elder care the responsibilities of a spouse/life partner may create conflicts.

- *Health medical:* Close physical proximity to others may present health challenges.
- *Lifestyle preferences:* The changes that were forced on many organizations in 2020 following the outbreak of the COVID-19 pandemic gave employees an opportunity to reflect on what sort of lifestyle they wished to have. They were presented with options that up until that time did not seem available, such as flexibility in relation to time, place, and synchronicity of their work with others.

Talent

In a world of co-location your talent pool is limited by an individual's ability and willingness to commute to your physical location. However, this limits the total available pool of talent and drives up the cost of that talent. In a world of hybrid or remote talent you significantly increase the available pool and could potentially drive down cost. Of course, one assumes that the task can be completed efficiently and effectively in a remote environment.

Also, due to an increase in the availability of hybrid and remote positions, a number of professionals have decided to move out of high-cost centers in search of either lower cost housing or a better quality of life. If this trend continues it could put increased pressure on the price and availability of talent in some locations.

Presence Model

A presence model is an applied strategy for cumulative proximity. It evaluates the results of the network audit in order to design a system on how individuals and teams can be present for each other – either virtually or physically – at the appropriate level in order to meet their organizational and personal goals. Below I will introduce some presence models and concepts; however, we will explore how we might add flexibility to presence in greater depth in the next chapter.

Co-Location Full Time

This is the model that most organizations used prior to the COVID-19 pandemic. It is the physical co-location of employees in the same physical location; in other words, they are gathered in the same building. This may still be a valid or even a required model for many organizations based on their purpose and infrastructure needs. It is difficult to imagine, given the current state of technology, hospital staff or warehouse workers working remotely. On the other hand, it is possible that there are specific roles – even in hospitals – that could be done from home, such as accountancy, scheduling, or the evaluation of medical images or tests.

Reduced Work Week

Around the globe some organizations are beginning to experiment with reducing the total number of hours that employees are required to work, while maintaining the same level of compensation.

In both the US and Europe, the discussion of a four-day work week was floated in the past as a way to increase overall employment. This was based on the assumption that the total number of man-hours would have to be achieved to accomplish the same level of output. However, studies carried out in Germany and France concluded that reduced work weeks had little effect on the total employment levels.

More recently companies have looked at the practice as a way of retaining workers. An unforeseen result of early experiments was that in many cases there was an increase in productivity. A study carried out in Belgium in 2013 suggested that employees who work between 25 and 35 hours are actually more productive than those who work 40 hours (Bindley, 2022). What was even more impressive was the success of a Microsoft trial whereby Japanese employees reduced their hours by 20% and saw a 40% increase in productivity.

It is important to note here that productivity is often a complex calculation, and that many factors contribute to it. One concern that has been raised is that changes might have a short-term positive effect; however, as those changes are assimilated, teams might fall back to previous levels of output/productivity per hour.

Remote Work

In the simplest sense remote work is when you are no longer sharing the same physical space with your team. So, in practical application there is a spectrum of presence models that could claim to be remote. Many companies begin by letting employees spend part of their time working remotely or allowing specific tasks or roles to be done remotely. Later the remote allowance might develop into remote preference, or even remote only.

Hybrid Work

By definition hybrid work is the combination of two things. In the case of presence models, it is the combination of remote and physical co-location. Coming out of the pandemic this is the model that the vast majority of organizations with knowledge intended to implement. As I have dedicated a significant part of the next chapter to the details of how and why this model may be implemented, I will defer most of the discussion of this until then. However, I think it might be helpful to accept that at its core hybrid work is just an acceptance that there is some value to being both remote and co-located.

GitLab, the developers of a successful development platform for professional programmers, has published 10 levels of remote work:

- *No remote:* Remote work is not allowed, often due to a leadership mandate or the nature of the business.
- *Remote time*: Also known as "remote tolerated," this stage allows employees to work some days from outside the office. This is commonly seen in organizations where "remote days" are offered as a hiring perk.
- *Remote exceptions*: Some employees can work remotely indefinitely, while most are required to work from a company office.
- *Remote allowed*: Anyone at the company can work remotely some of the time, with very few exceptions for roles that are location-dependent.
- *Hybrid-remote*: Some employees — but not all — are allowed to work remotely 100% of the time. The remainder work onsite in at least one physical office. This can be a tempting compromise, but has many downsides, which we'll talk more about in the next section.
- *Remote days*: The entire company (executives included) works remotely at the same time.
- *Remote-first*: The company is optimized for remote work with documentation, policies, and workflows that assume that 100% of the organization have prioritized remote working, even if some occasionally visit the office.
- *Remote only*: There is no co-located work in a common office. However, the work is still biased toward one time zone. Some companies maintain "core team hours."
- *All-remote*: In an all-remote company like GitLab, there is no office, and no preferred time zone. A bias toward asynchronous communication encourages documentation, discourages synchronous meetings, and provides greater flexibility.
- *Strictly remote*: A strictly remote company never meets in person and never permits synchronous meetings.

This is by no means an exhaustive list of all the subvariants of hybrid/remote work that are currently being bandied about, and as this general concept becomes more readily accepted more will likely be developed.

Virtual Proximity and Cumulative Proximity Implications

Virtual proximity is not a choice – just as your reputation is not a choice. It exists in relative terms to the environment in which you live and operate. Individually or as an organization we have a level of virtual proximity with every team member, supplier, partner, or collaborator that we currently have or could potentially have. However, just as your reputation can be managed and improved with time, vigilance, and effort so can your virtual proximity. Managers should realize that the majority of telecommunications traffic is local – be that phone calls, text messages, tweets, emails, social media posts, or whatever means of virtual communication your organization or network participates in. Virtual proximity is both a local and remote phenomenon.

In addition, if the historical data is to be believed, the engagement levels of resources can drop significantly in a matter of a few meters. The old adage "out of sight, out of mind" suggests that there is a constant erosion of our ability to stay aware of the resources and maintain our relationships. Virtual technologies are powerful tools that allow us to maintain our relations whether they are within our own organizations, across the street, or on the other side of the world.

Therefore, managers looking to capitalize on their innovation opportunities should have a proximity strategy. This strategy should at a minimum include the following:

- *Entropy and organizational culture*: If not attended to, relationships will fade over time. This will lead to less efficient communication and less efficient organizations. It is also important to remember that our organizations, and our organizational cultures, are in effect the cumulative relationships of the organization. If you improve your cumulative proximity, you will likely have a significant effect on your culture – and conversely if you reduce your cumulative proximity will also affect your culture – but maybe not the way you want.
- *Visual clues are critical*: If at all possible visual clues should be incorporated for key resources. Examples of this include ensuring that messaging platform profiles have up-to-date pictures and that there are regular posts to remind key resources of your existence. Also, simple tools that show presence are important, such as messaging tools or group collaboration tools that show the status of team members and could remind potential collaborators of each other's existence.
- *Combine proximities:* The effect that diversity has on innovation can be plotted as an inverse U-shaped curve. Initially, as diversity is added to a group, there is a marked improvement in innovation, and this continues to a point. However, eventually if their group is too diverse, it will lack a level of commonality that allows members to communicate efficiently. For example, suppose that everyone on the team spoke a different language. They would be very diverse, but likely also highly inefficient. So, it would seem only reasonable that

we would need to find resources that have some minimal level of proximity on multiple scales of proximity (cultural, cognitive, organizational, technological, or visual), and we should engage resources outside to firm to help to bolster the diversity of thought.

- *Use common tools*: It is important to develop familiarity with tools that enable virtual proximity. Virtual proximity can be developed using tools as simple as a text message or as complex as telepresence conference rooms; however, it is important that the users feel comfortable with whatever tools are chosen. Some of these tools will require training and all will require practice if they are to be used properly without excessive cognitive effort. So, there must be some agreement, whether overt or implied, as to which tools will be used and why.
- *Push the regular integration of new tools*: New tools are constantly being introduced in this area; however, managers must be careful that they are integrated carefully. New tools may have a technical advantage, but the advantage might be negated by the additional overhead cost that it takes to be competent with a new tool. The introduction of too many new tools, or tools that feel unnatural to the users, could actually be a detriment to the process. On the other hand, not introducing new capabilities that would improve the communication process and improve the level of virtual proximity could have the same effect.
- *Roll out new tools with closely knit teams*: Since familiarity with both the tools and the participants are important in reducing the cognitive overhead, when possible new tools should be first used by participants who are familiar with each other. This will reduce the cognitive overhead and allow faster integration of the tool into the innovation process with the least disruption.
- *Most of all experiment*: Virtual proximity is a broad principle and there are few hard edges to the concept. It is also likely that many of the key variables that surround virtual proximity will change over time and so will the specifics of virtual proximity. However, it is likely that the innovators will need to find power tools to maintain a broad set of relationships and expand their reach working with new collaborators and resources. In this sense it is likely that virtual proximity will increase in importance over time and it will be necessary to develop new skills, techniques, and capabilities in this area as our existing tools and techniques complete their life cycle.

Rules for Creating a Proximity Strategy

We have reached a point where we can no longer assume that our organizations, departments, or even our teams will share the same physical space or even the same work schedule. Therefore, in order to achieve our organizational goals we will need to consider how different types of proximity will affect our ability to effectively reach our goals.

- *Assess the network*: Assess how the network within your organization works.
  - Understand how information currently flows within the organization.
  - Understand the type of communication that is necessary (type 1, 2 or 3).
  - Evaluate the closeness of the relationships and what it would take to reach and maintain the proper hygiene.
- *Set proximity requirements*: Blanket solutions are likely to be suboptimal, so there is a need to understand team by team and role by role what the proximity requirements are.
- *Understand its dynamic*: Proximity requirements will likely change over time for all the reasons mentioned above, so be willing to reassess and change on a regular basis.

Chapter 5 Takeaways

Some of the key takeaways in this chapter include:

- Proximity is more than just the physical distance between individuals, it is often more of an emotional distance than anything else.
- Proximity is the result of shared communication, shared values, and a shared emotional connection.
- There are several types of communication: coordination, codified knowledge, and tacit knowledge.
- The richness of the media has a significant effect on both the efficiency and the effectiveness of the communication.
- The richness of the media needs to be strategically mapped to the goals of the communication, and the needs of the team, to allow for the success of the company's goals and initiatives.
- Geographic industrial clusters allow for logistical and communication efficiency; however, it might be possible to replicate some of this virtually.
- Virtual proximity is about leveraging ICT to build and maintain relationships – the emphasis being on the relationship and not the technology.
- Cumulative proximity is the connection you have developed with another person over time. When studying this type of proximity, we attempt to understand the nature of the relationship that is necessary for these individuals to function effectively in their shared roles. We

look to reach a hygiene level in the shared relationships that allow for the necessary level of efficiency in our communications. And we recognize that different media with differing levels of media richness will affect the amount of proximity we develop over time.

- The field of ONA has been developed to discover these relationships, and to analyze how they affect a number of factors including:

  - business culture;
  - innovation levels;
  - efficiency;
  - the level of effectiveness;
  - changes in implementation;
  - the distribution of knowledge and information.

- Presence models are an attempt by organizations to plan and develop the most effective and effective strategy for where employees are physically located – remote/home or co-located – and the amount of time they can or should spend in different states of presence (remote, co-located, office hours, digitally available).

References

Allen, T. J. (2007). Architecture and Communication Among Product Development Engineers. *California Management Review*, 49(2), 23–41. http://search.ebscohost.com/login.aspx?direct=true&db=bth&AN=24195457&site=ehost-live.

Amin, A., & Cohendet, P. (2005). Geography of Knowledge Formation in Firms. *Industry and Innovation*, 12(4), 465–486.

Beckerman, W. (1956). Distance and the Pattern of Intra-European Trade. *The Review of Economics and Statistics*, 38(1), 31–40.

Ben Letaifa, S., & Rabeau, Y. (2013). Too Close to Collaborate? How Geographic Proximity Could Impede Entrepreneurship and Innovation. *Journal of Business Research*, 66(10), 2071–2078. https://doi.org/10.1016/j.jbusres.2013.02.033.

Bhaskar-Shrinivas, P., Harrison, D. A., Shaffer, M. A., & Luk, D. M. (2005). Input-Based and Time-Based Models of International Adjustment: Meta-Analytic Evidence and Theoretical Extensions. *Academy of Management Journal*, 48(2), 257–281. https://doi.org/10.5465/AMJ.2005.16928400.

Bindley, K. (2022, April 15). California Considers the Four-Day Workweek. *Wall Street Journal*. https://www.wsj.com/articles/california-considers-the-four-day-workweek-11649994203.

Black, J. S., Gregersen, H. B., Mendenhall, M. E., & Stroh, L. (1998). *Globalizing People through International Assignments* (1st ed.). Prentice Hall.

Cairncross, F., & Cairncross, F. C. (2001). *The Death of Distance: How the Communications Revolution Is Changing our Lives* (rev. ed.). Harvard Business Review Press.

Cantu, C. (2010). Exploring the Role of Spatial Relationships to Transform Knowledge in a Business Idea: Beyond a Geographic Proximity. *Industrial Marketing Management*, 39(6), 887–897.

Carraher, S. M., Sullivan, S. E., & Carraher, C. E. (2004). Validation of a Measure of Expatriate Stress: Findings from Multinational Entrepreneurial Health Care Service Organization Professionals. *Journal of Applied Management and Entrepreneurship; Sheffield*, 9(3), 3–21. https://search.proquest.com/docview/2039163 80/abstract/E78D062F72064DB1PQ/1.

Coughlan, T. (2010). A Model for Quantifying Effects of Virtual Proximity on Innovation. *International Journal of Business, Marketing, and Decision Sciences*, 3(1), 138–152.

Coughlan, T., & Fogarty, D. (2016, March). *Using Virtual Proximity to Promote Expatriate Cultural Adjustment and Innovation.* Presented at the ISPIM Innovation Forum, Boston, MA.

Coughlan, T., Fogarty, D. J., & Fogarty, S. R. (2019). Virtual Proximity to Promote Expatriate Cultural Adjustment, Innovation, and the Reduction of Stress Levels. *International Journal of Applied Management and Technology*, 18(1). http://search. proquest.com/abicomplete/docview/2273114401/abstract/20AC83B683944222PQ/3.

Daft, R. L. (1984). *Information Richness. A New Approach to Managerial Behavior and Organization Design.* JAI Press.

Dennis, A. R., Fuller, R. M., & Valacich, J. S. (2008). Media, Tasks, and Communication Processes: A Theory of Media Synchronicity. *MIS Quarterly*, 32(3), 575–600.

Dennis, A. R., & Kinney, S. T. (1998). Testing Media Richness Theory in the New Media: The Effects of Cues, Feedback, and Task Equivocality. *Information Systems Research*, 9(3), 256–274.

Doloreux, D. (2004). Regional Networks of Small and Medium-Sized Enterprises: Evidence from the Metropolitan Area of Ottawa in Canada. *European Planning Studies*, 12(2), 173–189.

Dunbar, R. I. M. (1993). Neocortex Size, Group Size, and the Evolution of Language. *Current Anthropology*, 34(2), 184–193.

Dunbar, R. I. M. (2008). Cognitive Constraints on the Structure and Dynamics of Social Networks. *Group Dynamics: Theory, Research, and Practice*, 12(1), 7–16. https://doi.org/10.1037/1089-2699.12.1.7 7

Firth, B. M., Chen, G., Kirkman, B. L., & Kim, K. (2014). Newcomers Abroad: Expatriate Adaptation During Early Phases of International Assignments. *Academy of Management Journal*, 57(1), 280–300. https://doi.org/10.5465/amj. 2011.0574.

Friedman, T. L. (2005). *The World is Flat: A Brief History of the Twenty-First Century.* Farrar, Straus and Giroux.

Greunz, L. (2003). Geographically and Technologically Mediated Knowledge Spillovers Between European Regions. *The Annals of Regional Science*, 37(4), 657–680. https://doi.org/10.1007/s00168-003-0131-3.

Harrison, D. A., Shaffer, M. A., & Bhaskar-Shrinivas, P. (2004). Going Places: Roads More and Less Traveled in Research on Expatriate Experiences. In J. J. Martocchio (Ed.), *Research in Personnel and Human Resources Management* (vol. 23, pp. 199–247). Elsevier Science/JAI Press. https://doi.org/10.1016/ S0742-7301(04)23005-5.

Harvey, M., & Moeller, M. (2009). Expatriate Managers: A Historical Review. *International Journal of Management Reviews*, 11(3), 275–296. https://doi.org/ 10.1111/j.1468-2370.2009.00261.x.

Hofstede Insights (2023). *Intercultural Management*. https://www.hofstede-in sights.com/intercultural-management.

Jones, S. (2021, Oct 31). A 4-Day Week Pilot Is Underway in Ireland. Organizers Hope That It Will Act as a Template for Trials Elsewhere. *Business Insider*. http://rdas-p roxy.mercy.edu:2048/login?url=https://www.proquest.com/newspapers/4-day-week-pil ot-is-underway-ireland-organizers/docview/2589059836/se-2?accountid=12387.

Kelley, T. (2005). *The Ten Faces of Innovation: IDEO's Strategies for Defeating the Devil's Advocate and Driving Creativity Throughout Your Organization*. Random House.

Knoben, J. (2008). Localized Inter-organizational Linkages, Agglomeration Effects, and the Innovative Performance of Firms. *The Annals of Regional Science*, 43(3), 757–779. https://doi.org/10.1007/s00168-008-0229-8.

Knoben, J., & Oerlemans, L. A. G. (2006). Proximity and Inter-organizational Collaboration: A Literature Review. *International Journal of Management Reviews*, 8(2), 71–89. https://doi.org/10.1111/j.1468-2370.2006.00121.x.

Kraimer, M. L., & Wayne, S. J. (2004). An Examination of Perceived Organizational Support as a Multidimensional Construct in the Context of an Expatriate Assignment. *Journal of Management*, 30(2), 209–237. https://doi.org/10.1016/j.jm.2003.01.001.

McNulty, Y. (2015). Till Stress Do Us Part: The Causes and Consequences of Expatriate Divorce. *Journal of Global Mobility; Bingley*, 3(2), 106–136. http://dx.doi.org/10.1108/JGM-06-2014-0023.

Morgan, L. O., Winter, J., & Young, S. T. (2004). Operational Factors as Determinants of Expatriate and Repatriate Success. *International Journal of Operations & Production Management*, 24(11/12), 1247–1268. http://search.proquest.com.ezproxy.apollolibrary.com/docview/232324732/FF424684CA2B4539PQ/1?a ccountid=458.

Ning Shen, K., & Khalifa, M. (2008). Exploring Multidimensional Conceptualization of Social Presence in the Context of Online Communities. *International Journal of Human-Computer Interaction*, 24(7), 722–748. https://doi.org/10.1080/10447310802335789.

Nonaka, I., & Konno, N. (1998). The Concept of "Ba": Building a Foundation for Knowledge Creation. *California Management Review*, 40(3), 40–54. http://search.ebscohost.com/login.aspx?direct=true&db=bth&AN=738856&site=ehost-live.

Pentland, A. (2014). *Social Physics: How Ideas Turn into Action*. Penguin Books.

Pisano, G., & Shih, W. (2009). Restoring American Competitiveness. *Harvard Business Review*, 87(7/8), 114–125.

Porter, M. E. (1998). Clusters and the New Economics of Competition. *Harvard Business Review*, 76(6), 77–90. http://search.ebscohost.com/login.aspx?direct=true&db=bth&AN=1246493&site=ehost-live.

Porter, M. E. (2001). Innovation: Location Matters. *MIT Sloan Management Review*, 42(4), 28–36.

Saxenian, A. (1994). *Regional Advantage: Culture and Competition in Silicon Valley and Route 128*. Harvard University Press.

Scullion, H., & Collings, D. G. (2006). *Global Staffing* (1st ed.). Routledge.

Silbiger, A., & Pines, A. M. (2014). Expatriate Stress and Burnout. *International Journal of Human Resource Management*, 25(8), 1170–1183. https://doi.org/10.1080/09585192.2013.824911.

Sobel-Lojeski, K. (2015, April 8). The Subtle Ways Our Screens Are Pushing Us Apart. *Harvard Business Review*, 6.

Subel, S., Stepanek, M., & Roulet, T. (2022). How Shifts in Remote Behavior Affect Employee Well-Being. *MIT Sloan Management Review*. https://sloanreview.mit.edu/article/how-shifts-in-remote-behavior-affect-employee-well-being/.

Sousa, C. M. P., & Bradley, F. (2006). Cultural Distance and Psychic Distance: Two Peas in a Pod? *Journal of International Marketing*, 14(1), 49–70. https://doi.org/10.1509/jimk.14.1.49.

Suutari, V., & Brewster, C. (2003). Repatriation: Empirical Evidence from a Longitudinal Study of Careers and Expectations among Finnish Expatriates. *International Journal of Human Resource Management*, 14(7), 1132–1151. http://search.ebscohost.com/login.aspx?direct=true&db=bth&AN=10917482&site=ehost-live.

US Census Bureau (2019). *Overseas Citizen Population Analysis*. https://www.fvap.gov/info/reports-surveys/overseas-citizen-population-analysis.

Wuyts, S., Colombo, M. G., Dutta, S., & Nooteboom, B. (2005). Empirical Tests of Optimal Cognitive Distance. *Journal of Economic Behavior & Organization*, 58(2), 277–302. http://www.sciencedirect.com/science/article/pii/S0167268105001526.

Zaffron, S., & Unruh, G. (2018, July 10). Your Organization Is a Network of Conversations. *MIT Sloan Management Review*. https://sloanreview.mit.edu/article/your-organization-is-a-network-of-conversations/.

Chapter 6

Flexibility

Work Flexibility

As a teacher of graduate and undergraduate students at several colleges and universities, I am very fortunate to have deep conversations with dozens of millennial and Gen Z students every week. In doing so – even though my sample size is small relative to the population as a whole – over the past couple of years I have come the realization there has been a major shift in the expectations of those who are now entering the workforce and those of their mothers and fathers. That said, those who are outside looking in often change their perspectives once they gain a little experience.

However, I am not the only observer to see such a shift.

Why Flexibility?

Prior to the 1970s employees were considered either in the office or not – and there might even have been a good reason why they were not. There were of course positions that were based out in the field, on-site with a customer, or in a remote company location. However, through growing use of phones, fax machines, and computers from the 1970s onward, knowledge workers, whose jobs required presence in an office, could now begin to experiment with working remotely.

NASA has been credited with the development of the term *telecommuting* (commuting by phone), which today we might describe as remote working. Several progressive companies jumped onto the bandwagon early on too. IBM was creating fully remote positions as early as 1979, putting terminals in the home offices of five employees working for a laboratory in Silicon Valley. By 1983 the company had 2,000 fully remote employees, and by 2009 approximately 40% of its workforce was working remotely, saving about $2 billion in office rent.

However, like a lot of things in life, each of the major work modalities (office, remote, hybrid) by their very nature have advantages and

DOI: 10.4324/9781032646657-6

disadvantages – so your choice of modality inherently has its compromises. For example, from an employee perspective:

- If you are in the office, you have a shot at face time with the boss, but you have to suffer the commute.
- You might find you have fewer distractions at home, but you miss casual interactions with people both on your team and in other departments.
- You might have young children at home who can be a distraction – so the office is more productive – but you miss the flexibility of a work from home arrangement.
- You might face an awful commute, and remote work allows you to reduce, cost, time, and anxiety, while at the same time possibly giving you more productive time (business or personal) each workday.
- When working remotely you miss the close personal contacts, the water cooler conversations, and the ability to observe others.
- When working remotely you are able to constantly change your work location and gain a number of new experiences.
- Or if you are an employer or manager:
- Having people co-located makes it easier to monitor and manage employees.
- Co-location limits the potential pool of employees who are willing and able to join the firm.
- Many managers believe that co-location allows them to monitor and manage culture more easily.
- Going remote, or even hybrid, can help to make tremendous savings on the cost of office space.
- Foreign workers can work for the firm outside the US and eliminate visa issues.
- Many managers are concerned that collaboration and innovation might stagnate due to a decline in information flow.

Anyone who has taken even a cursory look at the presence issues realizes that the examples shown above are far from exhaustive. The issues are seemingly endless. However, in what follows we will introduce some of the major issues that must be confronted when deciding on the level of flexibility that is appropriate for your organization's situations.

The Nature of Work

One thing to consider regardless of the work modality (office, hybrid, remote) is the nature of what it is we are trying to accomplish, and what will and will not actually assist us in accomplishing our goals. In many ways the model for the modern office and its associated practices, which was built up over centuries, is a set of technologies that was developed for a very different time – often for a very different set of goals and for a very different workforce.

We now have an unprecedented opportunity to rethink or reevaluate the following:

- Our basic assumptions;
- Our goals;
- Our current methodologies;
- Our work-life balance;
- Where we and when we wish to work;
- Where and how we wish to live;
- And the communities we wish to be part of.

Far too often in the past we have fallen foul of equating work with hours of activity or perceived effort. In many organizations it was more important to be seen actively doing something rather than actually accomplishing something. In most cases these activities were happening between 9:00 am and 5:00 pm, within a 40-hour workweek, more by tradition and momentum than for any other reason.

Prior to the modern era, in many cultures workweeks could be 12 to 14 hours a day for six to seven days a week, or in the case of many hunter-gatherer societies as little as 15 hours per week. As late as 1900 it was not uncommon for the average workweek in Europe and the United Kingdom to exceed 50 or even 60 hours. The 40-hour workweek did not become standard in the US until around the end of World War II, decades later than in parts of Europe (Schein & Haruvi, 2017).

Over time, however, some have questioned the logic behind this and proposed alternatives. In 1930 John Maynard Keynes suggested that with the addition of productivity tools that would be developed over time, the average American worker would only need to work 15 hours per week by 2030. Earlier, Ben Franklin, who was famous for being highly productive and structured in his work habits, suggested that a man could meet all his wants and needs by undertaking only four hours per day of focused work.

Deep Work/Flow/Focus

There is a whole field of study that looks at productivity and effectiveness in knowledge work. Let's be clear here – we are not just exploring how busy you are, we are exploring the quality and quantity of what you are producing. The unfortunate part of many organizations' culture, and the general practice of many individuals, is to fill their day with frantic activity with little thought of how this activity is helping to reach a specific goal. They seem to equate activity with productivity – and nothing could be further from the truth.

There is a broad spectrum of tasks that the average knowledge worker is engaged in. Some are routine and almost mechanical in nature requiring very little focus, while others require some level of interaction with others and a modicum of focus, while others require what Cal Newport (2016) described as deep work (deep focus on the current task). For most people reaching deep focus requires limited to almost no competing stimulus, and this allows them to direct all their attention to the task at hand. Newport has the following theorem for knowledge workers: High-Quality Work Produced = (Time Spent) x (Intensity of Focus). However, many organizations have designed their organizations' structures and workflows to restrict, if not almost eliminate, highly focused work.

One common problem is how the organization's workspace is designed. Many organizations have opted for an open office, sold on the idea that it will foster a high number of interactions between employees, and result in higher innovation due to the increased flow of information and ideas. On top of this it also typically reduces the size and cost of office space. However, in practice what happens is most employees become overwhelmed with stimuli. Their concentration is constantly interrupted by the noise and activity around them, and they are constantly guarding their personal space and the confidentiality of their personal information. In his book *Focus*, Daniel Goleman (2013) suggests, "The more distracted we are, the more shallow our reflections; likewise, the shorter our reflections, the more trivial they are likely to be." Therefore, this structure results in the exact opposite of what it is attempting to promote.

So, how should we design our workflows? Newport (2016) points out that for most knowledge workers there needs to be a balance between deep work and shallow work. For each role, this balance is likely to be different. Therefore, in designing workflows we might consider a time budget for each type of task – and we might even go so far as to schedule specific blocks of time for both. Also, many of the most productive organizations have a hub and spoke type of structure, which means that employees spend their time in private spaces, or offices, but share common facilities (e.g., centralized restroom, common coffee area, common lobby). These common areas create those serendipitous interactions but allow for space for deep concentration and uninterrupted thought.

This hub and spoke and focused interaction concept could be extended to the work of hybrid presence. Tsedal Neeley (2022) points out that:

> To go into the office to stare at a screen all day, the way that you would at home, is not helpful. In fact, people resent that. The office is for connecting with one another, for innovative work during certain

phases, for onboarding people ... To treat the office as a tool and not a destination is a mindset shift that's going to be really helpful in using the space in a way that's productive for all.

(p. 16)

The amount of time spent in the office should be dependent on the team and the process. It is conceivable that there are teams, based on the type of process and work that they are engaged in, that should be co-present in an office at all times. However, if the COVID-19 pandemic has taught us anything it is that these teams are not the majority. Therefore, we should be designing our processes to include deep work time and places. Depending on the life situation and environment that individual employees find themselves in those deep work locations could be at home, at a co-working space, or in some private space within a traditional office.

It is difficult to have a discussion about a concept like deep work without discussing the concept of *flow* introduced by Mihaly Csikszent-mihalyi (1990). The core of Csikszentmihalyi's theory is that our best and most productive moments occur when we are stretched to the limits – both mentally and physically – but still within the outer limits of our ability. In these situations we enter a mental state of flow. Athletes and musicians often experience these states whereby they are in a state of deep concentration and at the highest level of their performance – at times like this things just seem to work and you feel on top of your game. However, this can also be experienced by knowledge workers. Csikszentmihalyi points out that there are some preconditions to this state:

First, the experience usually occurs when we confront tasks we have a chance of completing. Second, we must be able to concentrate on what we are doing. Third and fourth, the concentration is usually possible because the task undertaken has clear goals and provides immediate feedback. Fifth, one acts with a deep but effortless involvement that removes from awareness the worries and frustrations of everyday life. Sixth, enjoyable experiences allow people to exercise a sense of control over their actions. Seventh, concern for the self disappears, yet paradoxically the sense of self emerges stronger after the flow experience is over. Finally, the sense of the duration of time is altered; hours pass by in minutes, and minutes can stretch out to seem like hours. The combination of all these elements causes a sense of deep enjoyment that is so rewarding people feel that expending a great deal of energy is worthwhile simply to be able to feel it.

It is important that these are effortful states and therefore they can be both exhilarating and exhausting at the same time. Therefore, you cannot be in a state of flow all the time.

Newport points out that deep work is a skill and like any skill it can be built up over time. In the beginning you might only be able to reach a deep work or flow state for an hour a day; however, over time you might be able to go for four hours at a time. It would seem important to have a realistic set of expectations when designing a workflow that requires deep work. But if you are able to develop a well-designed workflow and build skills of deep work that result in several multi-hour sessions per week it is likely you will see a significant increase in the quantity and quality of your overall output.

Collaboration and Independent Work

> Is it a fact – or have I dreamed it – that, by means of electricity, the world of matter has become a great nerve, vibrating thousands of miles in a breathless point of time? Rather, the vast globe is a vast head, a brain, instinct with intelligence! Or, shall we say, it is itself a thought, nothing but thought, and no longer the substance which we dreamed it!
>
> (Hawthorne, 2013)

By its very nature there is some knowledge work that typically can be done well through a solo effort, while other knowledge work benefits greatly from collaborative effort. However, even those projects, tasks, or team efforts that benefit from collaboration have elements that should, or can, be done independently. For example, any team that regularly does some form of brainstorming knows it is often more productive if team members first go off to research and explores the topic on their own before getting together to discuss it.

So, structure does play a role in the success of collaboration. Many managers have expressed concern that in a remote and hybrid world the quality and quantity of collaboration will suffer. This would seem to be a legitimate concern. Innovation and collaboration are highly dependent on the flow of information and the quality of that information. In addition, we know from our discussion in this book about media richness, and that the richest form of communication is a face-to-face meeting. However, this might be an oversimplification of the issues at hand. The nature of the information, and the style of learning that the target individual prefers, will often dictate the best media choice. For example, there may be some technical information that is better delivered in a document, while more subtle information might need a meeting, and still others – say some training and development – should be in a video or app form.

Information Flow

When studying innovation, one of the key factors that determines the quality of new ideas and innovations a group develops is the diversity of the team members. Having team members who are in a different location, and who have different professional and life experiences, has historically been an advantage. However, to take advantage of this diversity there had to be a structural way to facilitate the movement of information between team members.

Those who study networks know that according to Metcalf's Law a network's impact is the square of the number of nodes in the network. Put another way, a network is an effective way of moving information and ideas. As we increase the size of the network it can increase not only the amount of information we have access to, but also the paths to that information. However, as the network grows, we might become overwhelmed and need help to navigate the resources of the network.

Having the information that you need, when you need it, in a way that you can easily consume and process it, is critical to the success of knowledge workers. The flow of this information between workers in both the office and remote locations must be a consideration when developing an organization's strategy on remote and hybrid work.

Bridging

In many multinational or global organizations this might have been partially supported by the use of expatriates, namely managers who have moved from the home country to a host country, or a remote international office, and who can act as a bridge between disparate elements of the organization. However, in the past you did not have to be a large international organization to see similar functions in action. Often, multi-site organizations domestically would have individuals who spent time at both the headquarters and the remote site, and one of their tasks (officially or unofficially) would be to act as bridge between groups. In remote or hybrid organizations this bridging role might be played by super-connectors in the organization, or by managers who understand and are aware of the need to facilitate this.

Box 6.1 Super Connector

Super connectors are individuals who have the ability and proclivity to develop a high number of relationships and connect disparate individuals. The term was made famous by Stanley Milgram in the 1960s as part of his small worlds experiment, which is known for the development of the six degrees of separation concept.

Milgram provided 160 people with envelopes with instructions to get the envelope to a specific stockbroker in Boston. However, the rules were they could only forward the envelope to people they knew personally, and then ask the recipients to forward it on to one of their personal contacts that might be able to get the envelope one step closer to the intended target.

> It was found that a disproportionate number of the envelopes went through one individual – the owner of a men's clothing store in Boston. This particular individual had a very large social network and was exceptional at making connections.

This skill is one that comes more naturally to some more than others, but it is a skill that all managers should recognize and develop. It can be a tremendous asset when attempting to foster information flow.

Socialization/Isolation

The ease, and efficiency, with which information moves between nodes of a network, or a group of people, will be heavily affected by the relationships that exist between the individuals within the network. The closer the relationship the more comfortable it is to share that information, and the easier it is to effectively communicate an idea.

It is easy for team members to begin to feel isolated. If this develops it has a negative effect on productivity and innovation. This is a significant risk for remote workers and increases correspondingly with the level of independence of the tasks that the worker performs (Orhan et al., 2016).

Infrastructure

For some reason there are managers who feel that all that is necessary to enable collaboration to happen is to put people in the same building. This could not be further from the truth. Having the proper communication infrastructure to facilitate a flow goes much deeper than that. Anyone who has had their team spread across multiple floors of a building or an open office infrastructure can attest to this.

No matter if you share the same physical location or are at different physical locations, the infrastructure you have in which to communicate is a critical factor in collaboration. In physical locations it should create places where people have time to themselves, places where people from different groups mix and can have chance encounters, and places where small teams can perform focused work together.

As a species we have a vast knowledge of how to socialize and communicate in person. For most individuals this takes as much conscious effort as breathing. However, the same cannot be said for digital communications. Digital communications by their nature are far more effortful, and the mediums of exchange less rich. On the other hand, digital communication often requires us to write, which may force us to think more deeply about what we wish to communicate.

The more important aspect that managers should consider is the norms. What are the norms that we have agreed to in our communications? As we move from the office to the remote locations there has to be an agreed set of tools, an agreed set of methods on how to use the tools, and a built-up level of competency in order to allow those tools to be effective.

Developing Collaboration Efficiency

Effective collaboration is often a function of your connection to your team both socially and through effective use of technology. We've collectively learned a great deal over the past couple of decades about how to leverage digital technology to develop and maintain relationships, and what we have learned is that it takes a great deal more than just installing hardware and software. There is a socialization process that should be respected. "Socialization refers to the process by which individuals acquire the behaviors, attitudes and knowledge necessary for participation in an organization. Through socialization, the norms, identity, and cohesion between team members develop, enabling team members to effectively communicate and perform" (Panteli & Chiasson, 2008, p. 22).

In her book *Remote Work Revolution* Tsedal Neeley (2021) points out that being remote is not a death knell to collaboration. She suggests that the main contributing factors are lack of trust, lack of well-established communications norms, and lack of social connections, i.e., things that are usually built into a socialization process. She suggests that organizations consider a reset or re-onboarding of employees to help to facilitate a change in the way they work and how they communicate. This reset or re-onboarding is not a one-and-done, but rather a regular part of the governance process that happens on a recurring basis (possibly multiple times a year).

Neeley suggests that their success will be built on several factors:

- *Mutual awareness*: There needs to be a set of commonly understood things that allow team members to place communications and decisions in context.
- *Social presence*: We need to understand how to use communication tools to communicate social cues, and understand the social cues of others, with the goal of creating social awareness.
- *Communications mix*: Mixing the level of media richness, synchronous and asynchronous channels, and alternating meetings (virtual and in-person) with other activities can help to reinforce the message. It may also be necessary to repeat the message in different channels for it to be assimilated into the consciousness of the organization.

- *Social distance*: Building social connections also builds trust and increases a willingness to share information and ideas. This can be done by implementing social tools such as Slack or Teams, but success with these tools goes far beyond installation. They need to become accepted by the team and become part of the social fabric.

The process of how and when to reset the team can and should vary widely based on the context of the situation the organization finds itself in. The process suggested by Keith Ferrazzi (2014) includes the following steps:

- *Build the right team*: Choose the right people to work remotely. Successful remote team members have "good communication skills, high emotional intelligence, an ability to work independently, and the resilience to recover from the snafus that inevitably arise" (p. 121). Also keep the team small – Ferrazzi suggests no more than 13 individuals.
- *Open dialogue and clear goals*: These seem to be obvious to most managers looking for new ideas, but unfortunately all too often they don't exist.
- *Kickoff*: The purpose is to set goals and expectations of the effort at hand. This should be either in-person or on video. The synchronous interaction and the visible body language goes a long way to building trust.
- *Onboarding*: When possible, this should be carried out in person, if not on video. This sets norms and expectations. It may also be helpful to pair new members with mentors to help to reinforce the message.
- *Milestones*: It is easy for virtual teams to drift and begin to feel disconnected. Regular celebrations of small successes go a long way in maintaining cohesion and direction.

Purpose of the Office

At the beginning of the COVID-19 pandemic there seemed to be a pervasive sentiment that organizational leaders, and even many workers, were looking forward to the day that we could all get back to the office, and return to business as usual. However, as the pandemic dragged on it became increasingly clear to many that there had been a fundamental change in the environment, and many organizations were being forced to rethink their previous assumptions about the use of, or even the need for an office.

It is important to remember that the office is a technology that is designed to solve a series of business problems – a technology that at its core has the sole purpose of helping the organization to achieve its goals. Many organizations have begun to reevaluate the following:

- What is it that the office should achieve?

  - Business process support;
  - Development of culture;
  - Monitoring of employees;
  - Social interaction and development of relationships;
  - Facilitation of collaboration;
  - Internal network development.

In addition, the format and use of space in the office had to be re-evaluated:

- The size and location of the office;
- Methods to facilitate information flow.

Visibility

Prior to the outbreak of the COVID-19 pandemic it is likely that anyone who spent a significant amount of time in a remote, or field-based position would have experienced some level of isolation while out of the office. Many would lament the increased difficulty they experienced in completing tasks that would have been far easier if they were in the office and could stand next to the desk of a colleague and make a request, or push something through the company workflow. Several studies carried out in the decade prior to the pandemic confirm that often remote employees felt like second-class corporate citizens (Grenny & Maxfield, 2017; Bernstein et al., 2020).

In addition, remote workers were far less likely to receive a promotion or a raise than those who had face time with the boss. In times past the default assumption of managers was if they could not see you then you were not working. Not only is this sort of management unfair, it leads to increased frustration among employees, decreased employee retention, and likely suboptimal organizational performance. In order to combat these issues, managers need to be more intentional in their management styles.

Managers can no longer count on running into an employee in the course of normal business. They need to find time to have regular check-ins with employees to make sure that they are aware about what is happening with that employee, to understand the challenges they are facing, to guide them on their direction, to provide the employee with frameworks with which to make decisions, and so on.

When working remotely employees need to communicate what they are doing, how they are doing it, who they need to coordinate with, and how they are helping the team to achieve its goals. If this is no longer done in the physical office, then the role of visibility needs to move to a new technology – more often not digital. Therefore, it is incumbent on the organizational leadership that this infrastructure exists, and that team members have both the proper skills to use it and understand the agreed upon uses of it.

Open Office

Over the past few decades a large number of companies have moved to an open office floor plan. Open office is an office layout that lacks interior walls and has multiple employees sharing a common space. Advocates of the open office cite among the advantages the free flow of information between employees, and a reduction in the space required for each employee resulting in higher levels of innovation, higher productivity, and lower cost to the company.

Unfortunately, in practice many companies find that the only real advantage is reduced space leading to lower cost. A number of studies have shown that if anything open offices create highly distracting environments leading to a dramatic reduction in overall interaction among employees (Sailer et al., 2021). A study by Bernstein and Turban (2018) suggested that the reduction in face-to-face interactions can be as high as 70%. In these environments many employees often replace face-to-face interactions with electronic communication.

In addition, the constant interruptions lead to far lower productivity per employee. Employees who are interrupted at work report higher levels of stress, and a higher likelihood of being in a bad mood. Furthermore, knowledge workers who become distracted and lose concentration often take more than 20 minutes to get that concentration back (Mark et al., 2008). In other words, open offices have sounded the death knell to tasks or processes that require serious thinking or creativity.

Hub and spoke models are small spaces where individuals or small groups can work and collaborate, and common areas where employees can come together for shared services and amenities. These spaces allow for those serendipitous encounters where unsought information happens your way, and the development of loose ties within the organization, while at the same time facilitating concentrated work and collaboration.

Strong and Weak Ties

The quality of the relationships formed both within and outside the organization have a significant effect on the quality of work, of employees, and innovation. This is particularly visible in relationships between team members, or people who work in close proximity to each other. In short, the more we talk with each other the more we trust each other (Bernstein et al., 2020). The stronger the relationship and the greater the trust, the more efficient the communication, the more likely sharing of information will occur, the more connected employees feel to the organization, and the higher the level of innovation in the firm.

However, in the decades prior to the pandemic we witnessed a steady decrease in the number of employees who reported having a good friend at work, and an increase in loneliness among employees. Several studies suggest that the rate of loneliness prior to the pandemic was over 40% of all employees, and many experts are concerned that the reduction in personal contact due the changes implemented following the outbreak of the COVID-19 pandemic will have detrimental effects (Murthy, 2017; Bernstein et al., 2020).

In the classic article "The Strength of Weak Ties," Mark Granovetter (1973) described strong ties as being a strong personal relationship or close friendship, and weak ties the opposite of strong ties. Weak ties are friendly, cordial, or professional relationships but lack the emotional or time commitment that would typically be present in a close tie. Granovetter pointed out that there are typically large groups of overlapping connections between individuals who share strong ties – so your close ties share a great deal of common knowledge – whereas weak ties often travel in different circles and have different sources and bodies of information.

To illustrate this point, Granovetter suggested that when looking for a new job you are likely to be more successful in your search if you tap weak ties for information than if you contact close ties. You are more likely to share the same sources of information regarding job availability with your close ties. Therefore, it is likely that they will only be able to tell you about job openings that you are already aware of or would have discovered without their help. On the other hand, weak ties travel in different social and professional circles and could provide you with information about jobs that you would otherwise miss.

Within organizations strong ties are usually people on your team, or with whom you interact on a regular basis, whereas weak ties are those with whom you are familiar but who are outside your team. These weak tie relationships could be developed and supported by chance encounters in a shared facility, or common area within a facility. Owing to the nature of our interactions in remote or virtual environments weak ties become more difficult to develop and maintain. The Microsoft 2021 Work Trend Index suggested that since the beginning of 2020 and the shift of employees to remote or hybrid working environments there has been an increase in the volume of electronic communication (phone calls, video chat, email, text messages) between team members; however, there has also been a dramatic reduction in the level of communication across teams.

Knowledge Flow

Lynda Gratton (2022), professor at the London Business School in the UK, reminds us that "in reality, people, the tasks they perform, and the jobs they do are embedded within networks of human connections. Through these connections flow knowledge, insight, and innovation."

When mapping or evaluating the flow of information or knowledge across an organization it is important to recognize that knowledge falls into two broad categories: knowledge that can be codified, and tacit knowledge. Knowledge that can be written down and shared is codified knowledge. This sort of knowledge can be easily shared in an electronic fashion. However, tacit knowledge is often difficult to write down or codify and is often only gained through experience and being in the environment in which it exists. A significant amount of any organization's knowledge is tacit, and some – such as cultural norms – is typically more efficiently shared by proximity with others or by being in a shared environment.

Gratton also points out that sometimes a large proportion of a firm's tacit knowledge could be codified if explicit efforts were made to do so. Firms moving from in-person models to remote or hybrid working might consider how much of the necessary knowledge flow is tacit, how much could be codified, and what would it take to do so.

One group that can help to facilitate the flow of information is those who Gratton calls "boundary spanners," i.e., employees who belong to two or more groups within the firm. They can help to share information across group boundaries. This sort of activity was also identified by Stanley McChrystal et al. (2015). In *Team of Teams* General McChrystal describes a team structure that he developed whereby each team member was responsible for maintaining connections with other teams, and for acting as a liaison for his/her primary team. His structure proved very successful in developing a network of informal information across a very broad organization.

Off-site (Reset/Kickoff)

Off-site meetings that take place outside the office have long been a staple for organizations looking to develop strategic plans, mark the beginning of a new project, or introduce a new initiative. The purpose of an off-site meeting is to break people out of their routines and shake things up, and to create a bonding experience or rallying point around a new idea or direction. What has changed is the definition of what is routine. Keswin (2022) points out that if we spend a significant amount of our time working remotely the office itself is a change of venue and can become a rallying point for a team.

Days in the Office

As the COVID-19 pandemic began to subside, and offices began to open up again, many companies began to evaluate the split between on-site and remote working. There have been many heated debates about the number of days that employees should be on-site with their teams. Unfortunately, many organizations did little analysis on the subject, and made decisions based on emotion or tradition. Worse, many organizations took a blanket policy approach covering most, if not all employees. For the reasons stated above most organizations find value in employees being physically co-present, but some of the questions leaders should ask are:

- Is there a point of diminishing return on co-location, and is there a value to independent work?
- How will the policy affect employee recruitment and retention?
- What types of tasks are better done in the same physical location?
- Which individuals are more effective in the office, and which are more effective when working remotely?
- How could a different technology infrastructure affect these decisions?
- How could a different organizational model affect these decisions?
- Could changes in the training and development of employees affect these decisions?
- Could training on management and leadership affect these decisions?

In order to maximize organizational results these and other considerations need to be taken into account. One place to start might be Organizational Network Analysis (ONA). An ONA assessment looks at the information and process flow of an organization and attempts to weigh those elements that could benefit from geographic proximity.

Like most network analysis techniques ONA begins by developing nodes which are most often individuals but could be teams or groups. It evaluates the tasks and roles that these nodes play in the network, and how the nodes are connected to other nodes of the network. Next, it looks at the following (Deloitte 2016):

- The nature of those connections;
- The types of inform shared;
- The volume of information;
- The frequency of sharing.

From this we can begin to recognize different categories of nodes:

- *Central*: Nodes that are broadly connected across the network.

- *Knowledge brokers*: Nodes that act as the boundary spanners (see above).
- *Peripheral*: Nodes that mostly work independently.

As we work through this analysis it may become clear which nodes should spend more time geographically co-located, and which could spend most if not all their time working remotely. However, there are few absolutes when it comes to defining the best in-office policy. What is clear is that the right plan will be highly dependent on context based on the individual, team, and organizational level.

Office Days

After performing an ONA, we might find that a hybrid model could work, so the next question might be how to coordinate the days on-site. If there is value in co-location, organizations should have guidelines in place regarding the days that employees should be in the office. Showing up to an empty office is far less valuable than one filled with your colleagues.

There are several good ways to approach this:

- Protect Mondays and Fridays as remote days to extend the weekend.
- Alternate days of the week to break up commuting days. For example, Mondays remote, Tuesday on-site, Wednesday remote, Thursday on-site, Friday remote.
- Create a pattern that spans multiple weeks. For example, be on-site on Tuesdays and Thursdays, and every other Wednesday.
- Create seasonal patterns. For example, accounting teams might want everyone on-site for month end, and during the tax season, but allow more remote days in the summer.
- Project-driven patterns might include meeting on-site at the beginning and the end of a project and require online checking in between. Clearly, there are a number of ways this could be organized, but the value of the alternatives will be highly dependent on the context.

Office Hours

To foster information flow some companies have experimented with requiring defined office hours – some defined by the company and others by the employee. During these office hours employees are available for colleagues to drop in physically, or virtually, to collaborate or ask questions. For example, an employee might set a time between 10:00 and noon as their office hours. They might reserve the early morning and afternoon for scheduled meetings or heads-down work.

Non-compliance

All this planning is great, but there must also be a plan for how to react when there is non-compliance. This is especially true in an environment in which there are many disengaged or actively disengaged employees. Blatant disregard for the rules could turn into a moral problem and affect the organization's productivity.

However, these rules should be treated as such, not as laws of nature. Exceptions should be made when and where appropriate.

Chapter 6 Takeaways

To most serious observers it is clear that the days of nine-to-five, five days a week in the office are fading away – if they haven't disappeared already. Not only are employees demanding it, but greater flexibility will be an advantage going forward in attracting and retaining talented knowledge workers.

However, to reap the benefits of this hybrid and remote work the devil is in the detail of how it is implemented. Blanket rules are likely to sub-optimize the opportunity for success. Managers need to understand and question the following:

- The nature of the work;
- The flow of the necessary information;
- The process of collaboration;
- Is the infrastructure in place to enable information flow and collaboration?
- What are the cultural imperatives and relationships between team members?
- How can the office space aid or detract from the business process? There needs to be a plan that is measured and reassessed on a regular basis to ensure success. It must be remembered that the office is a technology that can be used to further the business, and just like any other technology it has its advantages and disadvantages. In defining the goals of the office, we might consider:
- What is it that the office should achieve?

  - Business process support;
  - Development of culture;
  - Monitoring of employees;
  - - Social interaction and development of relationships;
  - Facilitation of collaboration;
  - Internal network development;

- In addition, the format and use of space in the office had to be re-evaluated.

    - The size and location;
    - Methods to facilitate information flow.

References

Bernstein, E. S., & Turban, S. (2018). The Impact of the "Open" Workspace on Human Collaboration. *Philosophical Transactions of the Royal Society B: Biological Sciences*, 373(1753), 20170239. https://doi.org/10.1098/rstb.2017.0239.

Bernstein, E., Blunden, H., Brodsky, A., Sohn, W., & Waber, B. (2020). July 15). The Implications of Working Without an Office. *Harvard Business Review*, 2–10.

Csikszentmihalyi, M. (1990). *Flow: The Psychology of Optimal Experience* (1st ed.). Harper Perennial Modern Classics.

Deloitte (2016). *Organizational Network Analysis*. https://www2.deloitte.com/us/en/pages/human-capital/articles/organizational-network-analysis.html.

Dhawan, E., & Chamorro-Premuzic, T. (2018). February 27). How to Collaborate Effectively if Your Team Is Remote. *Harvard Business Review*, 7.

Ferrazzi, K. (2014). Managing Yourself: Getting Virtual Teams Right. *Harvard Business Review*, 92(12), 120–123.

Goleman, D. (2013). *Focus: The Hidden Driver of Excellence* (illustrated ed.). Harper Business.

Granovetter, M. S. (1973). The Strength of Weak Ties. *American Journal of Sociology*, 78(6), 1360–1380.

Gratton, L. (2022, May 3). Maintaining Network Connections. *strategy+business*. https://www.strategy-business.com/article/Maintaining-network-connections.

Grenny, J., & Maxfield, D. (2017, November 2). A Study of 1,100 Employees Found That Remote Workers Feel Shunned and Left Out. *Harvard Business Review*. https://hbr.org/2017/11/a-study-of-1100-employees-found-that-remote-workers-feel-shunned-and-left-out.

Hawthorne, N. (2013). *The House of the Seven Gables*. Dover Publications, 183.

Keswin, E. (2022, January 6). In the Hybrid Era, On-Sites Are the New Off-Sites. *Harvard Business Review*. https://hbr.org/2022/01/in-the-hybrid-era-on-sites-are-the-new-off-sites.

Mark, G., Gudith, D., & Klocke, U. (2008). *The Cost of Interrupted Work: More Speed and Stress*. Proceeding of the Twenty-Sixth Annual CHI Conference on Human Factors in Computing Systems (April 6), 107. https://doi.org/10.1145/1357054.1357072.

McChrystal, G. S., Collins, T., Silverman, D., & Fussell, C. (2015). *Team of Teams: New Rules of Engagement for a Complex World*. Portfolio.

Murthy, V. (2017, September 26). Work and the Loneliness Epidemic. *Harvard Business Review*.

Neeley, T. (2021). *Remote Work Revolution: Succeeding from Anywhere* (illustrated ed.). Harper Business.

Neeley, T. (2022). *12 Questions About Hybrid Work, Answered*. Harvard Business School Cases, 16.

Newport, C. (2016). *Deep Work: Rules for Focused Success in a Distracted World* (1st ed.). Grand Central Publishing.

Orhan, M. A., Rijsman, J. B., & Van Dijk, G. M. (2016). Invisible, Therefore Isolated: Comparative Effects of Team Virtuality With Task Virtuality on Workplace Isolation and Work Outcomes. *Revista de Psicología Del Trabajo y de Las Organizaciones*, 32(2), 109–122.

Panteli, N., & Chiasson, M. (2008). *Exploring Virtuality Within and Beyond Organizations: Social, Global and Local Dimensions.* Palgrave Macmillan.

Sailer, K., Koutsolampros, P., & Pachilova, R. (2021). Differential Perceptions of Teamwork, Focused Work and Perceived Productivity as an Effect of Desk Characteristics within a Workplace Layout. *PLOS One*, 16(4), e0250058. https://doi.org/10.1371/journal.pone.0250058.

Schein, A., & Haruvi, N. (2017). The Relationship between the Average Work-week Length and Per Capita Gross Domestic Product (GDP). *International Studies of Management & Organization*, 47(4), 311–323. https://doi.org/10.1080/00208825.2017.1382268.

Chapter 7

People and Talent

Finding, Training, and Retaining the Right People

During the writing of this chapter my life crossed a new milestone. I became a grandpa again for both the second and third time, on the same day (my daughter in-law delivered twins). As you might imagine I was over the moon with joy, and I was proud to share the news with friends and family. As grand events often do, it led many of those in my circle who have been around the block a few times to reminisce about the *good ol' days*, and how *back in the day* we struggled through some of the challenges that such a blessed event presented.

Talking about maternity/parental leave one friend lamented, "I think when my son was born, I got a day off – but only because it was a Sunday – I was expected back at work the next day." Of course, he was kidding, but not by much. When I discussed this with someone else close to me – a partner in a firm with over 100 employees – he said,

> What we were expected to do back when we had kids was crazy. That time in your life is crazy enough without us adding to it. You're making me want to go back and revisit how we are handling that now. Not just because it's the right thing, but because we need to support our people if we want them to support us.

So, beyond the joy of these new additions to my family, I have a good reason for bringing up this topic. When faced with an inflection point in the environment managers have to reassess the ramifications thereof for their policies and procedures. This is especially true of those policies and procedures dealing with people, and is related to how we find them, train them, and retain them.

DOI: 10.4324/9781032646657-7

Finding

Recruiting

This week I had the chance to speak to a young woman who manages a technology recruiting team for one of the world's top ten recruiting firms. I asked what has changed since the start of the COVID-19 pandemic. Her response was clear: the demand for flexibility in where and when a candidate is expected to work. Candidates are looking for the ability to be in the office for a maximum of two to three days a week, and many would like to limit office time to the early stages of a project when high levels of coordination are required.

Flexibility

Of course, this is a small sample focused on candidates with a very specific set of skills; however, this trend seems to be supported by cross-industry data. Recent data from McKinsey and Company (2022) suggests that 87% of employees given the option to work hybrid or remotely take that opportunity. McKinsey also suggested that many of the recruiting techniques from the past may need to be reevaluated, due both to high levels of employment (particularly among some key roles) and differences in the demands of the candidates.

My recruiter friend also noticed an increase in firms willing to allow roles that in the past were on-site to shift to fully remote. This of course has broadened the geographic area in which she can recruit but has also led to a diaspora among existing employees searching for a lower cost of living or a better lifestyle – a concept that we discussed in Chapter 1. The real challenge that these companies are now facing is how to compensate these employees who have moved out of a commutable distance from the company offices, and how do they compensate fully remote employees.

Historically companies have paid employees in high-cost areas more than those in more remote areas with lower costs of living – and there are logical economic reasons for this practice. If companies were recruiting for a high-demand skill that needed to be on-site in a specific office, they needed to find candidates for that job within a commutable distance of the office. Often, they found themselves competing for a limited pool of candidates with a number of other competitive firms. Based on the simple laws of supply and demand they would often bid up the price (salary) paid to acquire that candidate. Candidates who had the necessary skills but who lived outside a commutable distance of a large metropolitan area often found it difficult to find opportunities; therefore, the price they demanded was lower.

Geography

Simply by broadening the acceptable geographic area you can dramatically increase the pool of candidates. In addition, candidates may be willing to accept less remuneration for a position that allows them to live where they want – especially if they can maintain a comparable lifestyle at a lower cost. However, companies may find that those with the knowledge, skills, and abilities (KSAs) that are in high demand may still demand the same salary no matter where they live, if they feel that their marketability is still strong. Attempting to negotiate a lower salary based on their geographic location could push them into the employment of a competitor.

Investing in the Future

Historically a draw for high-potential candidates was the ability to grow and develop. Firms like GE, IBM, Proctor & Gamble, McKinsey and Company, and Bain were magnets for talent due to their history of investing heavily in training and development. However, the social contract between employer and employee changed over time. Both sides of the equation demonstrated they were less committed to the contract. Employers were less willing to invest in their staff, and employees were willing to accept almost any new opportunity that arose outside the firm. However, many have noticed a marked change. Employers see training and development as a retention tool, and many employees are reacting positively to their efforts.

Open Talent

This may also be an opportunity for organizations to reassess their relationship with their talent. They may begin to reassess what talent is strategically important and which talent could be purchased as needed on the market. In past generations many employees were looking for stability and security. However, many in the current generation of employees are more concerned with engagement and meaning. They are more willing to move from project to project in search of personal fulfillment.

In an open talent world talent would span a spectrum:

- *Balance sheet*: Full-time, statutory employees;
- *Partnership talent*: Employees who are part of a partner or joint venture;
- *Borrowed talent*: Employees who are part of the value chain or ecosystem;
- *Freelance talent*: Independent workers or short-term contractors;

- *Open source talent*: People who volunteer their time and IP as part of a community.

(Liakopoulos et al., 2013)

Retaining

Onboarding

If left to sink or swim in their new role, new hires often take six months or more to reach peak productivity. The simplest description of onboarding is to reduce that peak productivity time to weeks instead of months. Historically this process was highly dependent on physical presence. Often even remote employees were brought into a company facility (often the company headquarters) for a boot camp-like experience. The value of these experiences hinged on the intensity of the experience and the ability to acquire the tacit knowledge that comes from immersion in the company culture.

As we move to a remote and hybrid world, these on-site experiences are often more difficult to coordinate, or logistically they become untenable. Often remote employees chose a remote role because of personal challenges that make it difficult if not impossible to be on-site, even on a temporary basis, and many hybrid worker would face similar challenges if the onboarding process lasted more than a few days.

Among the issues facing professionals responsible for onboarding, many would agree that the online process often takes longer than it would if carried out on-site, and many current practices are more challenging online. Processes that rely on tacit knowledge or the observation of other employees are more difficult to manage online.

Many organizations have included a mentor/buddy system. Such programs pair a newcomer with an organization veteran – someone who can instruct the newcomer in how the organization's processes and culture work and help them to avoid common traps or cultural gaffes. In a 2018 study conducted at Microsoft over 97% of the participants in such a program – who had met with their mentor more than eight times in the first 90 days – said that their mentors had helped them to come up to speed quickly. Microsoft's human resources team now describes this as an essential part of the onboarding process (Lublin, 2022).

It may also be important for managers to realize that this process should be planned, organized, led, and controlled over a period of months not days or weeks. The management of the process is even more critical when employees are remote. Unless there are processes and metrics to measure progress, employees could find themselves frustrated and directionless – leading to both a drop in productivity and adding to the probability that employees will leave the organization.

Belonging and Friendship at Work

Throughout my professional career I held roles that were either partially or fully remote, so I can draw on firsthand experience of the challenges that professionals face while working remotely. In decades past many salespeople, consultants, field technicians, and other professionals whose work takes them out of the office on a regular basis found that tasks that would be easy to do in the office suddenly took significant effort when working remotely. These challenges have now been more broadly felt. Therefore, since the start of the pandemic a number of academic studies and articles have codified these challenges.

Any remote professional will tell you that it is far easier to get problems resolved when you can look the person you need help from in the eye. My personal experience tells me that there are a number of reasons for this. Some of it is the social pressure to deal immediately with the present issue by the person in front of you; however, there are several other issues at play here. Among the issues are the:

- Quality of the relationship between team members;
- Engagement of the individuals involved;
- Richness of the media used to communicate;
- Quantity/quality of the information or knowledge transferred.

Whatever the reason there are often inherent advantages of co-location from a performance point of view.

Prior to the COVID-19 pandemic 40% of employees said that they felt isolated at work (Carr et al., 2019). This often leads to a reduction in commitment, engagement, and overall performance. The feeling of loneliness that results is extremely detrimental to the overall wellbeing of the employee. Some studies suggest that it is equivalent to smoking 15 cigarettes a day, and poses an even a greater risk than obesity (Murthy, 2017). What is of concern is that the rates of isolation and loneliness have doubled since the 1980s, and anecdotal data suggests that pandemic-related lockdowns and work from home initiatives have exacerbated the problem.

Conversely, we know that when employees score highly on belonging there are a number of other associated benefits. They typically have a:

- 56% higher job performance;
- 50% drop in turnover;
- 75% drop in the number of sick days;
- And those with higher belonging scores typically secure double the number of raises and promotions.

(Carr et al. 2019)

One of the advantages of co-location relates to the effort required to communicate and form relationships. Communication issues have a lot to do with the richness of the media, and the effort required to initiate dialogue and exchange knowledge and information. Media richness is a concept that we discussed earlier in the book. In short it is any given media's ability to carry the full content of a communication. An example of rich media would be an in-person conversation where body language and tone would add to the richness of the communication, while a text message would be a low richness media where much of the subtlety of a message is lost due to the omission of the elements that enrich the message. Unfortunately, when working remotely we are often forced into situations in which we use less rich media – or forego communication altogether.

In addition, when working remotely we often choose asynchronous communication methods for logistical reasons. This can create a series of problems in the efficiency of the communication. According to Media Synchronicity Theory (Dennis et al., 2008) there are advantages to both synchronous and asynchronous media – each has tasks that they are better suited to. In professional communication there are inherently two tasks: the conveyance of information, and the convergence of meaning of information. Conveyance is better served by asynchronous media, and convergence is better served by synchronous media. Synchronous media is also instrumental in the development of rapport and friendship among employees.

Any loss in the efficiency of the communication results in a loss of cumulative proximity (see Chapter 5 which discusses proximity). This loss in cumulative proximity could, and often does, lead to the loss of closeness in the relationship between team members. The strength of the relationship between individuals has a significant effect on the efficiency of the communication between them. Therefore, for efficiency alone – never mind the other positive effects on employee happiness and retention – there are ample reasons for inventing in internal employee relationships. In addition, if there is not a concerted effort to maintain internal relationships, when shifting to remote work organizations tend to become more siloed (Yang et al., 2022).

Commitment

Overemployment

The US Census Bureau released a report in 2019 that looked at data collected in 2013 and 2014 that suggested that 8.3% of workers in the US had more than one job, and that 6.9% had more than two jobs. Subsequent reports published by the US Bureau of Labor Statistics recognized that multiple job holders represent a significant percentage of the workforce. The Bureau estimated that an additional 320,000 workers joined the US labor force between 2020 and 2021. Holding multiple jobs is nothing new; however, the number of people participating in this activity has been trending upward for some time and it accelerated with the imposition of lockdowns intended to curb the spread of the COVID-19 pandemic and the resulting dramatic increase in remote workers.

In 2021 *Business Insider* noted that in a survey of over 1,200 remote workers over two-thirds held down two jobs, some had a part-time second gig or side hustle, but others held a second full-time job. They noted that few of these employees work 80 hours or more per week (the equivalent of two 40-hour per week jobs). When reporting on their productivity, they claimed to be as or more productive at work now than when holding only one job (Tan, 2021).

Others have reported that this has become so common that there are now websites such as Overemployed.com that chronicle the best practices of those involved. One topic that is frequently discussed on these websites is how not to get caught. What many find interesting is that in many cases this sort of duplicity may not be illegal. However, employers may be able to bring a lawsuit against such employees for issues such as:

- Confidentiality agreements;
- Non-compete agreements;
- Misrepresentation.

The general consensus seems to be that it is difficult to get caught if employees are careful to avoid self-incrimination (Feintzeig, 2021). However, there are several moral hazards that should be considered seriously before any such activity is undertaken.

Issues/Implications

The fact that over employment exists leads to several underlying issues and implications that managers might consider.

Culture of Productivity

There is an old aphorism that states that *if you want something done give it to your busiest person.* As counterintuitive as this sounds it is often true. Busy people are often highly focused and efficient.

The fact that overemployed people have enough time in their week to hold down two full-time jobs is anecdotal evidence that these people are likely more productive than the average employee. However, it might also be evidence that many companies have a culture of complacency and mediocrity – that over time we have begun to accept low levels of productivity as normal and acceptable.

This may be a reason for many managers to begin to question both the level of productivity that they are getting from their existing employees, and how many of their employees are either incompetent or coasting.

Job Definitions

If these jobs can be done by overemployed individuals, should they be contract positions? It seems you are getting contractor efforts, but you are paying benefits and taxes for an employee. Or should we assess the actual requirements of these jobs more carefully, and consider combining two or more jobs and their compensation to attract star employees who will be highly focused and efficient? Such a move might create a culture of efficiency and productivity.

Compliance versus Engagement

One common theme that appears with overemployed people is they are not looking to be superstar employees. They simply want to get by and not get fired. For them, the incentive is not praise or career opportunity. They are motivated by money.

One classical management theory that might apply here would be Hertzberg's two-factor theory. Hertzberg believed that when it comes to employee motivation there are factors that can by their nature increase satisfaction, and others that by their nature can cause dissatisfaction among employees. Among the factors that Hertzberg recognized as satisfiers would be:

- Recognition;
- Job status;
- Responsibility;
- Achievement;
- Opportunity for advancement;
- Personal growth.

These factors are likely to positively increase an employee's job satisfaction and lead to their greater commitment to the organization.

Among the factors that Hertzberg recognized as causing dissatisfaction were:

- Salary/compensation;
- Working conditions;
- Physical workplace relationship with colleagues;

- Relationship with supervisor;
- Quality of supervision;
- Policies and rules.

What is counterintuitive about these factors is they act very differently to the satisfiers. If increasing satisfiers is good, then simple logic might suggest that decreasing dissatisfiers would be a way to increase satisfaction; however, if we look at Hertzberg's list decreasing salary or having poor working conditions would seem to be a poor option. Rather, what Hertzberg suggests is that for all the dissatisfiers there is a hygiene level that must be achieved. If a factor is below hygiene level it has a negative effect on employee sanctification and engagement. If we increase the factor above the hygiene level there is little to no long-term effect.

So, if employees are not making a salary that they are comfortable with they will be dissatisfied or will look for ways to remedy the situation. Historically that might mean looking for a new job, or a side gig. If they are looking for strong relationships with colleagues or supervisors, moving to remote work often affects those relationships and possibly leads to a feeling of being disconnected from the organization. One could also argue that for a lot of people working from home could put them in environments that are not conducive to focused work (e.g., no dedicated work space and/or young children at home who need attention).

In working environments where low productivity is acceptable there it is likely to be low value generation; such companies are likely to lack the resources to remunerate their workforce to a level that would be expected by high-performing employees. In addition, given the number of relationship-oriented dissatisfiers that are affected by remote work, it is not surprising that many employees are finding themselves disconnected, unmotivated, and demotivated. These employees would look to meet the minimum requirements of a job and find a way to use their free time to meet their personal goals in other ways.

The Great Resignation

Beginning in the fall months of late 2020 a flurry of articles touting the beginning of the Great Resignation started to appear in the general business press. This flurry soon turned into a blizzard with an endless number of theories as to why the phenomenon was occurring. It might make sense to start with a description of what the Great Resignation is. Put simply, the number of American workers who were changing jobs, or considering changing jobs, skyrocketed. As of the summer months of mid-2022 the number of workers who were considering changing their jobs within the next six to 12 months was around 40%. Although the numbers were higher for younger workers than older workers this trend cut across demographics (Noonan, 2022).

Some observers have suggested that it might have been better to call this phenomenon the Great Reassessment or the Great Realignment because many workers were reevaluating their life and career tracks. One recent study suggested that approximately 65% of those changing jobs were either leaving the workforce (17%) or had changed industries (48%) (McKinsey & Company, 2022).

If we delve into the data pertaining to specific industries, we find that the attrition rates vary wildly. In early 2022 the rates varied among industries from as low as 2% or as high as 30%. Even within industries there were dramatic differences between companies. "Workers are 3.8 times more likely to leave Tesla than Ford, for example, and more than twice as likely to quit JetBlue than Southwest Airlines" (Sull et al., 2022).

By December 2021 Gartner Group noted that over 60% of corporate leaders "described themselves as significantly concerned about employee turnover." In addition, they predicted that the year-over-year turnover rate would to increase by 50%–75% compared to the level that managers are accustomed to and predicted that henceforth it would, on average, take 18% longer to fill open positions (Wiles, 2021).

Issues and Implications

Managers should of course evaluate the potential reasons why this phenomenon is occurring and attempt to mitigate their firm's exposure to these factors. Some of the most common themes are listed below.

Unemployment Rate

The strong economic conditions prior to the outbreak of the COVID-19 pandemic led to historically low unemployment. As of February 2020 the national unemployment rate stood at 3.5%. Following the imposition of a national lockdown the rate skyrocketed to 14.7% in April 2020, only to plummet to 3.5% by mid-2022 (US Bureau of Labor Statistics, 2022). However, national averages are just that – averages. Some states saw unemployment rates fall below 2% by mid-2022.

Organizational Culture

One of the most significant reasons given for an employee to tender their resignation was toxic organizational culture. This has been rated as "10.4 times more likely to contribute to attrition than compensation." However, other studies show that burnout, lack of recognition, and constant pressure to innovate are factors that strongly affect the rate of attrition. One interesting point is that many companies known for innovation – a fact that many employees would find exciting and inspiring at first blush – often had a higher attrition rate. The pressure to innovate creates a certain level of instability in the environment, and constant change makes a consistent vision of the probable future harder to agree on, so it often leads to long hours and grueling work schedules (Sull et al., 2022; Wiles, 2021).

Presence Policy

Now that the vast majority of employees have had an opportunity to work at home, and therefore have been able to avoid the time and expense of commuting, and to experience greater autonomy and greater flexibility in their lifestyles, many do not want to return to the office – or at least not full-time. This of course is in direct contrast to many corporate leaders who are concerned about factors such as company culture, innovation, and in some cases productivity, which are affected by co-location of employees. This has led to employees refusing to return and, in some cases, finding other employment that will allow them to continue to work remotely. In a recent ADP study 64% of workers said that they would look for a new job if required to return to the office full-time (ADP Research Institute, 2022).

Quiet Quitter

During the summer months of mid-2022, the term "quiet quitter" went viral on social media platforms and in the business press. It has been defined in several different ways: at best it is the development of clear work-life boundaries; at worst it is the act of doing the bare minimum required to keep a job (Ellis & Yang, 2022; Dill & Yang, 2022; Klotz & Bolino, 2022). Gallup suggested that these workers currently make up 50% or more of the US working population, and the proportion seems to be higher among younger employees (Harter, 2022).

Some observers have suggested that this is a fake crisis. Indeed, they have suggested that "disengagement is about as novel as cubicles," and the term quiet quitter is just an attempt to invent a new term (Thompson, 2022). It is generally agreed that it is merely a new term for something that has been happening since the start of time. Giving it a name allows us to track it. It makes it easier to define who quiet quitters are, understand what might be causing them to behave as they do, and hopefully define and execute a plan on how to fix it or at least slow the progress.

As discussed in Chapter 2, Gallup has been tracking employee engagement level for over 20 years, and divides employees into three categories: engaged, disengaged, and actively disengaged. Engaged employees are those who are excited about their jobs and are willing to go above and beyond when required to do so. Disengaged employees are those who do the minimum required and no more. Actively disengaged employees work against the organization for their own benefit. Recent Gallup studies have shown a marked increase in the number of disengaged and actively disengaged employees. Some of their key findings are as follows:

- The percentage of engaged employees under the age of 35 dropped by six percentage points from 2019 to 2022. And during the same time, the percentage of actively disengaged employees increased by six points.
- Younger workers have dropped 10 or more points in the percentage who strongly agree that someone cares about them, someone encourages their development, and they have opportunities to learn and grow.
- Fully remote and hybrid young workers dropped 12 points in strong agreement that someone encourages their development.
- Disturbingly, less than four in 10 young remote or hybrid employees clearly know what is expected of them at work.

(Harter, 2022)

This trend of employees setting limits on the level of effort that they are prepared to expend or demonstrating an unwillingness to go above and beyond what is required of them is troubling in many ways. In order to maintain their competitiveness employers need their employees occasionally to be willing to step up and take on additional tasks, initiatives, or projects. If there are a large number of disengaged employees unwilling to participate, it puts additional pressure on those who do – leading to a very unhealthy situation.

In the past employees did indeed go above and beyond in order to boost their careers. These extra efforts helped to create social capital that led to career opportunities. Some observers have suggested that this situation exists because in recent times, when employees have stepped up and taken on additional work and responsibility, there has been a lack of recognition or delivery on the promise of career success. They were not recognized, nor did they see any benefit (such as bonus, career opportunity, or even recognition) tied to the effort (Klotz & Bolino, 2022).

In the early days of the pandemic when it was clear that employees were as productive, or in some cases more productive, than before the pandemic many analysts feared that we had entered crisis mode whereby employees were putting in heroic efforts – and that these efforts might be unsustainable over time. This could be a contributing factor. In addition, when considering that remote employees have far fewer casual conversations with their managers and team members there is less affirmation of such heroic efforts. In many of those casual conversations in the past they would have received a verbal (and sometimes literal) pat on the back. The paucity of these conversations has possibly led to a feeling of disconnectedness. Gallup has also suggested that many employees feel that a reduced level of communication with leadership and management has led to a lack of clarity on goals and expectations, thereby creating additional stress (Harter, 2022).

Issues and Implications

Listening Tour

Before implementing this strategy managers should implement a listening tour of the organization, the goal of which is to understand where the organization is facing its biggest challenges, and where investment might have the greatest effect on both engagement and organizational success. Some areas of focus m ight be compensation, flexible work arrangements, and training and development. However, leaders should be looking to rebuild strained emotional and psychological connections to their teams.

Managers

What is even more damaging is that many managers – particularly front-line and mid-level managers – have themselves become disengaged. Some studies suggest that currently one in three are disengaged. Not only do we need to get to the root of the issues with these managers, we need to re-skill these managers to enable them to identify both their own issues and the issues facing their teams. Since the casual conversations are not happening there should be regular and frequent check-ins with employees (15–20 minutes) to surface issues and provide support.

Teams

In many cases teams are also feeling the pressure. In some cases teams may need to change their processes to create better information flow and collaboration. This might mean new hardware and software infrastructure, and/or it may mean that there is a need for training and leadership on how to effectively collaborate remotely. At the very least some attention should be paid to how to facilitate addition conversations between team members – both those who cover project- or task-related topics and those who exchange more casual information to facilitate personal connections. In general, purpose is becoming more important. Employees and teams need to understand and buy into the purpose of the organization, and their role in facilitating that purpose.

Job Definition

Since employees are not going beyond their job descriptions, one possible strategy that could help to mitigate the problem is to redefine their job descriptions so that they match what is really required of them to ensure organizational success. However, this strategy should be implemented cautiously. If implemented with too heavy a hand there could be significant pushback from disengaged employees, some of who may indeed decide to leave. This effort should include the careful crafting of employees' job responsibilities so as not to require the heroic efforts that have caused disaffected many employees to begin with.

Creation of Focus

I have had two managers in my life who taught me lessons about focus that I carry to this day, Vic Melfa, Sr. and John Hoffman. Vic was the founder of and my manager at Vitronix (a computer wholesale business in the late 1980s), and John was the founder of and my manager at Right Source (a tech marketing communications firm in the early and mid-1990s). Both firms grew at an outstanding rate. Vitronix appeared among the top 50 firms in the Inc. 500 list of the fastest-growing privately held companies in the US, and although Right Source never applied to be ranked on the list it grew even faster than Vitronix. In addition, both men made a successful exit in merger and acquisition deals after a few years of my work with them.

Due to their extremely high growth rates both firms were faced with the fact that systems, business processes, and skill sets were outgrown on a regular basis. This meant that management was constantly reassessing goals, training and development needs, recruiting requirements, and what tasks they should and should not be doing themselves.

For a while John started to ask me in our one-on-ones *what things I was going stop doing this week?* He was making a point that I had to constantly be aware of what was the *highest and best use of my time*. In a similar fashion, Vic would have me prepare a one-page report each week. It had three sections: *What were the top things you planned for last week? What were the top accomplishments for the last week? What are your plans for this week?* As you might imagine, my plans and accomplishments differed on a weekly basis. I was then asked to explain why my plans and my accomplishments were out of sync – which was sometimes very difficult. Vic's message was similar to John's: *There are plenty of thing you can fill you week with, but you have to ask yourself if they are the right things.*

I see parallels between what I experienced early on in my career and what many managers are facing today. Then and now these are times of unrepresented change. The business model, policies, and processes we started these eras with had been working fine at the time they were first implemented; however, as time went on they were becoming less and less effective. The trick is to recognize the change in requirements for success and to develop new policies, practices, systems, and skill sets to meet the challenges.

Even though I spent much of my professional career in small professional services firms where making such changes is far less challenging, my clients were all very large technology firms which had a significant level of bureaucracy. So, I saw at firsthand the difficulties large firms face when attempting to be agile. However, over 16 years ago I became a full-time academic. There are not many industries that can match education at the level of calcified bureaucracy – except maybe healthcare and government (case in point – these guys still use fax machines).

The post-COVID-19 environment is very different from the pre-COVID-19 era; therefore, adjustments are necessary. According to Robert Sutton (2022) of Stanford University, the default action seems to be to add things rather than take them away. He suggests:

> When leaders are undisciplined about piling on staff, gizmos, software, meetings, rules, training and management fads, organizations become too complicated, their people get overwhelmed and exhausted, and their resources are spread so thin that all their work suffers.

Sutton suggests that "less, less, less – is the key to success." My experience tells me that most people find comfort in their current routines and hang onto them even when they know they are not working as well as they should be. The longer you've been doing a task, the harder it is to let it go. However, there are only a limited number of hours in the week and a limited amount of mental capacity. Therefore, this process of reassessment is more than just a good idea, it is critical to efficacy and competitiveness.

The Shallows and Stolen Focus

In 2010 Nicholas Carr released *The Shallows*, a book that describes how the internet has been changing our brains. One of Carr's contentions was that given the nature of the tools now available to us (e.g., web browsers, email, social media) we often find ourselves being constantly interrupted. We find ourselves being drawn out of focused work to the intellectual equivalent of junk food. Over time this has developed into patterns of behavior that result in a decline in our ability to focus and concentrate.

John Culkin, a Jesuit priest, famously quipped in 1967 that "we shape our tools, and thereafter they shape us" (cited in Carr, 2010, p. 210). Carr suggests that we are facing an inflection point in our future mental ability, and that we need to create structures and disciplines that are structured to help us both to recover and to further develop our mental capacities, or we are surely facing a future that will be far less rich and fulfilling.

It is true that Carr penned his work over a decade ago. This might lead some readers to believe that this issue must have been resolved by now. However, evidence would suggest this is not the case. In 2022 Johann Hari published *Stolen Focus: Why You Can't Pay Attention – and How to Think Deeply Again* on basically the same theme as Carr.

Both works, and many others beside them, have suggestions on how we can overcome the issue of diminishing focus. However, the biggest hurdle is to recognize that focus is a skill, it is a skill that can be developed, and it is a skill that will atrophy if not attended to over time.

Training and Development

In Chapter 2 we introduced the concept of training and development and how prior to the COVID-19 pandemic many companies had been placing less emphasis on this area. Since these executives saw a reduction in the commitment and tenure of employees many were less inclined to invest in these employees, opting instead to hire the talent they needed as and when they needed it. This strategy worked well for a while; however, it has some inherent flaws.

There is an old adage that the way to develop trust is to start trusting people – it becomes a self-fulfilling prophecy. When you believe that there is low commitment on the part of your employees it is likely to become a self-fulfilling prophecy. Employees will sense the lack of commitment to them, and they will respond in kind. Also, the philosophy that you can just hire talent as and when you need it ignores the reality of the market. When unemployment is low this philosophy might work – but only for KSAs that are not in high demand. As the employment market tightens, or as you search for KSAs that are in high demand, this philosophy begins to falter.

Although the definition of a recession is not standard (Duggan, 2023) there is debate on whether or not the US is currently experiencing a recession. According to Duggan (2023), "US companies are hiring with a stunning 336,000 jobs added to the economy in September. Also, consumers are still spending." Moreover, in 2023 the US still had an exceptionally low unemployment rate, of 3.8% (US Bureau of Labor Statistics, 2023), even with the implementation of a number of rate hikes implemented by the Federal Reserve designed to dampen inflation and employment. And although the situation might change, according to my contacts in the recruiting world, candidates in demand are still looking for employers who are willing to invest in their development.

Why Learning and Development?

Noe (2023, p. 67) posits that companies must recognize the value of training and development activities as a part of their business strategy. The following key capabilities should be included in such a strategy:

1   Alignment of learning goals to business goals;
2   Measurement of the overall business impact of the learning function;
3   Movement of learning outside of the company to include customers, vendors, and suppliers;
4   A focus on developing competencies for the most critical jobs;
5   Integration of learning with other human resource functions, such as knowledge;
6   Delivery approaches that include classroom training as well as e-learning;
7   Design and delivery of leadership development sources.

In 2020 a total of $82.5 billion were spent on training, development, upskilling, and reskilling activities (Noe, 2023, p. 37), and a study by the Society of Human Resource Management predicted that two-thirds of the organizations that had responded to the survey would increase their budgets to include not only traditional training activities, but also mental health and wellbeing training (SHRM, 2022, p. 14). As a matter of fact, a report by LinkedIn (2023) indicates that 41% of learning and development (L&D) professionals expected an increase in spending power in 2023, with only 8% expecting their L&D budgets to decrease in that year.

What is The Difference Between Learning and Training?

Learning refers to the acquisition process of knowledge/skills/abilities along with competencies, attitudes, and behaviors (Noe, 2023, p. 6). Training is a planned and formalized activity developed by the organization. However, training can also be informal in nature and is best described as learner initiated (Noe, 2023, p. 7).

Upskilling

Asking employees to take on new opportunities, roles, and responsibilities necessitates individual, team, and organizational learning (Zajac et al., 2022) also known as upskilling and reskilling. Upskilling is defined as learning that improves or expands current skills, while reskilling is defined as the acquirement of new knowledge or skills (Noe, 2023). Finan (2020) posited that upskilling is a win-win because it helps employees to be better able to meet the demands of the business, changing customer needs, and their own career objectives, along with driving retention and making companies attractive to new hires (pp. 4–11). According to a Workplace Learning Report published by LinkedIn (2023, p. 6), the upskilling of employees has become a number one priority that involves the mapping of learning to business goals. During the pandemic, training and development took on a more important role with a link to support business strategies (Noe, 2023), and LinkedIn noted that L&D has never been better positioned to help (2023, p. 9). New technologies will force organizations to reevaluate the importance of work teams with various skills and the need to cross-train employees with different skill sets in order to fill roles based on requirements (LinkedIn, 2023, p. 35).

Training Modalities

Traditional face-to-face learning models have been thrown on their heads with the pandemic and created the need for other methods quickly. As noted by Noe (2023), "companies looked for digital learning solutions that extended learning beyond the traditional classroom, including online learning, simulations, virtual reality, games and virtual classrooms that provided the necessary environment for employees to learn" (p. 4). Artificial intelligence (AI) is just starting to enter the training and development space. The benefits of AI are being debated in the literature. According to Noe 2023, a recent study reported that 50% of manufacturers have already adopted AI technologies including robots and machine learning (p. 25). Exciting developments in the use of wearables are adding to the training repertoire and show promise in providing employees with hands-free, voice-activated access to procedures and checklists and live access to experts (Noe, 2023, p. 32). Recently, Chiang (2023) posited that the state of the workplace will become more unpredictable through the use of AI and virtual reality (p. 33).

Post Pandemic L&D

As the COVID-19 pandemic begins to recede, it is clear that L&D needs careful scrutiny to ensure that pre-pandemic financial success and wellness are maintained. Zajac et al. (2022) looked at how best to support individual L&D during times of operational challenge, especially a shift to a virtual or hybrid working structure that has impacted the inherently social nature of learning (p. 283). In a 2022 study by the SHRM, respondents indicated the importance of training in attracting and retaining talent. For example, 83% of respondents believed that training was beneficial to attracting talent and 86% believed that training was beneficial to retaining talent. The study found that L&D served a dual purpose for organizations in terms of reskilling and upskilling current employees as well as meeting business needs and new employees' desire for continuous learning (SHRM, 2022).

Workforce Composition

Employees are not a monolithic group, and a one-size-fits-all model is no longer effective, relevant, or impactful (MacCartney, 2023). In fact, the SHRM study published in 2022 found dissatisfaction and frustration with employer training:

- 33% of respondents stated that they found motivation difficult;
- 25% complained about the transfer of training concerns;
- 25% lacked the time to complete the training;
- 24% said that the training content was relevant to their role;
- 21% noted that the content was out of date.

The study's findings indicated that in addition to training being more relevant to actual jobs and having content that is current and up to date, employees want training to have a social element and they want more control over their training programs. In terms of talent management, employees considering a career move reported that they would leave their current jobs if opportunities to learn and develop new skills are missing (SHRM, 2022, p. 23).

MacCartney (2023) points out that we currently have more generations working side-by-side than ever before:

- Traditionalists (1925–1945)
- Baby Boomers (1946–1964)
- Gen X (1965–1980)
- Millennials (1981–1995)
- Gen Z (1996–)

Lowell and Morris (2019) referred to two definitions of generation. The oldest reference found in 1952 describes a generation as a group of people who share a similar worldview developed through exposure to social and historical events that occurred during the same period and during their formative years. A second definition purports that people are shaped by similar early life experiences (2019, p. 115). All this suggests that adults may require very different training approaches, and due to the number of generations currently working together this could be a real challenge for L&D administrators and managers.

MacCartney (2023) suggests that learning may be becoming increasingly personalized and highly experiential. Yousafzai (2022) noted that 77% of training and development experts believe that employee engagement depends on the ability to tailor instruction and to adopt a personalized approach. Data from the *Workplace Learning Report* published by LinkedIn (2023) indicated that the youngest employees (comprising 31% of the total US workforce) value opportunities for career growth, learning, and skills building. The same report posited that employees aged 35–49 (26% of the total workforce) value work-life balances, while employees over aged 50 (35% of the total workforce) will value challenging and impactful work (p. 24).

Agovino (2023) stated that as younger generations gain workplace influence, they will insist that employers offer flexible and hybrid work, strong mental health benefits, a commitment to diversity and social justice and good pay (p. 47). In fact, a debt of gratitude may be owed to millennials for forcing employers' hands in offering more benefits that improve workers' lives (Agovino, 2023, p. 49). In response to millennials' insistence, employers have recognize that there is a huge demand for workplace learning, and that development is vital (Yousafzai, 2022).

In the area of training and development, does research support the assumption that generational differences exist? According to Noe (2023), the assumptions regarding training show more similarities than differences resulting in an assumption of more fiction than fact and thus training designers should not attribute differences in employee behaviors and attitudes (p. 22). However, generational differences do exist and contribute to learning preferences and needs, as reported by Lowell and Morris (2019), who noted that training is usually offered on a specific topic and tends not to take into consideration the nuances of different generations, which can lead to ineffective training outcomes.

Lowell and Morris (2019) described Baby Boomers' preference for using technology in the training environment as a means to do something rather than simply adopting a new technology just because it's available (p. 117). Conversely, Gen X is interested in a work-life balance having seen the impact of their parents' focus on work and recognizing that they lacked sufficient pursuits beyond the workplace (p. 117). However, millennials have only known a world with computers and large amounts of accessible information, instant gratification, and quick responses (p. 117). In terms of desired training methods and technologies, Noe (2023) stated that Gen Z employees are more attracted to mobile phones and tablets. Generational differences may not be more fact than fiction, but an aging workforce is fact today. The labor force continues to work even though 40% of the labor pool eligible to retire have opted to continue working. By 2029 the Baby Boomer generation is expected to have increased from 5 million to 43 million (Noe, 2023, p. 21). It's a fact that age does not adversely affect work performance and learning (p. 21). A SHRM (2022) Learning and Development trends report found that 64% of respondents' preference was for training and learning through simulation closely followed by coaching/mentoring (51%), video conferencing (50%), webinars/lectures (38%), textbooks/print (34%), micro-learning (32%), audio/podcasts (25%), role play (19%), and finally blogs/internet resources (17%).

Changes in Training Methodologies

As discussed throughout this book, business practices have changed dramatically since the outbreak of the COVID-19 pandemic, especially where training and development activities are concerned. For example, prior to the pandemic 70% of all training was instructor-led, but afterwards it fell by approximately 50% (Yousafzai, 2022). However, one of the main criticisms expressed by employees was the failure to transfer training practices. MacCartney (2023) reported that 54% of respondents indicated that organizational leadership is frequently a barrier to expanding learning and development because leadership often see these activities as a cost rather than an investment. Kirkpatrick and Kirkpatrick's (2020) *Four Levels of Training Evaluation* and the integration of learning contracts are instruments that can help to ensure that the transfer of training to the workplace is more likely to occur.

In the future employers will need to consider these emerging trends: the demand for more agile ways of organizing work including creating continuous learning opportunities and empowering employees to comprehend and respond to new work situations; proactively developing skills that enable organizations to better navigate the future of work in the US; fostering individual success by creating employee-centric learning cultures; providing targeted learning experiences through broader use of learning experience platforms; integrating data-driven learning platforms with human resources information systems in order to improve and craft more personalized and relevant learner experiences; creating procedures and processes that thwart data security hacks which cause employees to questions trust of the security of their personal data; recognizing AI's influence on and its potential implications for the workplace; placing value on creating new sources of training content which may force training and development professions to repurpose training and generate user-generated content; considering ramifications of using generative AI in course content; providing development opportunities beyond the hard or technical skills and focus on supporting employees and their mental health and wellbeing (Valamis, 2023); and offering an annual personal learning stipend to support a learning culture (SHRM, 2022, p. 15).

There is no crystal ball to help organizations to work out how to stay competitive, but several predictions have been made that provide insights that will help to drive training and development strategies and practices. SHRM (2022) found that organizations must set learning and development goals including improving employee engagement, closing the skills gap, building a highly skilled workforce ready for change, and creating a workforce based on diversity, equity, and inclusion. It's important to determine the value proposition to a training and development program and to calculate a return on investment for training the workforce of tomorrow through the integration of organizational data and the integration of emerging technologies (MacCartney, 2023). As stated in the LinkedIn *Workforce Learning Report* (2023), employees who are top learners are top performers (p. 18).

For example, the e-learning market is predicted to expand by at least 200% between 2020 and 2025, and in particular an AI-powered e-learning platform will enhance the user experience by enabling learners to set their own personalized and individual learning paths (Koumadoraki 2022); meanwhile, training and development professionals must consider the potential implications of the increased array of AI systems (Valamis, 2023). Organizational agility and continuous learning will enhance adaption to changes in the market, but will require a commitment to continuous learning, empowering employees to rapidly comprehend new situations and respond effectively (Valamis, 2023). Companies needing to address the skills shortage will need to shift the focus of talent management from a recruiting mindset to investing in training for technical and soft skills, and hiring from a more diverse pool of talent and collaborating with educational institutions (SHRM, 2019). The LinkedIn (2023) *Workplace Learning Report* commented that "L&D's time in the spotlight is just beginning" (p. 16) and that strengthening the link between L&D and talent acquisition can help to propel companies into the future (p. 28).

L&D Conclusions

Clearly a number of changes that have been developing for some time have been accelerated by the COVID-19 pandemic and the trend toward hybrid/remote work. Famous old school corporate training centers like GE's Crotonville, where high potential individuals would take extended periods out of the field to participate in formal on-site training away from the office are fading from the forefront. Developing trends that managers should consider include:

- *Virtual instructor lead programs*: Think of these as Zoom-based courses that are led by an instructor in real time. Some of the advantages include the lack of travel, and the ability to schedule after hours training if necessary.
- *On the job mentoring*: This is similar to an apprenticeship program where more experienced employees lead the development of one or more apprentices.

- *Asynchronous online/self-paced*: Typically this involves computer-based learning, or some variant of a correspondence course.
- *Asynchronous online/instructor lead*: This is similar to traditional online learning which involves reading, discussion boards, simulations, assignments, and instructor asynchronous feedback
- *Virtual worlds/metaverse*: Although this is a simple variant of the above the distinguishing factor is the media. Here we are making use of new virtual worlds which could help to create a better feeling of presence and the ability to deliver different andragogical elements not available in the other typical media choices.

Chapter 7 Takeaways

When there are significant changes in the environment, whether they happen rapidly or slowly over time, there comes a point where adaptation is required if you are to stay viable or competitive. This point of required change is known as an inflection point. The COVID-19 pandemic was one of those inflection points on many levels – and this is especially true of talent and people management.

It has changed how companies find, train, manage, and retain talent on many levels. In addition, it has driven home the need to develop relationships, values, purpose, and communities within and around organizations.

Those organizations that fail to do this will find that they will either fail to gain commitment and engagement – often manifesting as a cadre of quiet quitters who will sap the effectiveness and competitiveness of the organization – or they will see large numbers of employees – likely the most talented ones – finding other opportunities more in line with their personal aspirations.

Finally, focus has developed into an issue that has become critical at both the organizational and individual level. Organizations and individuals must not only do things right – they must also do the right things, and work on the skill of mental focus to enable deeper thinking and more creative solutions.

References

ADP Research Institute (2022). *A Transformation in the World of Work*. https://www.adpri.org/assets/a-transformation-in-the-world-of-work/.

Agovino, T. (2023). Workforce: Rigid Workplace Rules Are Softening as Younger Generations Gain Influence. *HR Magazine*, 68(2).

Bolinger, A. R., Klotz, A. C., & Leavitt, K. (2018). Contributing from Inside the Outer Circle: The Identity-Based Effects of Noncore Role Incumbents on Relational Coordination and Organizational Climate. *Academy of Management Review*, 43(4), 680–703. https://doi.org/10.5465/amr.2016.0333.

Chiang, V. (2023). WORKPLACE Evolution: HR Has Undergone Global Change in the Past 75 Years. *HR Magazine*, 68(2), 32. https://link.gale.com/apps/doc/A755566940/ITBC?u=csudh&sid=bookmark-ITBC&xid=4eb40a88.

Carr, E. W., Reece, A., Kellerman, G. R., & Robichaux, A. (2019, December 16). The Value of Belonging at Work. *Harvard Business Review*, 7.

Carr, N. (2010). *The Shallows: What the Internet Is Doing to Our Brains*. W. W. Norton & Company.

Dennis, Alan R., Fuller, R. M., and Valacich, J. S. (2008). Media, Tasks, and Communication Processes: A Theory of Media Synchronicity. *MIS Quarterly*, 32(3), 575–600. https://doi.org/10.2307/25148857.

Dill, K., & Yang, A. (2022, August 25). The Backlash Against Quiet Quitting Is Getting Loud. *Wall Street Journal*. https://www.wsj.com/articles/the-backlash-against-quiet-quitting-is-getting-loud-11661391232.

Duggan, W. (2023). Recession or Soft Landing: What's Next for the US Economy? *Forbes*. https://www.forbes.com/advisor/investing/is-a-recession-coming/.

Ellis, L., & Yang, A. (2022, August 12). If Your Co-Workers Are "Quiet Quitting," Here's What That Means. *Wall Street Journal*. https://www.wsj.com/articles/if-your-gen-z-co-workers-are-quiet-quitting-heres-what-that-means-11660260608?mod=article_inline.

Feintzeig, R. (2021, August 13). These People Who Work From Home Have a Secret: They Have Two Jobs. *Wall Street Journal*. https://www.wsj.com/articles/these-people-who-work-from-home-have-a-secret-they-have-two-jobs-11628866529.

Finan, T. (2020, June 10). *After COVID-19: Cyber and the Coming Remote Work Revolution*. https://www.willistowerswatson.com/en-US/Insights/2020/06/after-covid-19-cyber-and-the-coming-remote-work-revolution.

Fosslein, L., & West-Duffy, M. (2019, February 8). How to Create Belonging for Remote Workers. *MIT Sloan Management Review*. https://sloanreview.mit.edu/article/how-to-create-belonging-for-remote-workers/.

Hadley, C. N. and Mortensen, M. (2020, December 8). Are Your Team Members Lonely? *MIT Sloan Management Review*. https://sloanreview.mit.edu/article/are-your-team-members-lonely/.

Hari, J. (2022). *Stolen Focus: Why You Can't Pay Attention – and How to Think Deeply Again*. Crown.

Harter, J. (2022, January 7). U.S. Employee Engagement Drops for First Year in a Decade. Gallup. https://www.gallup.com/workplace/388481/employee-engagement-drops-first-year-decade.aspx.

Harter, J. (2022, September 6). Is Quiet Quitting Real? Gallup. https://www.gallup.com/workplace/398306/quiet-quitting-real.aspx.

Kirkpatrick, J. D., & Kirkpatrick, W. K. (2016). *Kirkpatrick's Four Levels of Evaluation*. ATD Press.

Klotz, A. C., & Bolino, M. C. (2022, September 15). When Quiet Quitting Is Worse Than the Real Thing. *Harvard Business Review*. https://hbr.org/2022/09/when-quiet-quitting-is-worse-than-the-real-thing.

Knight, C., Olaru, D., Lee, J. A., & Parker, S. K. (2022). The Loneliness of the Hybrid Worker. *MIT Sloan Management Review*, 63(4), 10–12.

Koumadoraki, A. (2022). 10 eLearning Trends that Will Go Big in 2023. LearnWorlds Blog. https://www.learnworlds.com/elearning-trends/.

Liakopoulos, A., Barry, L., & Schwartz, J. (2013). *Human Capital*. Deloitte. http://www2.deloitte.com/global/en/pages/human-capital/articles/open-talent-econom y1.html.

LinkedIn (2023). Building the Agile Future: L&D Puts People and Skills at the Center of Organizational Success. *LinkedIn Workplace Learning Report*. https://learning.linkedin.com/resources/workplace-learning-report?src=go-pa&trk=sem -ga_campid.12612599681_asid.123631661727_crid.647037612424_kw.workplace %20learning%20report_d.c_tid.kwd-1173743060144_n.g_mt.p_geo.9031084&m cid=6841846450872315944&cid=&gclid=EAIaIQobChMI_oO0xaGAggM VeM3CBB0XNwvIEAAYASAAEgJHqfD_BwE&gclsrc=aw.ds.

Lowell, V., & Morris, J. (2019). Leading Changes to Professional Training in the Multigenerational Office: Generational Attitudes and Preferences Toward Learning and Technology. *Performance Improvement Quarterly*, 32(2).

Lublin, J. S. (2022, May 17). The Do's and Don'ts of Onboarding "Buddies"; The First Rule: Don't Force Somebody to Be a Buddy. It Probably Won't End Well. *Wall Street Journal* (online). http://www.proquest.com/abicomplete/docview/2665077452/citation/B8D981BEBEA0427DPQ/1.

MacCartney, T. (2023). *The Great Reset: Key Trends That Will Shape Learning and Development in 2023*. Society of Human Resource Management. https://www.shrm.org/executive/resources/pages/learning-development-2023.aspx.

Moss, J. (2018). Helping Remote Workers Avoid Loneliness and Burnout. *Harvard Business Review Digital Articles*, 1–6.

Murthy, V. (2017, September 26). Work and the Loneliness Epidemic. *Harvard Business Review*. https://hbr.org/2017/09/work-and-the-loneliness-epidemic.

McKinsey & Company (2022, June 23). *Is Remote Work Effective: We Finally Have the Data*. https://www.mckinsey.com/industries/real-estate/our-insights/am ericans-are-embracing-flexible-work-and-they-want-more-of-it?cid=other-eml-s hl-mip-mck&hlkid=58469f95ca6a44549ce32e67d52503f6&hctky=11879482&hd pid=22ec38c7-3ff8-4003-8e92-02216c8d12af.

McKinsey & Company (2022, September 8). *Greener Pastures?*https://www.mckin sey.com/featured-insights/coronavirus-leading-through-the-crisis/charting-the-p ath-to-the-next-normal/greener-pastures.

Noe, R. (2023). *Employee Training and Development* (9th ed.). McGraw Hill.

Noonan, P. (2022, July 21). The "Great Resignation" Started Long Ago. *Wall Street Journal*. https://www.wsj.com/articles/the-great-resignation-started-long-a go-economy-pandemic-labor-force-participation-workforce-men-mothers-stimu lus-welfare-11658440164.

Seppälä, E., & McNichols, N. K. (2022). June 21). The Power of Healthy Relationships at Work. *Harvard Business Review*, 7.

Smith, R. A. (2022, September 7). Quiet Quitters Make Up Half the U.S. Work-force, Gallup Says. *Wall Street Journal*. https://www.wsj.com/articles/quiet-quit ters-make-up-half-the-u-s-workforce-gallup-says-11662517806.

Society of Human Resource Management (SHRM) (2019). *State of the Work-place: Exploring the Impact of the Skills Gap and Employment-Based Immigra-tion*. https://www.shrm.org/about-shrm/Documents/SHRM%20State%20of%20Workplace_Bridging%20the%20Talent%20Gap.pdf.

Society of Human Resource Management (SHRM) (2022). *Workplace Learning and Development Trends*. https://www.shrm.org/hr-today/trends-and-foreca

sting/research-and-surveys/pages/2022-workplace-learning-and-development-tre
nds.aspx.

Sull, D., Sull, C., & Zweig, B. (2022). Toxic Culture Is Driving the Great Resignation. *MIT Sloan Management Review.* https://sloanreview.mit.edu/article/tox
ic-culture-is-driving-the-great-resignation.

Sutton, R. (2022, September 25). Why Bosses Should Ask Employees to Do
Less—Not More. *Wall Street Journal.* https://www.wsj.com/articles/bosses-sta
ff-employees-less-work-11663790432.

Tan, H. (2021, November 2). Over Two-Thirds of Remote Employees in the US
Work 2 Jobs, According to a Survey. Half of Them Say They Are More Productive Than When Working Just One Job. *Business Insider.* https://www.pro
quest.com/abicomplete/docview/2591121108/citation/44F7714FB9774965PQ/10.

Thompson, D. (2022, September 16). Quiet Quitting Is a Fake Trend. *The Atlan-
tic.* https://www.theatlantic.com/newsletters/archive/2022/09/quiet-quitting-tren
d-employee-disengagement/671436/.

US Bureau of Labor Statistics (2022). *Civilian Unemployment Rate.* https://www.
bls.gov/charts/employment-situation/civilian-unemployment-rate.htm.

US Bureau of Labor Statistics (2022). *Unemployment Rates Lower in All 50 States
and the District of Columbia from June 2021 to June 2022.* https://www.bls.gov/
opub/ted/2022/unemployment-rates-lower-in-all-50-states-and-the-district-of-col
umbia-from-june-2021-to-june-2022.htm.

US Bureau of Labor Statistics (2023). *The Employment Situation – September
2023.* https://www.bls.gov/news.release/pdf/empsit.pdf.

Valamis (2023). *Trends in Employee Learning and Development 2023 and Beyond:
Future-Ready Workforce.* https://www.valamis.com/blog/trends-in-learning-a
nd-development.

Wiles, J. (2021, December 9). Great Resignation or Not, Compensation Won't Fix
Everything. Gartner. https://www.gartner.com/en/articles/great-resignatio
n-or-not-money-won-t-fix-all-your-talent-problems.

Yang, L., Holtz, D., Jaffe, S., Suri, S., Sinha, S., Weston, J., Joyce, C. et al. (2022).
The Effects of Remote Work on Collaboration among Information Workers.
Nature Human Behaviour, 6(1),43–54. https://doi.org/10.1038/s41562-021-01196-4.

Yousafzai, D. (2022). The Future Trends of Corporate Training: Stepping into
Another Dimension. LinkedIn. https://www.linkedin.com/pulse/future-trends-c
orporate-training-stepping-another-khan-yousafzai/.

Zajac, S., Randall, J., & Holladay, C. (2022). Promoting Virtual, Informal
Learning Now to Thrive in a Post-Pandemic World. *Business and Society
Review.* doi:doi:10:1111/basr.12260.

Technology and Communication

Technology and Communication

Technology seems to be one of those things you either love or fear. I have generally been on the love side. One of my daughters recently described me as a tinkerer. It could be with computers, brewing beer, my sailboat, or home improvements – I'm one of those guys who likes to get his hands dirty. I spent most of my professional career working for technology companies, where I loved to get into the detail of how everything worked. So, it should be no surprise that I have some bias toward technological solutions (but at least I'm aware of my bias at an intellectual level). I get excited when I can leverage technology to make my life and the lives of my clients, my students, or my family and friends better in some measurable way.

However, real technologists are aware of the dangers of the Gartner Hype Cycle described in Chapter 1. There are times when we get caught up in the promise of what could be and miss the reality of what the technology really is today – or miss the unexpected consequences of the implementation of a technological solution. Engineers and technologists tend to fall in love with specific technologies and get excited about the finer details which, although fascinating to them, are of little interest or value to others outside their world. When applying technology, it is important to remember what the problem is, and to realize when we are using technology for the sake of our interest in the technology, and not as a viable solution to the problem itself.

The other side of the coin here is that technologies rarely reach their potential on their first implementation. Often we are several generations in before we truly understand the potential of any technology. There may be several generations of a specific technology that simply are not worth the effort of installing and maintaining, which eventually, when it matures, becomes highly valuable. We may also be relying on an aging technology that is past its prime, or awkward for the problem at hand. Often these technologies were better than alternatives in the past, and we

DOI: 10.4324/9781032646657-8

have become both familiar and comfortable with them; however, they may be less effective than more modern alternatives. The trick is being clear-headed and realistic about the future potential of technologies (those currently in use, and those we might attempt to move to), and to understand when to invest and when to cut loose and move on.

When attempting to understand the technology issues facing managers in a hybrid and remote world, we need to have an understanding of what we wish to achieve with the technology. This would also require an understanding of what the technology is capable of. For example, you cannot expect a text message to replace an in-person meeting, nor can you expect a team communications platform such as Teams or Slack to solve all the communication issues by themselves. As managers and team members, we need to take the responsibility to create an enabling environment, and to guide others in the best use of the technology options available to us.

Technology Elements/Platforms

In order to develop a cohesive strategy, it is important to have a clear understanding of the key characteristics and limitations of each of the technological elements available to us. In addition, we should be assessing the prerequisites, training, and trends that might affect the viability of these technologies over time.

Email

The earliest email systems date back to the 1960s, and by the 1970s were a staple in large mainframe systems. By the 1990s email had become pervasive across US businesses both large and small. Given its long history and pervasive use it is not surprising that most businesspeople are extremely comfortable with this technology and often choose it even when there are better options available.

One of email's great strengths is its level of flexibility and ability to connect to people or groups both within and outside the firm. Also, it can be used to send everything from a quick one-line message to the full text of a book, or a single photo to a folder full of files. However, due to its pervasive use most inboxes are extremely cluttered. This often makes it difficult to track ongoing conversations, or to find the files or content we need for an ongoing project.

Team Messaging Platforms

Team messaging platforms include products such as Teams and Slack. These platforms have evolved significantly over the past decade as platforms that organize team data and allow for electronic team communication. There are several advantages to these platforms over email. The most significant advantage is the ability to create channels or places where there is a common theme to the conversation. Unlike email where individuals are typically added to an ongoing thread at the beginning of the conversation, channels enable individuals to join a conversation in progress and see all the messages in one place. Often finding past email conversation in an active inbox can be a challenge. This is far less of a problem with a channel. Also, the platforms are arguably better for the short messages that are necessary for coordination. The messages can be related to a topic and do not have to be related to a past email to create context.

In addition, these platforms have the added ability to have voice calls, video chats, and @ mentions (the ability to tag an individual on a message or to create a private message within the platforms). If used as intended these features can go a long way toward facilitating a feeling of presence and team camaraderie, but many would argue they lack some of the serendipity that happens with physical co-presence.

Products such as Discord are making inroads in the gaming and some online technology aficionado communities. It creates a feeling of presence based on a combination of text, voice, and video-based forums where communities connect over shared interests. These products are still in the early adopter stage but could be a harbinger of things to come in more traditional organizations.

Video Chat

Desktop video chat has a history that goes back to at least the 1964 World's Fair in New York. However, most would argue that mainstream popularity did not happen until the early 2000s. Current market leader Zoom has significantly improved the usability and reliability over earlier products in this space. However, many organizations are still learning about group video chat etiquette, such as:

- When is it appropriate to have cameras off?
- Should photos be required to be displayed when cameras are off?
- Should camera requirements be dependent on how many people are on the call, or the likelihood of that participant being required to speak?
- Could meetings be split into camera required meetings, meetings where speakers are required on camera, and all cameras on?
- How do we make sure that all voices are heard?
- How do we prevent the loudest or most senior members from dominating the conversation?
- What is the technology required for remote participation?

One of the great advantages of video chat is that you can get some visual cues from the other participants. Even though there is some loss in the fidelity of these cues, it creates a stronger feeling of proximity and contentedness than a conference call, or other types of audio-only group conversations.

Due to the limitations of the media, it is far harder to pick up social cues on camera than during regular in-person conversations. Therefore, the conversation can easily be dominated by only a few individuals, and there is some loss of fidelity in the message due to the lack of some subtle body language. In addition, due to the nature of the media it is easy to multitask during a video chat. This causes participants to lose focus and results in less effective meetings.

One consideration missed by many senior managers is that many employees experience camera anxiety. This problem can happen to many different types of people but is most common among young, inexperienced employees. In this case it seems to be due to a constant fear of being judged and having to prove themselves. It is particularly common among women. As a group women tend to be more conscious of their appearance than men and more concerned about being judged on how they look (Gabriel et al., 2021).

Project Management Platforms

Project management has come a long way in the past decade and continues to develop rapidly. Leaders in the space change on a regular basis; however, current players include Monday.com, Jira, ClickUp, Basecamp, Asana, Wrike, Trello, and many others.

These systems allow teams to break down projects into tasks, assign them to individuals or teams, and track their progress. Most also allow for some or all of the following:

- Reporting of outstanding tasks by team, and individuals;
- Tracking of conversations relative to tasks or projects (similar in principle to channels in team messaging platforms);
- Reporting or displaying task progress in standard project management formats, such as Gantt charts and Kanban boards;
- Tracking cost to budget;
- Storing common files and linking them to projects and tasks;
- Providing chat (text, voice, video);
- Indicating who might currently be online.

In addition to providing direction and workflow, they provide a reason for team members to connect. One of the problems that remote workers face is anxiety over when it is appropriate to interrupt colleagues. These systems provide a stimulus and a topic for conversation. However, these systems are like gym memberships. Gym memberships don't make you healthy – making proper use of the gym does. Similarly, these systems don't make you productive or well connected with your team, but they do provide you with a platform from which to do the work.

Virtual Reality and Augmented Reality Work Environments

Futurists seem to have come to agreement that the metaverse is real, and it is the logical extension, and evolution, of a group of communications and internet-related technologies. There are as many definitions of what the metaverse actually is as there are technology pundits. However, one definition that has gained traction comes from the technology research and advisory firm Gartner:

> A metaverse is a collective virtual shared space, created by the con-vergence of virtually enhanced physical and digital reality. It is per-sistent, providing enhanced immersive experiences, as well as device independent and accessible through any type of device, from tablets to head-mounted displays.
>
> (Gupta, 2022)

As of the writing of this book, the way most people have experienced the metaverse is through virtual reality headsets, such as the consumer-focused Oculus headsets from Meta (formerly Facebook), and through the commercially focused HoloLens headsets from Microsoft. However, there have been rumors of augmented reality products from a variety of companies that seem to be expanding on the foundational work done by Google with its Glass project. This technology is still at a very early stage, and it is difficult to say what kind of role it will play as it develops, or even how long this development will take. However, there does seem to be a consensus that this technology is likely to be as disruptive as the internet itself has proven to have been over the past few decades.

Some of the advantages that have emerged for business use include the ability to facilitate deep focus as well as a more immersive remote com-munication and collaboration experience. Early products in the facilita-tion of deep focus include the solo experience from Immersed. This product creates a virtual world of limited distractions, provided by the user bringing their computer and keyboard into a multi-screen computing environment. Immersed, along with Meta, Arthur, Special, and many others have created shared collaboration environments for teams. These spaces create a feeling of 3D co-presence with other participants, and the ability to share desktops, whiteboards, and other digital assets. In most cases individual participants are represented by avatars that can move and interact with the environment and each other. In addition, spatial audio helps to support the illusion of a shared space.

As of 2023 much of the technology seems at every early stage. There is a sense that the avatars are a bit clunky and reminiscent of an old-school video game. This might lead some to discount their viability for real work, or even as a future way to satisfy a need such as entertainment or shopping. However, when considering the effects of Moore's Law and the speed at which technology has advanced over the past few decades, it is easy to envision a future where future versions of these technologies are likely to be a significant component of future work environments. Gartner suggests that "[b]y 2026, 25% of people will spend at least one hour a day in the metaverse for work, shopping, education, social and/or entertainment," and that "30% of the organizations in the world will have products and services ready for the metaverse" (Gupta, 2022).

Another area that shows significant potential for the metaverse is training and education – specifically employee training and development and graduate education. Over the past few decades both areas have leveraged technology to replace a significant amount of training and graduate education with asynchronous courses using instructor-led and independent study formats. Following the outbreak of the COVID-19 pandemic, we saw a significant shift in volume from the remaining traditional on-ground/in-person classes to synchronous online (e.g., Zoom, Teams, and similar technologies). The metaverse and its related technologies will provide an opportunity to migrate even more of the remaining traditional classroom-based courses to a location independent format, as well as providing a rich experience to students who otherwise would have taken an asynchronous course.

Box 8.1 Virtual Reality versus Reality

René Descartes (1596 – 650) suggested that if there is an all-powerful God who is all good, there might also be an extremely powerful evil daemon who manipulates us by building a simulated world that he places us in, wiping our memory of any reality, and feeding us feelings, emotions, and perceptions that are directed by him to his ends.

Under Descartes' premise we can never be sure that we are not living in a simulated world, because all the evidence that you are not in a simulation could itself be simulated. This might lead a philosopher to question if virtual reality itself is in fact reality. Will we in the future spend significant parts of our lives in virtual reality? Many question whether this will be a net positive or a net negative for those involved.

There is also the question of whether or not virtual reality is reality. Chalmers (2022) suggests that virtual reality is as real as physical reality. One is made of bits, and one is not. An analogy might be is a robot dog real? For most

> people the answer would be that it is a real device – even if it is not a real dog. It affects the environment around it and exists whether or not you are looking at it. In the same way virtual reality exists – maybe not the same way in which we experience *normal reality*, but nevertheless it is real.

Strategic Issues

Fast Follower

Communication technologies can have immeasurable effects on the culture and productivity of an organization. However, the implementation of new technologies takes both time and money. It is often difficult to decide which technology mix would be appropriate for the organization today, and which will position it best for the future. Therefore, managers should carefully weigh up their decisions. Sometimes making bold technology moves provides the firm with a competitive advantage; however, at other times it may make sense to be a fast follower – observing what the first movers do and learning from their mistakes so as to better position the firm for the long term.

Workplace Analytics

The implementation of modern workplace technologies often allows for new opportunities to gather analytics. For example, when implementing many metaverse environments companies can gather thousands of data points per hour; however, it is possible to collect even more data using new employee monitoring software (Boutenko et al., 2022). The effect on productivity should be weighed up with the legal, cultural, and moral factors that could be at play in this area.

Management by Algorithm

Many managers may find it useful to have a machine filter the endless stream of data that they face every day to find potential trouble spots, or to highlight areas for potential improvement. Data is extremely important to the management decision-making process. Modern managers should be using data to help them to step away from emotional decisions to ones that are more logical.

However, it is always important to remember that business is a social science and many of the models that good managers use to help them are incomplete. They simply can't capture all the relevant necessary data or put the data that is captured in context with the world in which it was gathered.

Location Independence

As we have mentioned elsewhere in this book, the human race has been striving toward location independence for a very long time, and for the most part we have not achieved it. The best we can hope for is to reduce the advantages of location, and supplement co-location with technologies which have sufficient media richness to allow for the maintenance of relationships – or indeed to build them more slowly. Many leading technology companies – some of which actually design tools for remote work – are still including co-location are a critical part of their strategy. They see the above tools as a supplement to their physical location strategy (Boutenko et al., 2022).

Employee Monitoring

The majority of large organizations monitor emails, many also track phone calls, text messages, and even the location of employees. Recently companies have started to track even more metrics including login/logout times, keyboard and mouse activity, screenshots of employee computers, and some have gone so far as to track biometric information. Although there was a growing trend in the deployment of such systems prior to the COVID-19 pandemic, in early 2020 the sales of employment tracking software doubled. In addition, the invasiveness of such systems has increased markedly over time. Microsoft reportedly captures biological data such as heart rate or blood pressure to create an employee "anxiety score."

Although the idea of tracking employees' every movement may appeal to some managers there are some significant issues that should be considered before implementing and operating such systems. There are various legal, moral, ethical, and leadership issues that must be considered. Organizations should obtain legal advice on what sort of data can be captured, how long that data can be kept, who can have access to that data, how the data can be used and, if you are in a regulated industry, what data do you need for compliance. Over the past decade data capture and data privacy have become political hot buttons, resulting in both national and local legislation at a global level.

At a minimum organizations should provide transparency, informing employees about the kind of data that is being collected, which metrics are being used, and how the data will be analyzed. There should be clear boundaries on what the data will be used for and why. This should be delivered in writing to employees, and employees should sign an acknowledgement of the receipt of this information. As part of this transparency effort employees should be given access to their own data, and the aggregated data of their team. If there is a clear business logic for the collection and use of the data employees are less likely to feel threatened and to assist in the process.

However, studies show that poorly handled implementation has significant negative effects. In a study by Accenture only 30% of senior executives found that their organizations always handled data responsibly, and over 50% of employees were concerned that mishandling of data could create trust issues (Blackman, 2020). Unfortunately, an additional study by the Society for Human Resource Management (SHRM) found that over 70% of employees believed that electronic monitoring is detrimental to trust (Zielinski, 2020).

Managers should be wary of the potential of micromanagement. Micromanagement gives the illusion of control at the cost of employee morale, productivity, and employee retention. Self-Determination Theory has been around since the mid-1980s and posits that in order to be motivated people need to feel competent, have autonomy, and to have a level of relatedness with those with whom they work. Micromanagement cuts against all of these (McNulty, 2022). Depriving employees of these three factors leads to stress, loss of productivity, and, if taken to an extreme, high employee turnover.

Poorly implemented employee monitoring systems and micromanagement often lead to employees feeling a loss of personal agency and autonomy. Consequently, employees feel less responsible for their own actions which results in unethical and immoral behavior. Studies by Thiel et al. (2022) suggest that "monitored employees were substantially more likely to take unapproved breaks, disregard instructions, damage workplace property, steal office equipment, and purposefully work at a slow pace, among other rule-breaking behaviors."

There may be legitimate reasons to implement employee monitoring; however, managers should proceed with caution and reassess the effectiveness of such programs on a regular basis.

Technology-Based Communication

This morning I had a lovely video chat with a former student who is now living in Nigeria. It's been a couple of years since we have shared the same classroom; however, we do share a friendship and a connection. I would not say we talk all that often, but there have been several LinkedIn messages and a couple of video chats over the past year, all of which made today's conversation easy and fun. I have been coaching her on applications to a doctoral program, and it is possible I will work with her as a research mentor. Needless to say, I believe that I will have a professional relationship with her for some time and am fond of her as both a person and a colleague.

But, as with my former student, sharing information is not just about physical distance – it is about a shared connection. To truly understand these connections, and in turn how professional relationships, productivity, and innovation happens, it is important to understand the concepts of proximity (discussed in Chapter 5), effective communication, information architecture, and some of the properties of the media used for interpersonal and intraorganizational communications.

In Chapter 5 we discussed how for centuries the human race has predicted the death of distance. We explored how simply implementing technology does not eliminate a sense of distance, and the element of proximity we feel is based on a number of factors that include physical distance, emotional connections (psychic distance, common interests, and culture (national, regional, industrial, company, and team).

Information flow, productivity, and innovation are often a function of recombining ideas and resources that often already exist or building on the ideas of others – who may exist both inside and outside your organization (Kelley, 2005). Unfortunately, given the pace of modern lifestyles, our ability to travel, and the required commitments of many of our potential collaborators, it is often difficult if not impossible to be in the same place at the same time – and of course recently there has been the issue of public health. However, some level of proximity is necessary in order for ideas to flow and collide, and for serendipity to occur. Therefore, as we discussed earlier in the book, we need to develop a new virtual type of proximity that allows our collaborators to be aware of the new ideas or potential resources when and where they could be useful. This awareness could lead to the development of a feeling of presence and possibly engagement, which could very well result in productivity and innovation.

We need to leverage our proximity, create new forms of proximity, and structure an information flow that supports the company's relationship and business process goals. So, in this section we will:

- Discuss how communication creates a feeling of proximity;
- Identify the key elements of effective communication and media use;
- Outline the key factors surrounding regional clusters and their effect on innovation;
- Explore how our relationship with our communication tools have changed and will continue to change;
- Changes in the etiquette of business communications
- Relations rules for moving forward.

Foundations of Communication

In business schools we love to teach the concept of communication using the communication model. The great thing about the model is it shows that there are a number of places where the fidelity of the communication

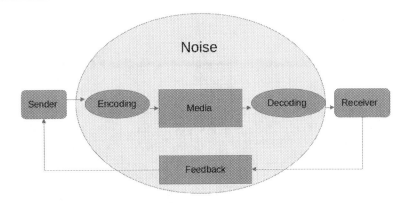

Figure 8.1 Communication Model
Source: Adler & Towne (1978).

breaks down. If a sender has an idea, he encodes that idea into words, which are then transported by some form of media. When it reaches its intended target, the words are then decoded, and the receiver now has a message.

So where does this communication break down? First, this is seen in the encoding. If the sender chooses a set of words that do not capture the idea, if there is room for equivocation, or words that could mean something different to the receiver, there is a loss in the fidelity of the message. Next is the quality of the media, which might not be rich enough to capture the complete message (see Chapter 5 on media richness), or some subtle part of the message. A mitigating factor to this is noise. This could be physical noise or competing messages. Finally, as the receiver you would hope to have feedback on your message from the receiver; however, this is subject to all the same issues as the original message.

Changes in Communication Norms

The effectiveness of one's choice of media and communication styles are affected by a number of factors, including culture, technology familiarity, business process needs, supporting infrastructure, and inertia (what has been used in the past and is most familiar). For many organizations, prior to the COVID-19 pandemic, it seems that the choice of media was often the least common denominator. Little thought was given to choosing the right tool for the job at hand. The default choice became just using what was easiest for the most technology-challenged individual involved in the conversation. So, for example, we used conference calls to review spreadsheets when a desktop sharing tool would have been far more efficient –

or we used email for short back and forth conversations that might have been more efficient in chat mode of some type.

The great reset that has resulted from the pandemic has forced many professionals to be far more deliberate in their choice of media. What is difficult for managers in the transition is to avoid the inevitable knee-jerk reactions, or making long-term commitments with a limited understanding of the available options. An example of this can be seen in the way every interaction has been turned into a Zoom call or a video chat on Teams, Slack, or similar platforms. In many cases teams have recognized that the environment is different – but they have failed to recognize how different. Far too often they are just plugging in a new technology – with limited understanding of the ramifications – into an existing business process. Zoom and other video chat products are not a drop-in replacement for being co-located in the same office. We can see this in the way video chat was used in the first year of the pandemic. If you find that most of the people on the call have their camera turned off and are not actively participating in the conversation – or if you are significantly more fatigued after a meeting – you have to wonder if this was the right media for the communication. We need a reassessment of the business process, the communication needs and the goals of the organization.

When looking at companies that have a long history of remote-first culture (e.g., GitHub, Automattic, Basecamp), or those that have recently changed their culture to focus on virtual-first culture (e.g., Dropbox), it is clear that there has to be a different approach to the tools we use, how we internalize the use of those tools, commitment to new processes, and an awareness of changing cultural norms in the use of our tools. Companies like Basecamp publish a checklist of over 30 points on how to select the appropriate communication media. Although I appreciate the effort, and agree with most of the points made, it seems a bit unwieldy as a framework for decision-making. Also, it is important to remember that Basecamp publishes an online suite of tools that help organizations to communicate asynchronously both internally and with clients. You would not be faulted if you were a little suspect of their recommendation that companies shift over 90% of their communication to asynchronous communication (like the ones they sell). However, this theme is pervasive across other leading companies that have gone almost fully remote. Synchronous communication is often preferred, but is not always necessary or efficient. In this changing environment, there will be a portfolio of communication options and the proper choice will be highly dependent on context.

It has become clear that there will be no textbook answers to what your communication should look like; however, there should be a set of principles that should drive those decisions, and possibly frameworks to help us to organize our thoughts and decision-making processes. It might be helpful to think along the lines of the agile movement used in software development and organization structures.

Agile and Scrum

The agile methodology has become extremely popular. However, there is no central authority that defines what is agile, and what is not. Because of that many people have modified the concept of agile, and the definition thereof, to fit their own needs. Here I will define it not as a methodology, but rather as a set of principles that help to guide decisions in particular circumstances. The core of agility is a willingness to change – both as an organization and as a professional. There is a need to be willing to move beyond what we have and what has made us successful in the past to a new world where our past processes and assumptions will be challenged. All this is done with the goal of allowing the organization to move faster and deliver products and services that match the needs of the customer better.

Once we accept that the world has changed, is continuing to change, and that *what got us where we are might not get us to where we need to be*, we can begin to reassess the current environment with a new eye. In an agile world leadership and management changes. In an agile world teams typically have much more autonomy and responsibility for making their own decisions and executing their own plans. Therefore, in order to keep the team on track toward its goals, the need for transparency and seamless communication dramatically increases. It is incumbent on the leader to make the context of the team's decisions, and the goals for completion, clear.

When we begin to apply the principles of agility, we might find that the processes we have in place are in fact better suited for more stable environments, and our past communication practices are far too resource-heavy for the task at hand. It is common in agile environments to implement the scrum process when working on processes. Scrum, like agile, is actually closer to a set of principles than to a pure methodology. It is typically used in project-based environments such as software development, where professionals are often working independently – but have a need for a high degree of coordination, and need to deliver on short timelines. Under scrum there is an upfront meeting that helps to set the context for the teams' decisions and provide a clear understanding of the needs of the customers and stakeholders. Teams discuss goals and timelines. Teams then choose their deliverables and begin work. The work sessions, called sprints, cover a specific length of time, typically under two weeks. Each morning there is a short meeting – usually lasting 15 minutes or less – where teams check in with each other to describe what they have recently accomplished, what they will do that day, and any roadblocks that are slowing them down. At the end of the sprint there will be a review of the project status – usually lasting an hour or less – with the customer representative. And, at the end of the project an after-action report is produced that reviews what went well and what could have been done better.

In an agile and scrum world organizations cannot waste their time on endless video calls that suck up man-hours that could have been used more productively. Meetings need to be far shorter and much more focused on the goals and deliverables of the team. In a pre-pandemic world teams were often in the same team room which allowed rapid, short, in-person communication to facilitate coordination. In a post-pandemic or highly remote team these team rooms might be simulated by some form of technology. Here the choice may be dictated by a first principles approach looking at what the media needs to facilitate.

MAAD Communications Framework

In choosing the proper media, it may be helpful to take a structured approach in addressing the multiple challenges faced in each choice. Therefore, we are devised the Managing at a Distance (MAAD) Communications Framework:

> WHAT: The content you are looking to convey.
> CONTEXT: What factors affect the meaning of the message?
> WHY: The purpose or process needs.
> CLARITY: Will the message be understood?
> WHEN: The effect of timing on the message.
> COMMUNITY: Could the message work to build community?

Content will dictate the level of richness necessary to ensure effective communication. However, this is affected by the conditions under which that content is communicated. For example, if the relationships are not strong, and familiarity between individuals is low, the content of the message needs to be more complete and more explicit. This will also often suggest the need for richer media with the ability for feedback. On the other hand, if we are dealing with strong relationships, and high familiarity, communication can often be achieved in shorthand with lower equivocality – and requiring less rich media.

The purpose of the message has to be a factor. For example, there is a difference between informing and persuading. If we are simply informing a team member of a non-equivocal fact (e.g., the time of a meeting) you might choose an asynchronous media with low richness. If persuading them on a contested point you might choose a synchronous rich media to avoid equivocality.

Finally, communication often has a shelf life. There is a period of time in which the message becomes less relevant or even useless. Often coupled with the timing of communication is an ability to create a feeling of community. How quickly you respond is often affected by or leads to a feeling of community and connectedness. It is an unspoken rule that if you are important to me, I will respond to you in what the community deems to be an acceptable time frame.

Remote and Hybrid Communication

It is hard to say how long it has been since business professionals started to hold meetings with others in different physical locations, but we could probably agree that this challenge would rival the age of business itself. In telecommunications there is general consensus that AT&T's Bell Labs developed the first commercial speaker phone in the late 1940s, but there are stories of Alexander Graham Bell hooking up speakers to phones as early as 1876. So, clearly even Bell saw the need for group communication.

However, as we began to apply technology to meet the challenges of multi-location meetings, we quickly realized that there were a number of challenges to overcome. Anyone who spent time as a knowledge worker over the past few decades can appreciate how frustrating it could be to even get a three-way call connected, never mind having people working across sophisticated video conferencing systems. The technology challenges often limit the flow of information.

Limits of Technology

It has been a common challenge to have teams fully recognize and engage with participants meeting remotely. Historically there has been a problem with enabling remote employees to be full participants in meetings. When implementing technology solutions, we run into at least two challenges: the media richness theory challenges we discussed in Chapter 5, and the technology acceptance model (TAM) which suggests that the use of technology is dependent on the perception of the user base. The TAM hypothesizes that the level of use of a technology is determined by the perception of the user base of its usefulness and the ease of this use (Standaert et al., 2016).

When new communication technologies become available the initial versions fall short in usefulness and ease of use. We also know from the diffusion of innovation theory that some groups (innovators and early adopter) will be more accepting of taking on the challenge of learning and using new technologies; however, the majority of users need to see clear evidence that the promises made by the technology can be met. We also know that there is a cognitive load that using a new technology creates until the technology has been assimilated into the daily routine of the users. This adds to both a reduction of cognitive resources to deal with the issues being discussed, resulting in a drop of productivity in the conversation.

When the pandemic forced people to work remotely, there was a dramatic increase in the number of meetings being held, leading to Zoom fatigue. The mistaken assumption was that managers should look to replicate the office environment in an electronic environment. This would seem to be a misguided assumption. Managers need to be more aware of the appropriate media for sending a message or implementing a business process. In a remote or hybrid environment there should be much greater use of asynchronous media or tools. Allowing for fewer meetings and more discretion on when and how an employee addresses an issue. This would likely make greater use of messaging platforms such as Teams or Slack.

Social Issues

Adding to this is the media richness problem. Most experts agree that when employees are required to be in the same room with other participants, all technologies limit the conversation in some way. The flow is also affected by seniority and the personalities involved. Under the current technology limitations, video chats suffer from the risk of the conversation being dominated by the most senior people on the call and those who are the most extroverted. Meeting facilitators should be conscious of this and look to moderate the conversation to ensure that all voices are heard.

Meeting Engagement

Among the issues we are now facing in a hybrid and remote world is a reduction in engagement. It is far easier to multitask when in a video meeting than in a meeting where you are co-located. Even when on camera participants could be checking their emails, working on the deliverables for their next meeting, or even playing a video game, and with a little effort they appear to be fully involved in the meeting. However, when cameras are off participants can dedicate the majority of their focus to tasks beyond the meeting. This has led some managers to suggest that cameras should be on in all meetings.

With cameras on and mute off information often seems to flow much more easily. Also, nothing kills the mood more than when a facilitator makes a joke, or some attempt at humor, and there is dead silence because everyone is on mute. Mute should be used appropriately, such as when you are in a very noisy environment – one where an individual's background noise could disrupt the meeting. However, if mute is the default setting it can slow or even kill the conversation and collaboration.

Just like mute, cameras on/off should be used appropriately. Given the amount of communication that is transmitted through facial expressions and body language, camera can positively affect communication flow and engagement. Therefore, a number of analysts and consultants recommend that this should be the default setting (Frisch & Greene, 2020). However, some groups of employees – usually woman or those in lower power roles – who can feel like they are being watched and judged, and therefore become very self-conscious. This results in higher levels of fatigue and a loss of focus on the issues at hand for the affected employees (Shockley et al., 2021).

Rules for Engagement

Develop Relationships

As we have mentioned several times in this book, relationships are key to the quality and efficiency of communication. Therefore, there should be a concerted effort to develop both inter-team and intra-team relationships. In addition to developing greater efficiency and information flow, it often aids in the retention of employees. Employees who have at least one friend at work are more likely to stay.

Action Steps

- *In person meetings*: When logistically possible there should be some regular all-hands meetings in person. Situational context will drive the particulars of these meetings; however, in most cases this should be done at the beginning of major projects or initiatives, and at least annually (if not quarterly or monthly). The point of the meeting is to reduce the social distance between team members.
- *Smaller meetings*: The default is to keep the meetings as small as possible (remember the Amazon two pizza rule). In small meetings it is easier for managers or facilitators to recognize who is not engaged or participating. Often the meetings can be recorded, or notes can be published so that others who are not on the required attendee list can access the content.
- *Fewer and shorter meetings*: Meetings will have more impact and elicit stronger engagement if there are fewer of them. Therefore, managers and facilitators should work toward meeting efficiency. In addition, they should work toward better information/media planning. Information to be delivered should be analyzed to assess if it might be better delivered in an asynchronous manner (e.g., Slack or Teams).

- *One-on-one*: managers should have a formal check-in on direct reports on a regular basis. Since they are less likely to simply bump into direct reports in the office formal scheduled meetings have developed a greater importance in maintaining strong managerial/mentoring relationships.
- *Presence*: Within the technology portfolio there should be a tool for signaling online presence and availability. This is often accomplished with messaging platforms; however, success requires that all team members are logged into the tool and know how to use it.
- *Office hours*: Part of signaling availability could be a standard set of office hours. These hours are a time when the employee is available to be contacted by team members.

Communications Charter

Rules for communication should be outlined and agreed upon. In most cases this should be supported by a formal communications charter. This charter should set a baseline for acceptable communication behavior and be updated on a regular basis to stay consistent with the changes in the organizational needs. Items in the charter should include:

- *Media selection*: There are rules for matching information to the appropriate media. For example, when should:
  - There be a meeting;
  - The content be posted to a shared platform (e.g., Slack, Teams);
  - Chat be used; and
  - Is an email appropriate?

- *Format*: The appropriate message format changes according to the media used. There should be an outline of an appropriate format with examples provided.
- *Time*: Are there times when you should not communicate. Some countries (particularly those in Europe) have laws that prohibit companies from communicating with employees during non-working hours. Many companies in the US have adopted these rules as well, as a way of promoting a healthy work-life-balance.
- *Frequency*: How often and when should employees communicate with managers and team members?
- *Tone/Voice*: What is considered the appropriate framing of the message?
- *Emergencies*: Define what does and does not constitute an emergency. Clearly you want employees to err on the side of caution; however, we all know the story of the boy who cried wolf.

Action Steps

- *Task force*: This should be a group effort with representatives from across the constituencies affected.
- *Roll out meeting*: There should be an all-hands meeting to roll out the charter to employees. Facilitators should start with the goals and follow with the strategies and tactics suggested in the charter.
- *Training*: There should be training on the tools and appropriate use. This training might be synchronous; however, well-structured asynchronous training may prove more appropriate.
- *Enforcement*: There will be growing pains in the adjustment of the embedded communication practices. This needs to be a group effort with team members coaching others on their use of proper communication channels. However, a group of advocates or managers should lead the effort.

Meeting Structure

For many organizations the structure of meetings should change to ensure the participation and engagement of all team members. As mentioned earlier, in the past remote participants were often treated as second-class meeting participants. Given that most organizations will often have a significant number of their team members working remotely, two classes of participants can no longer be tolerated. There are several tactics that can be implemented to level the playing field.

Action Steps

- *BYOL (bring your own laptop)*: One tactic is to have all co-located participants bring their own laptop to the meeting and log in as if they were working remotely. This allows remote participants to be able to see and interact will all the individuates in the meeting
- *Video conference rooms*: Sophisticated video conference rooms were once the purview of only the largest organizations, but this is no longer the case. New cameras and audio tools designed for conference/team rooms are now within the reach of even modest-sized organizations. These tools make use of AI technology to:
  - Intelligently isolate and highlight the individuals who are speaking;
  - Track the movement of individuals in the room;
  - Some even create a gallery of images of those in the room so that all participants can be identified on screen.

- *Capture meeting content*: Capture content for those who could not attend the meeting. This could be a recording of the meeting, or a simple set of notes on a shared platform.

Shared Office

In a hybrid environment companies have shifted away from dedicated offices, and toward shared spaces. Some pre-pandemic experiments in this area resulted in employees adopting tactics that were counterproductive. Many would make great efforts to stake out prime locations, would take to hording supplies in their cars, and spend far too much time finding places to store files and personal effects. Often teams found themselves spread across the office, thus defeating the purpose of being on-site.

Action Steps

- *Storage*: Have secure storage for each employee who will regularly be in the office.
- *Reservation*: Develop space reservation policies that are equitable and create a feeling of community. This might lead to defining which days an employee should, or should not, be in the office. In addition, these systems should consider the purpose of the office visit. Consideration should be given to keeping teams in close physical proximity.
- *Purpose*: The office is just another business tool, and like any tool there is both proper and improper usage thereof. Proper use of the office should be outlined, and guidance provided on how to accomplish those purposes.
- *Design*: In many cases the floor plan of the office should be reconfigured. Organizations are finding that in a hybrid office typically:

  - More shared spaces are required;
  - Investment should be made in video conference rooms;
  - Private spaces are necessary for certain types of work;
  - Common amenities and facilities that encourage casual interaction should be provided;
  - Open offices should be avoided where possible.

Chapter 8 Takeaways

Some of the key takeaways from this chapter include:

- Keep your focus on the business issue and be realistic about what the technology can be expected to accomplish.
- Technologies have a life cycle, and it is important to understand where your infrastructure is on that life cycle curve.
- There is a tendency to err on the side of choosing the familiar tool over the unfamiliar one – even when the unfamiliar tool is better suited for the task.

- As teams move to hybrid and remote presence structures, the use of team messaging platforms and project management systems take on a new significance.
- Gym memberships do not make you healthy – making proper use of the gym does. Similarly, these systems do not make you productive or well connected with your team, but they provide you with a platform from which to do the work.
- Although nascent at the time of this writing, many believe that the metaverse (either virtual reality or augmented reality) will play a role in professional presence.
- Technology has provided us with an endless ability to capture information about the performance of our teams, our customers, and even personal information about employees. This will lead to moral and ethical issues relating to what data should be captured and what should not.
- Special attention should be paid to information flow within the organization. The moment we stop sharing a physical space we need to develop new information infrastructures and the proper skills to leverage them. If not, information will not flow freely and there will be a number of resulting issues which will cause the organization to underperform.

References

Adler, R., & Towne, N. (1978). *Looking Out/Looking In* (2nd ed.). Holt, Rinehart and Winston.

Blackman, R. (2020, May 28). How to Monitor Your Employees – While Respecting Their Privacy. *Harvard Business Review*, 8.

Boutenko, V., Florida, R., & Jacobson, J. (2022, August 16). The Metaverse Will Enhance – Not Replace – Companies' Physical Locations. *Harvard Business Review*, 10.

Chalmers, D. J. (2022). *Reality+: Virtual Worlds and the Problems of Philosophy*. W. W. Norton & Company.

Frisch, B., & Greene, C. (2020, March 5). What It Takes to Run a Great Virtual Meeting. *Harvard Business Review*. https://hbr.org/2020/03/what-it-takes-to-run-a-great-virtual-meeting.

Gabriel, A. S., Robertson, D., & Shockley, K. (2021, October 26). Research: Cameras On or Off? *Harvard Business Review*, 6.

Gupta, A. (2022, January 8). *What Is a Metaverse?* Gartner. https://www.gartner.com/en/articles/what-is-a-metaverse.

Kelley, T. (2005). *The Ten Faces of Innovation: IDEO's Strategies for Defeating the Devil's Advocate and Driving Creativity Throughout Your Organization*. Random House.

McNulty, E. J. (2022, January 3). Micromanagement is Not the Answer. *strategy +business*. https://www.strategy-business.com/blog/Micromanagement-is-not-the-answer.

Shockley, K. M., Gabriel, A. S., Robertson, D., Rosen, C. C., Chawla, N., Ganster, M. L., & Ezerins, M. E. (2021). The Fatiguing Effects of Camera Use in Virtual Meetings: A Within-Person Field Experiment. *Journal of Applied Psychology*, 106(8), 1137–1155. https://doi.org/10.1037/apl0000948.

Standaert, W., Muylle, S., & Basu, A. (2016). An Empirical Study of the Effectiveness of Telepresence as a Business Meeting Mode. *Information Technology and Management*, 17(4), 323–339. http://dx.doi.org.rdas-proxy.mercy.edu:2048/10.1007/s10799-015-0221-9.

Thiel, C., Bonner, J. M., Bush, J., Welsh, D., & Garud, N. (2022, June 27). Monitoring Employees Makes Them More Likely to Break Rules. *Harvard Business Review*.

Zielinski, D. (2020, August 8). *Monitoring Remote Workers*. Society for Human Resource Management (SHRM). https://www.shrm.org/hr-today/news/all-things-work/pages/monitoring-remote-workers.aspx.

Chapter 9

Changes in Leadership and Management

Changes in Leadership and Management

As with our organizational models, our leadership and management practices were often developed in a different era with a different set of environmental variables and challenges. This is most evident in professional organizations. Many of the variables that influence the probability of success within an organization have shifted in recent years – in some cases radically. For example, in the last 50 years the percentage of Americans over the age of 25 with a bachelor's degree has more than tripled. In the past 20 years the number of bachelor's degree holders rose from about 31.5 million to 52.8 million. Also, there has been an explosion in the number of knowledge workers. According to Gartner, the world has crossed the threshold of having over 1 billion knowledge workers, and those are more likely to be working remotely than not (Roth, 2019).

When dealing with a well-educated remote workforce, the elements of trust, autonomy, transparency, and community become even more important than they have been in the past. Of course, good management practices are still vital to success; however, in such an environment leadership is even more important. Even more than managers, leaders provide vision and engagement – the vision to see what the future could be, and the engagement that excites employees and fosters commitment to the cause. With this in place you enable good decision-making, and you allow employees to see how their decisions affect the success of the team and the organization.

This chapter seeks to align these practices with the current situation in which a firm finds itself. Topics include:

- Management versus leadership;
- Theoretical framework for leadership;
- Some of the environmental issues facing leaders;
- Some strategies and tactics for successful remote leadership;

DOI: 10.4324/9781032646657-9

Preparing this chapter brought to mind the words of Heraclitus: "no man ever steps into the same river twice, for it's not the same river and he's not the same man." The reality is that the world is in constant motion, and there are a lot of moving parts. Even if you are successful is halting some of those parts you will never halt all of them, and the tide of change around you will eventually overwhelm you and force a change.

Also, you yourself are changing – you are not the same person you were in the past, nor are you the same person you will be in the future. Or, as Marcus Aurelius put it, "Everything is transitory – the knower and the known." Therefore, how we lead needs to change in response to changes in the environment and the people in it. Insisting that the old ways are best is shorted-sighted. They may have been, and they may be even now, but at some point in time it is likely that we will have to change.

Management versus Leadership

In the mid-1990s I was working for a marketing consulting firm that specialized in supporting live marketing events for the technology industry. The firm's employees had no official titles, however, and there was a clear unofficial hierarchy. There were those who most would consider managers. They were people in charge of functional areas such as account management, sales, or operations, and there were those who supported these leaders' efforts. I was the lead for several of the largest projects, with the highest profiles, and I recruited team members from across the company to be part of my team.

After I had been there for several years, and participated in what was an incredible period of growth, the founder brought on a new team member, who elsewhere would have been called the chief operations officer (COO). He had extensive experience as a senior operations executive in very large companies and was brought in to help to improve the operations process across the company. In the COO's first couple of weeks, he spent most of his time meeting with employees getting the lay of the land and learning about the cultural dynamics.

As I was confident in my role and position within the company I hardly noticed that I was not interviewed immediately. When we finally met the new COO told me that my name had come up early and often in his survey of the firm, and he decided that he wanted to save my interview for last. He told me it was clear that I was one of the more influential people in the company, and someone who was not only a manager but was a real leader. However, it was clear that I was a polarizing individual. There were people who both loved and hated me within the firm. His description of me was quite apt: "there are people here who would follow you into hell – and a few who would like to see you go there."

I have to admit that the comment made me smile, and I took it as a compliment, which is how I think it was intended. The new COO and I had a very friendly relationship for as long as we were both associated with the firm. It's not that I really wanted anyone to dislike me, but I stood up for my principles and the causes I believed in. This sometimes led to conflicts with people who had a different perspective on things, and more often than not they were people on different teams who had a vested interest in the status quo. Even more importantly, by sticking to my principles – even when it was difficult to do so – I helped my team to see a purpose in our projects. We had a cause. We had a shared purpose. And this bred fierce loyalty among the team members.

The point of this story is there is a big distinction between being a manager and a leader. Management is usually defined as planning, organizing, leading, and controlling, or as planning, organizing, directing, and controlling. Most management scholars consider both of these modern frameworks to have their roots in the works of Henri Fayol (1841–1925).

> **Box 9.1 Elements of Management**
>
> *Planning*: Developing an organized plan to meet a clear set of objectives;
> *Organizing*: Mustering the resources and talent to complete a process or set of tasks;
> *Directing*: Communicating the goals and objectives, and providing instruction on how, when, and where the tasks should be completed to those participating;
> *Leading*: Providing a vision of the future, fostering adoption of the vision, and gaining the buy-in and engagement of those involved;
> *Controlling*: Developing and administering a system of measures, metrics, and corrective actions to keep a process on track to an agreed set of goals and objectives.

Although *leading* is more commonly used in describing management today, the inclusion may be more aspirational than accurate. In many ways the use of the word *directing* may be more accurate in how many managers go about their daily routines. Or to paraphrase the COO's words: "a manager can prepare you to go to hell, but a leader makes you look forward to the trip."

Leadership

Leadership is very different from management, and over time the definition of what scholars have considered leadership has changed. In antiquity more often than not the term leader was used to describe someone who held a formal position of power: head of state, military commander, king. And the term *leader* was in common use at least as far back as the year 1300. However, the term *leadership* did not appear to be in common use until the 19th century (Bass, 1990).

Some could argue that there is a core to leadership that does not change. Peter Drucker (the most prolific writer on the subject of management in the 20th century) was quick to point out that leadership has nothing to do with charisma or personality traits. Some US presidents were severely lacking in charisma but were extremely effective leaders – he cited as examples Eisenhower and Truman. Meanwhile, the president with bucket loads of charisma, John F. Kennedy, got very little done (Drucker, 2001). According to Drucker, the essence of leadership is as follows:

> The foundation of effective leadership is thinking through the organization's mission, defining it, and establishing it, clearly and visibly. The leader sets the goals, sets the priorities, and sets and maintains the standards. He makes compromises, of course; indeed, effective leaders are painfully aware they are not in control of the universe. (Only misleaders – the Stalins, Hitlers, Maos – suffer from that delusion.) But before accepting a compromise, the effective leader has thought through what is right and desirable. The leader's first task is to be the trumpet that sounds a clear sound.
>
> (2001, p. 270)

However, Drucker never directly defined leadership as needing a formal role. In modern definitions, the term leadership now embraces those who do not hold official organizational positions of authority. Although those in formal positions of organizational authority are often leaders, leadership is more about influence and commitment. When at their best leaders provide a *vision of the future* and the path to get there. The act of leadership is in:

- Effectively communicating a vision to potential followers;
- Obtaining buy-in and the commitment of the group to a cause;
- Moving the group beyond compliance to engagement;
- Inspiring action to help to enable the vision and make it a reality;
- Provide focus on how to achieve the cause or vision;
- The power of persuasion and inspiration – not threat or coercion;
- The development of empathy by the leader for the group being led;
- The demonstration of their commitment to the cause through action.

Box 9.2 US Presidents on Leadership

The quality of leadership is often publicly demonstrated by people in positions of power. Below are a few quotes by US presidents that help to demonstrate some of the qualities of leadership:

"If your actions inspire others to dream more, learn more, do more and become more, you are a leader" (John Quincy Adams).

"Leadership is the ability to decide what is to be done, and then to get others to want to do it" (Dwight Eisenhower).

"A leader is a man who has the ability to get other people to do what they don't want to do, and like it" (Harry Truman).

"You are not here merely to make a living. You are here in order to enable the world to live more amply, with greater vision, with a finer spirit of hope and achievement. You are here to enrich the world, and you impoverish yourself if you forget the errand" (Woodrow Wilson).

"You cannot escape the responsibility of tomorrow by evading it today" (Abraham Lincoln).

"It is hard to fail, but it is worse never to have tried to succeed" (Theodore Roosevelt).

Leadership Theories

As we analyze the changes in management and leadership brought on by remote and hybrid work it might be useful to examine existing leadership and explore how it might be applied or modified to address the current situation.

Honor the Room

In his book *The Leader's Checklist* (2011), Michael Useem calls out a skill necessary for leadership that has long been used by politicians, professional speakers, and top salespeople, or indeed by anyone who seeking to make a persuasive argument – honoring the room. Useem points out that leaders need to clearly express their respect and confidence in the people they work with and who work for them. In addition, they need to have empathy for the challenges they are facing, and what the leaders' vision means to them both personally and professionally.

What is troubling, at the time of writing in early 2023 many companies are changing their policies on hybrid and remote work. Often there is a good reason to change these policies – issues such as company culture, ease of collaboration, coordination of projects and work efforts. However, the way this is being handled at some companies may lead to new and possibly even more difficult issues. Many of these leaders are approaching this kind of work model as a command-and-control issue by demanding compliance with a far more stringent set of rules concerning time on-site and giving employees very little advance notice of the changes afoot.

When interviewed on these issues such leaders often take a hardline approach, reflected in comments like "this is what the business requires, and therefore, this is what we will do." In a broader sense this logic might be sound in some ways but could lead to severe loss of corporate values and possibly the loss of key talent.

If these leaders were to honor the room, they might begin to have a very different perspective. They might realize that during the early stages of the COVID-19 pandemic, contrary to what many predicted, productivity did not drop – and in some cases it increased. These employees did prove that remote work is an option for many tasks – and they might see blanket rules as not honoring their efforts.

Such employees might have personal/life situations that might make these new, more stringent rules untenable – or they simply may not see the point of commuting and incurring the expense of travel and loss of time. This could result in the loss of talent – especially in times when unemployment rates are low, and new jobs are easy to find, especially if these new potential employers are taking a more liberal approach to on-site requirements.

McGregor's Theory X and Theory Y

Put simply, Douglas McGregor's Theory X and Theory Y questions whether or not a manager believes in the core goodness of people. Popularized in the 1960s McGregor suggested that there was a continuum that managers sat on. At one end are those who believe that employees are basically lazy and left to their own devices would do nothing, unless they are closely monitored and forced to work (Theory X). At the other end are those who believe that people are basically good and want to reach self-actualization (an idea that McGregor borrowed from Maslow's hierarchy of needs), and all a manager has to do is to help take the roadblocks out of the way (Theory Y; see also the servant leadership style).

In remote work environments there are both types of managers. The Theory X managers will have tools designed to capture employee activity such as employee monitoring software or call monitoring systems. They often equate activity with productivity. At the extreme they have a set of metrics that will trigger either rewards or disciplinary actions based on reaching a threshold or the failure to do so. Theory Y managers will focus more on relationship building and leadership activities. They will have regular check-ins with their employees, focus on the development of transparent information flows, and ensure the delivery of adequate resources to ensure success.

Managers may gravitate toward one or the other of these styles; however, neither is always correct or always wrong. The choice of where a manager sits on the spectrum is driven by a number of factors, including culture (national, regional, industry, company, team), industry norms, goals, timelines, and the gravitas of the manager. That said, you are more likely to see effective firms with high levels of engagement inclining toward a Theory Y approach.

Theory P and Theory Z

Theory Y drove the development of additional humanistic management theories. These theories focused on the self-actualization of individual, greater emphasis on self-direction, and meritocracy and fairness in employee evaluations. These qualities are seen in the United Kingdom (Theory P), and in Japan (Theory Z). With Theory P there is more of an emphasis on a consultative management style, and with Theory Z long-term employment and distributed decision-making are the end goals (Bass, 1990)

Transformational Leadership

Transformational leadership is one of the many theories that have grown out of Maslow's concept of self-actualization. Transformation leaders provide a dual focus, namely achieving a collective vision while at the same time achieving self-actualization. Leaders operating under this theory look to provide a clear vision for both the organization and the individual, develop the resources necessary for achievement of the vision, set high expectations for individual and group performance, and develop a culture of transparency and inclusivity.

Key attributes of a transformational leadership plan would include:

- *Vision*: There is a clear and compelling vision for both the organization and the individual.
- *Inspiration*: Team members buy in to the vision and are inspired to go above and beyond in their efforts.
- *Support*: There are adequate resources and emotional support from the leader and among the team members.
- *Innovation*: A culture of innovation is supported. There is a willingness to try new ideas, and failure is seen as an acceptable part of the process.
- *Empowerment*: There is a high level of autonomy and team members can make decisions on what to do and how, within a well-established set of parameters.

Servant Leadership

Another theory that leans heavily on the concept of self-actualization, and on McGregor's Theory X and Theory Y, is servant leadership. Servant leadership believes that people are basically good and looking to self-actualize. The servant leader puts the needs of the team first, works to remove roadblocks, and enables team members to succeed for both the team and themselves. In the case of remote employees this will often manifest itself as managers look to ensure that team members have the resources and support services they need, have adequate information and context to make informed decisions, and feel that they are part of a community that cares about them and values their contributions.

Situational Leadership

There exists in the cannons of leadership the concept that leadership is situational, that leadership is thrust upon individuals whose personal attributes are aligned with the needs of the time, place, and circumstances. As an example, Bass (1990, pp. 38–40) used the life of Ulysses S. Grant who had been a successive failure in private life before becoming one of the most celebrated generals of all time, only to become a lackluster president. He presents this theory as an extension of the great man theory.

The great man theory suggests that leaders are endowed with a collection of traits that foster their leadership ability. Situational leadership takes this concept a bit further suggesting that there are three parts: the personality traits; the nature of the group; and the events confronting the group. Although the different version of the great man theory has fallen out of favor with leadership scholars, some of the base concepts might be interesting to consider in our current situation.

It is not unreasonable to assume that the group you are leading, and the situation you find yourself in, might have a bearing on the effectiveness of whatever leadership techniques or tools you might be using. Therefore, as we enter a world where much of our leadership efforts will be done remotely, we need to reassess the need for trust in us by the people in our environment and the people we are leading.

Authentic Leadership

In the world of leadership, the term authentic has come to be accepted as meaning that the leader is being true to their nature and expressing themselves in line with their own inner thoughts and feelings – in other words being transparent and honest. It is this honesty coupled with a vision that the leader is willing to act on, a genuine concern for their team, and strong ability to communicate that can result in a powerful leadership style. This style can be very helpful when managers are looking to build community and team spirit.

A recent study by Microsoft (2022) drove home the need for "open, honest, empathetic" leadership as a foundation for creating an authentic culture and earning employee engagement. The findings of the study included the following:

> **Box 9.3 Microsoft 2022**
>
> Employees *with an authentic manager* are:
>
> - more inclined to go into the office for one-on-ones with them (82%, or +25 percentage points);
> - slightly more open to working on-site (1.80 days versus 1.66 days on average);
> - more likely to meet at least weekly (60%, or +16 percentage points);
> - more likely to discuss their wellbeing/mental health during their one-on-ones (32%, or +14 percentage points).
>
> Employees *without an authentic manager* are:
>
> - less motivated to go into the office;
> - more likely to disagree that they're given flexibility (44% disagree, or +32 percentage points);
> - more likely to agree that they face challenges in learning and development, especially that it's not a priority for their manager (65%, or +19 percentage points) and senior leadership (63%, or +16 percentage points).
>
> (Microsoft, 2022)

Emotional Intelligence

Originally developed by Danial Goleman in the 1990s, emotional intelligence (EI) relates to the ability to recognize and manage feelings in both one's self and others. Goleman's 1995 book on the subject suggests that one's emotional intelligence quotient (EQ) is as important, if not more important, to professional success as one's intelligence quotient (IQ). Managers and leaders with high EQs will be better able to understand, communicate with, and motivate their teams.

Key elements of EI include:

- *Self-awareness*: Consciousness of one's own feeling and emotions, and how they are manifest themselves in one's actions;

- *Self-regulation*: Being able to use your self-awareness to manage your feelings, actions, and reactions;
- *Motivation*: Leveraging your understanding of your feelings and emotions to motivate yourself and others to help you to meet your goals;
- *Empathy*: Understanding how others are feeling and how to motivate them;
- *Social skills*: The ability to build trust and relationships.

Management by Walking Around

In a hybrid and remote world one significant challenge many mangers face if being aware of what is happening with their employees, what they are working on, what challenges they are facing, and how they can best support the efforts of those who report to them. Many managers were brought up on techniques that assumed co-location.

Popularized by the bestselling business book of the 1980s, *In Search of Excellence* by Tom Peters and Robert Waterman, the roots of management by walking around (MBWA) date back to at least the 1970s. It has been credited to the management team at Hewlett Packard, who have also been credited with several other techniques including the very popular objectives and key results framework.

One common mistake that managers make when they first hear of this technique is to assume that it is just another name for aimlessly wandering the halls; however, this is not the case. It is true that under this technique the managers do make unscheduled appearances, and that route through the office and the agenda are fluid. However, there should be clear goals that drive the process. Some of these goals are:

- To capture tacit knowledge of what is happening within the organization;
- To understand which processes are working and which are not;
- To keep in touch with the moral and culture of the team;
- To judge the effectiveness of the information flow within the company in real time;
- To enable serendipity through proximity.

To be truly effective at this process requires the manager to develop some enabling skills:

Observation: Managers need to step back and attempt to look at the organization, team, and business processes with fresh eyes. Often, they have longstanding assumptions about how things are within their company, with their customers, and within their business environment. In almost every case managers have some assumptions that are not true. Also, when we find ourselves in the midst of significant changes, as we have seen in the past few years, it may be a good time to question our assumptions.

Listening: We should take this opportunity to practice active listening (discussed more in the next section). Many of us have been taught the basic principles of active listening since childhood; however, many of us are still not very good at it. One of the main goals of MBWA is to develop understanding, of the company, the customers, the partners/vendors, and the business environment.

Recognition and inclusivity: Part of this process should be to hear all the voices – not just those with the most access to the management structure – and to recognize those who are making significant efforts and accomplishing significant results.

Accountability and coaching in real time: If done well this provides the manager with the ability to hold team members accountable for results, and to provide coaching in real time as issues surface – and not wait for a formal employee review that may be months away.

Approachable: If we are able to increase casual contact between managers and those who report to them, it may make them seem more approachable. This may enable an information flow that could have a positive effect on the business overall.

Presence: For many the most difficult skill to develop in a remote and hybrid world is presence. The only way MBWA works is if you are casually bumping into people, which is far easier if you are in the same physical space.

The manager will have to make more of a concerted effort to make this happen as we move to more remote and hybrid work. I have heard some suggest that MBWA is impossible in the current environment; however, I am not convinced. Yes, it is far harder but not impossible. I think it is important to remember that not so long ago *not being in the office* meant *not working*. Over the past few decades changes in technology have made tasks that in the past could only be done in the office now location independent. Why can't this work for presence?

Box 9.4 Gemba Walk

It is important here to discuss a connected concept that is very often used in Japanese organizational management – the Gemba Walk. Roughly translated *gemba* means going to the real place. In this case, it means going to the place where the work is actually being done. When exploring this topic, I came across a quote from Gen. Dwight D. Eisenhower who said, "Farming is easy when your pencil is the plow and you're 1,000 miles from the field." As with

MBWA, Gemba Walks are intended to move past our assumptions and develop real understanding.

These two management styles involve more than merely going to the work location. As part of the process, similarly to MBWA, the manager attempts to understand the work process, why employees preform the tasks the way that they do, the challenges employees are facing as they perform the work, and to understand the environment in which the work is performed. In other words, they are not just looking at the output, they are attempting to understand the entire system in which the work is performed, and how the system might be improved.

The Age of Empathy and Authentic Leaders

Rita Gunther McGrath (2014) suggested there were three management eras: execution, expertise, and empathy. She defines these ages in the following ways:

Execution: This era was born during the industrial revolution when managers were focused on mass production, labor specialization, standardization, quality, workflow, and the measurement of it all. It "emphasized efficiency, lack of variation, consistency of production, and predictability."
Expertise: This era witnessed the rise of the knowledge worker, and the introduction of new disciplines that helped to professionalize the process, such as operations management, management by objectives, process reengineering, Six Sigma, and waterfall development processes in software.
Empathy: In a world of abundance organizations need to go beyond execution and advanced services. Managers are tasked with the development of "meaningful experiences" that drive engagement and communities.
Leaders need to drive this empathy through authenticity. According to Edmondson & Chamorro-Premuzic (2020), in an era of constant and dramatic change (such as now) it would be impossible for one person (a manager or a leader) to have all the information and all the skills necessary to be the fount of all knowledge and good decision-making. Therefore, it becomes incumbent upon the leader to be humble, honest, and open to criticism and advice. Examples of such a leader might include Satya Nedella of Microsoft or Howard Schultz of Starbucks. Behaviors that these leaders demonstrate include:

- Start by being honest: Being forthright and honest and admitting to your weaknesses and vulnerabilities is a sure sign of confidence and strength.

- Ask for help: This gives the leader an opportunity to leverage the strengths of the group and foster commitment.
- Try something new: You should be afraid to go outside your comfort zone. If the environment is changing the solutions currently in use may no longer be viable.
- Admit your mistakes and apologize: Everyone makes mistakes, but to deal with the issues caused by them, to resolve them, and foster future commitment, it is important to admit them and apologize.
- Focus on self-improvement: In a world of change it is important to develop new skills and techniques to simply stay competitive.

Zeitgebers

Significant changes in the environment, such as moving your work environment from a traditional office to a remote office or home office, significantly affect the cadence of our workday and the routines we develop. This also brings to consideration the necessary balance between structure and flexibility we need in a successful organization. Too much structure could stifle creativity and morale, too little could leave your team feeling isolated and adrift.

According to Jain and Brennan (2021) "Zeitgebers [time givers] are external environmental cues that humans use to regulate their internal biological rhythms … [they are] things that affect energy levels and send physiological signals to the body to be alert." In the broadest sense this could be the sunrise, sunset, and the changing seasons. In the sense of an organization, it could be the routines that we set up to foster communications and inclusion; such as weekly team meetings, one-on-ones with a manager or team member, check-ins, happy hours, holiday celebrations, and so on.

Managers working on long-term projects might set up milestones to celebrate, meetings to communicate progress toward short-term goals, or simply events to celebrate the end of a week, or end of a project. The important part of these zeitgebers is to foster a small level of structure to the existence of team members, create the feeling of inclusion, and foster the flow of information and connectedness. However, the other role of zeitgebers is to help to foster healthy behaviors for the long term. So, some companies have developed zeitgebers to foster healthy boundary-setting behaviors, such as setting rules on when the workday should start and end.

Workforce Ecosystem

Throughout the book we have referenced the changes in the workforce, and how these changes affect the structure of the organization. One model that might be useful in developing a leadership strategy in such an environment is the workforce ecosystem (Altman et al., 2021). In a recent global study over 75% of managers viewed their workforce as comprising both employees and non-employees. The non-employees included "contractors, gig workers, professional service providers, application developers, crowdsourced contributors, and others" (p. 1). Leaders in these cases have to deal with the conflicting goals of both individual non-employees, and non-employee organizations (partners, contractors, outsourcing groups). According to Altman et al. (2021), there are four major shifts that leaders should account for in their strategy:

Box 9.5 Workforce Ecosystem Shifts

- Shift 1: More non-employees are doing more work for the business.
- Shift 2: The nature of work is evolving. Job descriptions anchor traditional management systems. Semi-annual reviews and annual merit increases are predicated on employees remaining in jobs for extended periods and generally pursuing prescribed, linear career paths.
- Shift 3: There is growing recognition that a diverse and inclusive workforce can deliver more value.
- Shift 4: Workforce management is becoming more complex. Responsibility for internal employees rests with HR, while procurement and other departments orchestrate external workers. Few companies manage or can see their entire workforce in an integrated way.

Multi-Modal Leadership

Not all tasks, or for that matter all jobs, are created equal. By their very nature some tasks or jobs are highly independent affairs, while others require close collaboration. In addition, personality attributes and work styles should be considered when evaluating how and where tasks should or can be done successfully.

As a general rule of thumb tasks that are straightforward such as reporting, performing administrative tasks, making simple decisions, and sharing information are all good candidates for being carried out remotely. In addition, there are solo creative tasks that are often best done alone such as drafting documents, writing code, and performing financial analyses.

On the other hand, some types of design, new product development, and other creative work are best done in a collaborative team environment. These collaborative environments often work better in person – or at least partially in person (Hooijberg & Watkins, 2021; Trevor & Holweg, 2022).

Personal experience and several well-documented highly collaborative firms have proven that there are no absolutes in this situation. This often comes down to weighing the team's needs and preferences, how the work and team communications platforms are organized, and the firm's culture.

Many firms will find that they will have employees working on different parts of the *on-site — hybrid – remote* spectrum. In addition, some team members will be direct employees and some part of their workforce eco-system. It is likely that these conditions will require managers taking different approaches to deal with the different leadership needs.

For example, in the past there may have been a requirement to always be present for team meetings. The feeling at the time may have been that this was the best way to keep team members on track. This still may still be true for hybrid and on-site workers; however, for remote team members there may be a need to set up forums where all the key information is kept to allow asynchronous consumption of the material, or you might have to allow for some electronic workers who find it difficult to be on-site to find some other way of staying connected.

Recent studies carried out by MIT suggest that going forward over 60% of meetings will be online. Furthermore, although most knowledge workers will return to the office for at least two days a week, managers believe that over 60% of tasks can be completed successfully remotely.

Box 9.6 Organizational Network Analysis

In Chapter 5 we discussed the concepts behind Organizational Network Analysis and how it could be used to implement hybrid policies. This assessment could also be used to better understand how to implement a leadership plan.

Agile/Scrum Leadership

As we discussed in Chapter 8 agile and scrum are a set of governance principles that are often used in project-based organizations and software development. Among the principles that are most relevant are the assumptions that:

- Your team is made up of professionals who will work hard and make good decisions if given the opportunity.
- There should be a free flow of information, and a very high level of transparency to the status of all aspects of the project.

- Leaders need to provide a clear vision and regularly schedule short structured team meetings.
- Leaders and team members should regularly meet to share the status of projects, honest clear feedback, challenges, and plans to their parts of the initiatives in process.
- There should be honest after-action meetings to assess the quality of the team's work and to plan adjustments on future initiatives.
- Given the complexity and fluidity of most knowledge work today, structures like these, and other adaptive structures, would seem to be a good governance choice and it is likely that we will see more of them going forward.

Commander's Intent

When developing an environment of autonomy and self-direction, the military term *commander's intent* is often useful in setting a context for individual decisions. When a decision is being made, it asks the individual to question if following an instruction or order to the letter actually achieves what the commander intended when issuing the order. Applied more broadly it might question what the intention is of a specific goal, i.e., what might that goal actually intend to achieve?

As organizations move to hybrid and remote work environments, the volume of contact with individual employees is often reduced, and there is an increase in the need for remote and hybrid employees to make regular decisions that could affect the organization's progress toward an objective. Therefore, the intent of short-term goals and larger objectives must be crystal clear to even the lowest level employees.

Chapter 9 Takeaways

It might be helpful to look at leadership today using the *gardener* concept proposed by Gen. Stanley McCrystal outlined in Chapter 1 – the idea of creating a fertile environment that allows things to grow. This is based on a culture where there is a bias toward action, team members have autonomy in their daily actions, and where responsibility is encouraged, and where failure is seen as part of the process (so long as it is not reckless).

In an environment of rapid change, a healthy culture and sound leadership become essential elements of success. Leadership should be based on the communication of a vision and goals, the creation of purpose for the organization, and fostering commitment and engagement. This vision should act as a north star, or touchstone, for the team to go back to as they make their daily decisions.

As part of communicating the vision and goals, there should be a clear *commander's intent*, a high level of information transparency, coupled with extreme candor and honesty. If these elements are in place the team can be agile and make decisions in the proper context, understanding whether or not they are furthering the team's efforts.

References

Altman, E. J., Kiron, D., Schwartz, J., & Jones, R. (2021). The Future of Work Is Through Workforce Ecosystems. *MIT Sloan Management Review*, 62(2), 1–4.

Bass, B. M. (1990). *Bass & Stogdill's Handbook of Leadership: Theory, Research & Managerial Applications* (subsequent ed.). Free Press.

Drucker, P. F. (2001). *The Essential Drucker: In One Volume the Best of Sixty Years of Peter Drucker's Essential Writings on Management* (1st ed.). Harper Business.

Edmondson, A. C., & Chamorro-Premuzic, T. (2020, October 19). Today's Leaders Need Vulnerability, Not Bravado. *Harvard Business Review*, 6.

Gartner (2021, June 22). Gartner Forecasts 51% of Global Knowledge Workers Will Be Remote by the End of 2021. https://www.gartner.com/en/newsroom/press-releases/2021-06-22-gartner-forecasts-51-percent-of-global-knowledge-workers-will-be-remote-by-2021.

Goleman, D. (1995). *Emotional Intelligence*. Bantam Books.

Hooijberg, R., & Watkins, M. (2021). The Future of Team Leadership Is Multimodal. *MIT Sloan Management Review*. https://sloanreview.mit.edu/article/the-future-of-team-leadership-is-multimodal/.

Jain, T., & Brennan, L. (2021, November 16). What Space Missions Can Teach Us About Remote Work. *MIT Sloan Management Review*. https://sloanreview.mit.edu/article/what-space-missions-can-teach-us-about-remote-work/.

McGrath, R. G. (2014, July 30). *Management's Three Eras: A Brief History*. *Harvard Business Review*, 4.

Microsoft (2022, September 22). *Work Trend Index: Microsoft's Latest Research on the Ways We Work*. https://www.microsoft.com/en-us/worklab/work-trend-index.

Roth, C. (2019, December 11). *When We Exceeded 1 Billion Knowledge Workers*. https://blogs.gartner.com/craig-roth/2019/12/11/2019-exceeded-1-billion-knowledge-workers/.

Trevor, J., & Holweg, M. (2022). Managing the New Tensions of Hybrid Work. *MIT Sloan Management Review*, 64(2). https://sloanreview.mit.edu/article/managing-the-new-tensions-of-hybrid-work/.

Chapter 10

Analytics and Managing at a Distance

Introduction

The history of analytics in the workplace as it is currently known (defined as predictive analytics) probably started in ancient Roman times when the concept of insurance was first created. While the previous example showed that analytics for business had been around for some time, it is only relatively recently that there has been an increased emphasis on the use of analytics in the modern firm. Credit card firms and retail catalog companies relied on analytics to drive their business models for most of the latter half of the 20th century. The use of advanced analytics for business also grew around the millennium with the widespread use of data warehousing and relational databases on client servers. Moreover, machine learning and artificial intelligence (AI) techniques, which have been around for many decades, have had very few breakthrough success-ful applications up until recently when cloud computing and being able to take advantage of the infrastructure of companies such as Amazon and Google with their cloud services enabled these algorithms to be used to their full extent in firms. The availability of this powerful infrastructure combined with big data is creating breakthrough applications across many business models on a consistent basis. In addition to providing a historical context on the history of analytics in the workplace this chapter explores the use of the Managing at a Distance framework to maximize the analytics labor force around the globe. It will also explore the use of analytics and AI techniques to manage all workers more effectively from a distance and not just analytics workers. Finally, it will examine how ana-lytics changes the way we think about work and our ability to manage and lead employees who are not in the physical workspace. One of the key contributions that this chapter makes is that it recognizes and documents further evidence of the contribution of analytics to remote work. This is in addition to technology which traditionally has received the bulk of the credit.

DOI: 10.4324/9781032646657-10

Global Analytics including the Outsourcing and Offshoring of Your Analytics

Overview of Global Analytics

The surge of interest in big data has led to recognition of the need to develop analytics teams with the ability to extract meaningful and perhaps strategic insights from data. Developing analytics teams, however, is not easy: *Fortune* (May 10, 2013) reported that "Online help-wanted ads for data analysis mavens have shot up 46% since April 2011, and 246% since April 2009, to over 31,000 openings now, according to job-market trackers." A shortage of analysts and particularly those who can develop and lead a world-class team that might enable a firm to create a competitive advantage from its data and analytics is incentivizing firms to look to outsourcing their analytics. In addition, many firms are facing global competition today which may facilitate the need to have global talent pools and be able to use analytics strategically to help firms grow their global and domestic operations.

Gent (2019) points out that hidden behind every voice command you give Alexa, every Google search you run and every YouTube video you watch is the work of thousands of "invisible humans, sometimes continents away, who help build and maintain these technologies that we use every day. This kind of 'ghost work' is crucial for the biggest tech companies to function."

Workers crowdsourced over the internet are paid to label data to train algorithms. Contractors screen our social media feeds to keep them free of violence, hate speech and sexual exploitation. But a technology industry keen to portray itself as based on technical wizardry rather than human labor has kept its crucial contributions hidden, aided by automated workflows that treat humans as just another step in a computational pipeline.

Gent (2019) states that these tech companies are some of the most powerful on Earth. They are figuring out a way to marry the intense demands of rapidly evolving technologies with the support systems of traditional employment could be one of the most pressing human labor issues facing the modern workplace. These challenges represent a category named "global analytics." The following section will explore and document this branch of analytics in more depth through a series of case studies.

Global Analytics

Fogarty and Bell (2013, 2021) reported that as communication with the emerging markets began to improve during the telecommunications boom which began in the late 1990s, multinationals were able to take advantage of labor arbitrage opportunities between these markets and the developed world by locating their call centers in countries like India and the Philippines. India was particularly attractive for this type of activity due to the availability of an English-speaking highly educated labor force. With call centers including customer service and telesales firmly in place, firms began to innovate on other activities that could also be outsourced and/or offshored. These tasks included information technology (IT) services, computer programming, legal research, application processing, and accounting. Many of these offshored tasks could be split off from larger processes: for example, lawyers in the US might handle a case in its entirety but farm off the legal research to the offshore location. The offshore providers were mostly established by local nationals who were working in the US in places like Silicon Valley and Boston's Route 128 and the industry became known as business process outsourcing (BPO).

BPO is an outsourcing arrangement either through equity or contract which allows an external vendor or partner to perform an entire business function for a client organization (Dibbern et al., 2004; Beverakis et al., 2008). The driver of BPO is to outsource and/or offshore back-office processes, usually noncore, to a vendor who has "superior structural and human capital in the areas of business process and specific expertise" (Willcocks et al., 2004; Beverakis et al., 2008).

Analytics was a later arrival to the BPO menu. Analytics was a natural for places like India due to its history and focus on mathematics and statistical training. Gilliland and Ramamoorthi (2010) interviewed James Hannan who described taking PhD classes in the US with students from India as early as the 1950s and how well they were prepared for the statistics classes. Many of the offshore analytic BPOs (ABPOs) started as captives of multinational firms who already possessed infrastructure in the emerging markets. While some are still captives (Dell Global Analytics is an Indian-based captive of Dell Inc.), others were eventually spun off or acquired by other firms and offered to third parties that did not have a presence in India or the scale to set up their own captive operation. American Express was early in setting up a captive BPO center for analytics in India, while General Electric Company (GE) set up centers in India, the People's Republic of China, and eventually Hungary taking advantage of the focus on education in mathematical sciences that these countries offer. Many other firms, especially financial firms like Citigroup and HSBC, set up their own captives in India, China, and Hungary and poached many of the managers from the early trailblazers like GE and American Express. By the turn of the 21st century the birth of the offshore ABPO was firmly established. Firms today that are outsourcing and offshoring some or all of their analytics include Walmart, Allstate, Goldman Sachs, HSBC, Citibank, and Royal Bank of Scotland.

There is very limited research on corporate use of ABPOs although there is research literature on IT and other BPO operations. Dibbern et al. (2004) discuss success factors related to IT offshoring/BPO where there are partnerships and alliances in which the client and vendor share risk and reward including variants such as value-based outsourcing and equity-based outsourcing. Many Fortune 500 firms employ offshore firms on a pay-for-performance basis whereby the BPO is paid a percentage of the benefits realized only if there is a real ongoing cost saving associated with the project. Often successful offshore partnerships require the transfer of assets, contracts, and staff (see Beverakis et al., 2008). In a rapidly changing market, offshoring allows organizations to increase their flexibility by making fixed costs variable, and this can boost other success factors as discussed by Devata et al. (2005) who also reported that the success of BPO partnerships is dependent on factors such as the geographic distance between onshore and offshore hubs, having adequate infrastructure and connectivity, having adequate language and technical skills as well as proper contingency planning. They also point out the need to conduct thorough and appropriate research in advance of the project and for management to fully communicate the important decisions to all affected parties.

Willcocks et al. (2004) observe that businesses must be careful not to lose their expertise or their core intellectual property (IP) in this offshore transfer, suggesting that firms should first to a thorough job of identifying which capabilities are core and which capabilities could be better served by an offshore provider who can enhance in the firm rather than simply perform the same process at a lower cost.

While these findings relate to offshoring/outsourcing IT activities, there are direct comparisons from analytics. For example, Fogarty and Bell (2013, 2021) provide a case study that illustrates the importance of care in making decisions that reflect IP ownership and access. However, there are features of analytics where the comparison with IT is less obvious. For example, it is well known that the firm can create long-term competitive advantages through its use of analytics (see Bell and Zaric, 2012, for example); consequently, there is an opportunity for research into ABPO/offshoring as a facilitator of the creation and maintenance of competitive advantage. In addition, some firms already have in-house domestic world-class analytics functions, while other multinationals are looking at analytics for the first time. Should these firms approach outsourcing/offshoring analytics differently? An interesting question is whether the analytically naive firm can "buy" itself a world-class analytics function by outsourcing analytics.

In addition to APBO organizations and creating analytics value chains there is also an interest in firms creating a global analytics capability. The major question to be asked is what constitutes global analytics. Global analytics is a concept that I coined in the last decade of the 20th century when I worked for a large multinational consumer finance company which was expanding globally. The power of analytics and data-driven decisions is well documented. But what is the process of doing this globally and how has this led to the management of remote teams and the global analytics value chain? While most firms look to offshore their analytics to the ABPO to conduct labor arbitrage or to capitalize on the global workforce in their home countries I purport that an additional benefit of offshoring is to be able to conduct global analytics. Global analytics can be realized in many ways but the overall purpose for a firm is to use the power of globalization and analytics combined to grow the firm. This comes from a combination of offshoring and the center of excellence (COE) concepts. The offshoring component is about labor arbitrage and competing in the global labor marketplace for firms. The COE concept is about having hubs of talent to be exported into areas of the business where talent is needed most. They come together due to the fact that offshore centers do not just have to be low-cost centers taking cost out of a home country but instead can become global centers of competency. Gartner's Chris Pemberton (2016) defines a COE as a "physical or virtual center of knowledge concentrating existing expertise and resources in a discipline or capability to attain and sustain world-class performance and value." This definition can be broken down into four key elements, as follows:

> First, COEs need to focus on a tight scope defined around a specific capability such as marketing analytics or digital commerce. Next, consider the location of the COE (physical vs. virtual). Third, COEs should optimize and leverage resources internal to the organization, not external vendors or agencies. Lastly, COEs should focus on pushing beyond standard performance norms to deliver incremental value to the organization. COEs should not conduct business as usual around a capability. Instead, drive toward excellence in a medium or a channel.

Other terms for COEs include center of competency, knowledge hubs, experience centers, centers of expertise, hub of excellence, pole of excellence and capability center. The major question around any COE is its power and authority to get things done. Some COEs have literally no authority over their constituencies and can only share best practices or train individuals on more efficient and effective ways to do things by sharing knowledge across the organization. This is perfectly acceptable provided that the organization has autonomous and high-performing business units capable of evolving and learning independently. However, there are inefficiencies in every business in terms of individual business units being able to hire the top talent. For example, in analytics, individual country businesses in a large global firm do not have to hire modeling analysts to build models as this would not be a full-time job. However, a COE could spread out the modeling work over an entire region or abroad, thereby keeping a centralized team of model developers busy. Moreover, they could reach a consistency in terms of centralized training and level of quality that would be just too difficult to replicate in small country teams. Quality could be measured in many ways; for instance, from a model development perspective or ongoing quality monitoring. There are certain COEs which lend themselves to being more successful than others. Global analytics COEs developing statistical products like models are definitely included on this list as these are not task items that businesses build on a continuous basis in each business unit. Therefore, businesses can take advantage of a modeling COE which can manage utilization better for the firm on an enterprise basis. If a business doesn't have predictive models to build it could be an additional analytics product such as segmentation, and even the strategic analysis and insight extraction from raw data can sometimes be done more efficiently in a COE provided that the members of the COE know the business being analyzed. The COE also serves as a hub for talent sourcing and deploying key talent in local markets. For example, when the author worked for GE one of the firm's large retail credit clients in Australia requested a specific individual to come out to Australia to assist with the firm's retail analytics. It was the COE led by the author that vetted and did all the processing to send an individual with the right skills overseas. The COE continued to mentor and establish a reporting relationship with that employee and eventually repatriated them back to the US. This ensured that there was the adequate repatriation of expatriates. For companies that depend on the use of expatriate talent it's important to have the COEs source and manage this talent for their respective areas of expertise. Another task that falls to the COE is the sharing of best practices. The model I like to use is the Subway Sandwich Model. Subway has a COE that searches for best practices in each of its 37,000 stores worldwide. The Subway footlong, which retails for $5, was actually discovered in an individual store located in Jacksonville, Florida, owned by a franchisee. The Subway headquarters COE actually found the best practice when they heard that people were lining up outside the door of this particular Subway sandwich shop so they went to investigate and found that this was indeed a great best practice. Having thousands of independent franchises represents a test lab for a company like Subway so long as they are able to effectively and efficiently capture all the ideas being created in the individual franchise operations. Of course, there also needs to be freedom on the part of the franchise operator to come up with and implement new ideas. If restrictions are imposed by the corporation, then this can stifle the innovative ideas coming from franchisees trying to grow their revenues. Instead, the franchisor (in this case Subway) should actually provide incentives to encourage innovation. In order to do this, there probably needs to be an innovation team within the marketing department which is tasked with spearheading global innovation. It could also be within the strategy team or the product team. Regardless, this team needs to find ways to achieve innovation and add value to franchisees. After all, Subway owners can just start a family deli with low barriers to entry, so the franchisor has to add incremental value with the brand. One of the value propositions should be innovations around the pricing and marketing of the product/service. My family ran several successful local delis with their own local brand and without the backing of a corporate entity. It was difficult to differentiate themselves from the competition. This included not only sandwich shops, but other retail food outlets where people shopped for their breakfast, lunch, and dinner. Only a firm with the kind of financial power like that of Subway can work to change consumer perceptions. Subway has the resources through market conditioning to convince people that sandwiches are preferable for lunch over other food items. This lifts all boats including private competitors. In 2023 Subway announced that it would equip all its stores with meat slicers. Originally, the meat was sliced centrally, and this made for more consistent sandwiches. However, transportation costs have significantly increased post-pandemic and political forces are pushing for new sources of renewable energy. Also, many of Subway's competitors, such as Jersey Mike's, slice the meat in front of customers and display it in a fresh-looking, fluffed-up way. These types of decisions are what makes a scale corporation effective. Investors in the 1980s suggested that Proctor & Gamble had peaked and that most of its products were outdated for the millennial generation. Thirty years later we have Tide Pods and the Swiffer Vacuum which the millennials have adopted as their own. Never bet against companies that have core values of innovation and the ability to hire top talent. Apple is another company that continues to innovate. Some companies like Microsoft have such a good core product that they just need to innovate around their core. When they try to go too far into innovation there are complaints from users. Windows is an example of the saying "Build a better mousetrap, and the world will beat a path to your door." Whenever Microsoft tries to do a makeover of a new product its users react negatively. This actually happened during a release called Microsoft Vista and Microsoft 8 where users complained and wanted Microsoft to return to some of the older features. The Coca-Cola Company did the same back in the 1980s with the launch of New Coke. At that time Pepsi was gaining market share against Coke with their effective blind taste test commercials in which Coke was not named but was implied to be losing out to Pepsi in a direct taste test. I can remember participating in a study at a local Sears. In the test I chose Pepsi. After this I thought that the demise of Coke was inevitable because everybody who drank cola learned that Pepsi tasted better – myself included. Coke must have sensed that Pepsi was gaining momentum with the taste test, since the original Coca-Cola formula is treated like the holy grail. Amid all this pressure the Coca-Cola Company responded by creating a new formula. This formula was supposed to taste like Pepsi. When Coke introduced a new version of its cola, which like Pepsi was sweeter, the new campaign backfired with customers launching serious complaints and demands to bring back the traditional Coca-Cola. It is also noteworthy that at this exact time Pepsi was on the verge of catching up with Coke in terms of annual sales. What Coke decided to do was bring back the old Coke which it called Coca-Cola Classic. It then ran both products in parallel. Coca-Cola Classic gained massive market share after the reintroduction and basically knocked Pepsi off its growth trajectory, from which to this day it has never recovered. After a while, Coke discontinued its new Coke and brought back the old Coke Classic. Shortly afterwards it dropped the Classic label, having done permanent damage to its archrival Pepsi. It was as if the whole New Coke and Classic Coke follow-up history had never happened. Meanwhile, Coke gained critical market share which Pepsi was never able to reclaim. Now Coke has a new challenge in terms of a generation of consumers who are not accustomed to drinking Cola as a beverage. This is a similar problem experienced by some of the automotive firms like GM whose iconic brands such as Cadillac and Buick fell out of favor with successive generations. The Cadillac Escalade and Buick Enclave were the saviors for these firms since they appealed to younger generations who favored SUVs. Of course, the truck divisions at these car companies were always doing well. Trucks and SUVs are the biggest selling vehicles in the US today. These are what most Americans prefer to drive and if not then they choose hybrids or at least all-wheel drive vehicles, especially during winter. The sedan market has gone to luxury car manufacturers such as Mercedes and BMW. Buyers of these vehicles are looking for performance and/or luxury which typically comes from sedan or coupe-style vehicles. The Porsche Panamera is an example of a vehicle combining both luxury and performance. Porsche dealers and fans alike were at first off put by the thought of a sedan Porsche but quickly learned that it combined practicality with performance. Plus, this opened up the market to drivers who sought performance but needed additional room for passengers. Porsches tend to retain their value and to be driven for longer than traditional vehicles. We have yet to see if these vehicles follow the same economics. Porsche always like to quote that 70% of all its vehicles ever made are still on the road today. This sends a powerful message from a branding perspective which I am sure the firm wants to maintain. I have visited several Porsche dealerships and can attest to the pride that the staff have in the brand. They all understand the brand values and think that Porsche cars live up to them. When confronted with something different they are innovative in seeking solutions.

My first experience with global analytics was in the early 1990s when I was working as a risk analyst at GE Capital. I took a trip with my brother and friends backpacking across Europe. Beside day trips to Canada while skiing in Northern Vermont, I had never left the country before this trip. We started our trip in Paris, France, and then made our way down to Venice, Italy, via passenger rail transportation. After several weeks of going from country to country I grew weary of travel and started thinking about returning home. I certainly had no intention of ever leaving the US again. On the morning of our departure we went to check out of our hotel in Venice when the hotel clerk indicated that there was a message for me at the front desk. The message stated that GE Capital was contemplating its first international acquisition in Paris and that I was to book a flight and report to the due diligence team on the ground at a Paris hotel the next morning. The message also instructed me to purchase business attire including a suit and shoes from the department store Printemps that same evening when I arrived in Paris. The next day when I arrived at the due diligence meeting in Paris I was instructed to "run the numbers" and make sure that the business did indeed have the number of active customers it claimed it had, and that these customers were not currently in arrears. I used my statistical programming and data analysis skills to do this, and to my delight received a lot of attention from the senior leaders in the sessions due to the fact that the analysis I conducted was critical to the viability of the acquisition. In fact, GE Capital never did that acquisition in France, which I attribute to be partly related to my analysis which showed that this investment would yield a negative return.

I then returned home to my normal domestic job as a statistical analyst, but was determined to have a global job thereafter. I eventually relocated from the GE headquarters in Connecticut to Cincinnati, Ohio. Having originally come from the New York metropolitan area I began to feel stifled by my experience of living and working in the Midwest. At this point in time GE Capital had been doing a few acquisitions in consumer finance in Asia and Europe and this business had been growing rapidly. It had recently done a huge acquisition in the United Kingdom and the leaders there remembered my work in France and decided to ask me to help to set up the first international analytics team in Leeds, UK. The mission was based on the fact that GE had good analytics skills in the US and that these could be transferred to help to grow newly acquired businesses overseas. Therefore, the idea was to set up a COE in the UK which would then be used to execute projects in subsidiary businesses all around the globe. As the Cold War ended and Central European business opportunities expanded in countries like Poland and the Czech Republic there were many acquisition opportunities for GE. I arrived in Leeds first as an analyst with the goal of transferring best practices from the US. Over time, I became the center manager and as GE Capital expanded its footprint I and my team worked with local teams and carried out analytical projects including the development of statistical models which would help to grow the newly acquired businesses.

Eventually, GE Capital moved its analytical work from the UK out to India and China as offshore operations and to Hungary and Canada as nearshore operations. These offshore and nearshore teams were critical for the GE acquisition growth engine and as one securities analyst put it, "GE Capital consumer finance has the ability to keep growing in the future partly due to armies of statistical analysts located in India and China who evaluate all of the data and help newly acquired businesses to grow their top and bottom line." This statement represents the unofficial registration by Wall Street of the birth of global analytics.

I then moved back to the US and was charged with managing the remote teams in order to continue to grow the global business. Eventually, the team was also used to provide remote analytical services to the US. At its peak the team had over 1000 analysts working remotely.

At GE global analytics was all about the management of remote centralized teams that helped a global business to grow its international startups and acquisitions by providing analytic support to these subsidiaries. There was a gap in skills across the markets which could be arbitraged via global analytics and this created huge value for global firms such as GE Capital.

This key business driver would have not been possible without the creation of remote working teams and the management processes that led them.

Of course, ABPOs and COEs require one to manage by acting local but thinking global. Managers must be able to attend meetings late at night or early in the morning. The COVID-19 pandemic certainly accelerated the process of moving jobs offshore and created the need for managers to adapt their working schedules to meet offshore needs. One such adaptation is working earlier in the US and having the offshore business begin work earlier and end work later in order to cater for the overlap in time. This is especially necessary for analytics teams who are often working on programming or building models and there are handoffs which need to take place.

Analytics and AI for Human Resources: Employee Monitoring

Overview of Analytics and AI for HR

Human resources (HR) is just starting to scratch the surface in terms of using analytics to improve employee retention, productivity, recruitment, and even employee health and wellness. I conducted one of the first analytic projects for HR at GE in the early 2000s when population demographics and analytics were used to predict what the workforce would look like at GE in 2020. The application of analytics in HR is also known as people analytics, and is receiving considerable attention and additional investment in firms today. Agarwal et al. (2018) reported that companies are starting to realize that people data is just as important as other forms of analytics in firms and that a majority of organizations are building integrated systems to analyze worker-related data, and have accurate, timely data with data security policies in place. Moreover, they reported that these organizations are mining this rich variety of sources to provide unique insights about the entire employee experience as well as data on job progression, career mobility, and performance.

Analytics for HR and Employee Monitoring

The employee data being tracked includes data harvested from personal interactions, voice communications, and video interviews. Even the sentiment of employee emails is measured and monitored. Agarwal et al. (2018) also reported that organizational network analysis software can now interpret email traffic, monitor employees' stress levels, and help to spot abuse, fraud, and poor management. These tools can also analyze employee feedback and performance to identify management challenges, send coaching tips to different leaders, and identify key subject matter experts, knowledge management resources, and organizational influencers based on their interactions and relationships – not necessarily their titles and roles. However, HR organizations need to be aware of the purpose of workplace monitoring and their employees' perception of the activity. Thiel et al. (2023) studied employee monitoring and found emerging evidence suggesting that monitored employees may actually engage in higher levels of deviance. By this they meant employees deviating from corporate policies. They then drew upon social cognitive theory to examine the self-regulatory consequences of employee monitoring and theorized that "monitoring paradoxically creates conditions for more (not less) deviance by diminishing employees' sense of agency, thereby facilitating moral disengagement via displacement of responsibility." HR teams need to treat this research as a practical insight and develop programs to address how monitoring can be used effectively without also promoting unintended consequences.

With this background and context now let's talk about how HR can use analytics to monitor remote workers. Studies have shown that US firms have a lead in remote working because these firms tend to be the most advanced in terms of the performance measurement and evaluation systems (e.g., Scur et al., 2021 and Patnaik et al., 2021) that are critical for remote work when employees cannot be directly observed in the office. So, the question then becomes how can analytics and technology be an enabler and facilitator for remote working? First, because meetings take place via electronic meeting software and most work is being conducted via VPN or via a smartphone provided by the employer. HR analytics teams typically focus on employee retention, acquisition, promotion, etc. During the pandemic many companies and their employees were convinced that remote was the new normal. Many companies during this time were 90% remote. Post-pandemic many firms are calling employees back which range from pre-pandemic more than 50% of employees working five days per week to hybrid situations where the majority of the time will be spent in the office and the rest will be remote. These adaptations which are now being implemented are not optimized. Yang et al. (2021) used rich data on the emails, calendars, instant messages, video/audio calls and workweek hours of 61,182 US Microsoft employees over the first six months of 2020 to estimate the causal effects of firm-wide remote work on collaboration and communication. Their results show evidence that the shift to firm-wide remote work caused business groups to become less interconnected. It also reduced the number of ties bridging structural holes in the company's informal collaboration network and caused individuals to spend less time collaborating with the bridging ties that remained. Finally, their study showed that employees were spending a greater share of their collaboration time with their stronger ties, which are better suited to information transfer, and a smaller share of their time with their weaker ties, which are more likely to provide access to new information.

We are calling for HR to now have their analytics teams focus on remote employee monitoring and even interactions at work in order to optimize the hybrid environment. This can even be done by business sector or for that matter can even go down to the department level. Such an HR team could be called the hybrid working analytics team or the workplace optimization team.

Optimization will improve employee satisfaction and at the same time will ensure that the company is optimizing the management of their talent. This analytics application is a new one coming out of the pandemic and is very interesting since it's something that emerged from an event, unlike the majority of existing analytics applications which have already been established for many years. The statistical and management science techniques one would use for these applications could include mathematical programming, correlation and regression analysis, cluster analysis, factor analysis and structural equation modeling. We expect this to create additional job opportunities for statistical analysts and quantitative scientists.

How Are Analytics, Machine Learning and Big Data Changing the Way We Manage Remote Workers?

Overview of Analytics and Remote Working

Analytics, big data, machine learning and AI have changed the way we think about work and have led to an increase in the presence of remote workers. The idea is that a business which is run on analytics needs to have less interactions among workers and hence workers can do their jobs remotely. This is partially true; however, there are still requirements for managing remote analytics workers. As discussed earlier, there are now gigantic teams in India and other developing countries doing remote analytics work. These teams must be managed remotely by default and the premise of the section that follows is that we can learn from this forced "managing at a distance," in order to gain best practices for managing at a distance in general.

Analytics and Remote Workers

One of the key challenges of managing remote analytics workers is getting them the proper supervision for their analytics techniques. Similarly to the health professions it's good to get a second opinion or review from peers on a diagnosis – in this case the development of a model. However, it's difficult to do this when one is managing employees on a remote basis. One of the ways to do this is to create templates for how analytic projects or models can be displayed. If these templates are standardized across the globe then this will make it easier for peer reviews and for management or the chief analytics officer to evaluate the quality and efficacy of the models. One modeling template we used to follow was the credit score template created by the Fair Isaac Company. Fair Isaac set the standard for credit scoring (including the ubiquitous FICO Score) and always delivered a standardized document whenever it developed a custom score for a financial services firm. This standardized document included a business brief, sampling frame, dependent variable definition, independent variable definition, performance observation, model results, key variables, insights from the model, model fit statistics, performance graphs and charts, and pseudocode for model implementation. With this documentation such as a standardized financial report including an income statement, balance sheet, or statement of cash flows the data science and statistical community will have a common language from which to communicate the results of their models and analytics. This facilitates better teamwork and creates an organization where people can learn a standardized craft form instead of each person conducting a separate set of operations in order to complete a task. When I started in analytics building credit scores in the early 1990s I was given the task of developing a credit score but was not shown how to do it. Of course, not knowing differently I used linear discriminant analysis as I had been trained to do during my applied statistics program. Then one day I was printing out copies of my output and a model developer from another department looked at my output and made a comment on some of the fit statistics. It was at this point I started to wonder how people gained specific skills in this area. Although I was a trained master's degree level statistician when I started my career (I went on to receive my PhD later) I still didn't exactly know how to develop a risk scorecard in the industry so I fell back on my formal training and developed a linear discriminant analysis of the data. This seemed to be the right approach from a statistical standpoint and was consistent with what others were doing. It would have been nice to have a training course in how to build risk models (aka scorecards) but it was expected that you were able to learn this from more senior analysts under a sort of apprentice role. However, there was nothing formalized in the business and because I was working in an independently operated subsidiary of a huge firm it meant that I didn't have the exposure to some of the firm's main analysis resources. Therefore, the resulting analytical product (the score) was the result of a compilation of my formal academic training in statistics and what I discerned from the senior analysts in the firm from cafeteria meetings and other business social activities. Eventually, I worked closely on a project with another analyst who had a practice developing risk models and who had also written some SAS macros. I transferred the macros to my own storage device and then proceeded to use and study them. Eventually, I began to understand what was happening and started to integrate my classical statistical training into the practice because at first it seemed like a foreign language that was not related to any of the statistical techniques I had learned in my classes. However, I slowly learned that this type of statistical process required a unique type of data transformation which actually lowered the information value of the data in order to stabilize the model. The technique was referred to as fine classing and course classing and was a form of binning transformations. Once I had learned the context for performing this type of transformation it became easy for me to learn more and to become more highly skilled in this area. Today, there are algorithms that automate this classing but I always carry my wooden ruler ready to show employees or students learning how to build models how to do it the old-school way. The rulers allow one to precisely choose where the cuts for the binning will occur right at the points of inflection for the distribution. I pride myself on being able to transform any variable by eye using the old-school fine classing method better than any binning algorithm in production use today. The machines can probably beat me in the long run, especially with the expansion of AI but so far my old-school knowledge is still in the lead.

Similarly to new drivers learning how to drive a car with a manual transmission I urge all analysts to learn fine classing when building a model so that they fully understand how the binning is conducted and how it can create a better model. With control over the fine classing analysts now have greater self-confidence when running a machine learning algorithm because they can then compare the output of the machine with the work their own brain could have accomplished. This gives them a greater insight into the linkage between data and insights. The more the analysts can understand the logic of how these algorithms work the more effective they will eventually become as data analysts/analytics professionals. The same held true for me when I was working toward my master's degree in statistics and was required by the school to calculate all the equations by hand. Some of these multivariate equations, including factor analysis and discriminant analysis, were so complex that it was virtually impossible not to make at least one calculation mistake. However, one learned the inner workings of the algorithms and this allowed one to envision a higher framework for statistics. Thus, one is then able to apply the framework and to learn and link all of the new techniques related to statistics. This is key since the theoretical distributions of statistics represent basically everything besides the work of John Tukey. Tukey took a different approach and instead made it all about the data. However, it's still difficult to understand a data-driven approach if one cannot grasp probability distributions. Probability distributions explain how likely or unlikely it is that an event will occur. This can be done either mathematically or visually, which appeals to all types of learners. Using the normal curve or chi-square distribution curve to display the critical region can be very intuitive to visual learners especially when they cannot seem to comprehend the tabular information provided. Sometimes one will get questions on where the distribution came from. Today, it is easier to explain this by utilizing computer simulations which used the bootstrap method that was originally developed by Bradley Efron in 1979. With bootstrapping one can simulate the central limit theorem on a real-time basis using a computer. You can also simulate the same thing with a Gaussian machine as displayed on YouTube. The Gaussian machine uses ball bearings which bounce off rods using gravity and are randomized as they hit the rods. This is similar to the operation of a pinball machine. This is essentially a mechanical version of the applet which proves the central limit theorem which states that regardless of the underlying distribution the means calculated from multiple samples of the distribution selected at random with replacement will always be normally distributed. It acts like a giant pinball machine and when watching this amazing phenomenon, I now realize why I hated pinball so much when I was a kid. What I hated most about it was that even with the greatest skill there is still an element of probability associated with pinball. There are all

types of tricks one can learn to become a true pinball wizard. A lot has to
with trapping the ball and slowing the ball down to reduce its randomness. This can be done by using the arms on the machine to propel the
ball upward. However, the normal distribution machine reminds us of
just how much skill can be overridden by chance and the same hold true
for pinball machines. Maybe someone can gain the advantage over the
other. However, they are still subject to some of the randomness or friction interacting with the laws of gravity, which is why no matter how
skilled a player is it is impossible to gauge where the ball will eventually
end up in the machine. For example, there are applets which perform
bootstrapping and which actually prove the central limit theorem; this
used to be done by hand up until computers could simulate it. These
applets are an electronic version of the central limit machine much like
the difference between an analog and digital timepiece. Like time they
both represent probabilities in the real and virtual world which actually
coexist in the virtual and physical world.

The key to the above is that in the past success as an analyst was
achieved through a combination of working with peers and formal statistical training. In the world of remote work there are fewer face-to-face
peer interactions so manuals and how-to guides can serve to facilitate this
interaction. The need for manuals to facilitate the proper use of quantitative
analysis techniques is not a new idea. It was first proposed by John Tukey
(1954) and is now even more critical in the age of remote work. The good
news is that in Tukey's time this information needed to be transmitted through
print text via libraries. Today this knowledge can be transmitted through
internet links or PDF files sent via email.

Analytics in the Workplace Creating the Opportunity for MAAAD

Historical Overview of Analytics in the Workplace

While the awareness of probability has been observed in ancient cultures
through the discovery of primitive dice games made with animal bones
the history of analytics in the workplace as it is currently defined (defined
as predictive analytics) probably started in ancient Roman times when the
concept of insurance was first created. The Romans were particularly
concerned with the rituals around death and dying and therefore created
the concept of funeral insurance. Today the selling of funeral insurance
through direct TV is often viewed by the regulators and the public alike as
a deceptive substitute for life insurance targeted at seniors on low fixed
incomes. Little do they realize that the product has been around for literally thousands of years! The growth of analytics in business was probably stunted during the next several centuries due to the formation of

Christianity (see Bernstein, 1998). However, the process of diversifying risk through insurance gradually advanced until the concept of life tables was introduced by Edmund Halley of Halley's comet fame in 1693. Halley's work followed that of John Graunt, a London draper who in 1662 discovered that patterns of longevity and death in a defined group, or cohort, followed predictable patterns. This was the case despite the uncertainty about the future longevity or mortality of any one person. Life tables made it possible to set up an insurance product or policy in order to be able to provide life insurance or pensions for a group of people, and to calculate with some degree of accuracy how much each person in the group should contribute to a common fund assumed to earn a fixed rate of interest. Halley not only constructed the first known life table but also demonstrated a method of calculating a premium using it. A premium refers to the amount of money someone of a given age (or other attributes) should pay to purchase a life annuity.

While the previous examples have shown that analytics for business has been around for some time, it is only relatively recently that there has been an increased emphasis on the use of analytics in the modern firm (Fogarty, 2017).

The use of advanced analytics in business has followed the data trail and has grown since the widespread use of data warehousing and relational databases on client servers. At first analytics was primarily used by mail order catalog companies desiring to target new customers who would make purchases and existing customers who will purchase more. It was also used by credit card companies who needed to assess a customer or credit prospect's creditworthiness before extending unsecured revolving credit. Eventually, however, most firms, even the packaged goods companies, were able to gather enough data to be able to conduct more advanced analytics. Today companies like Proctor & Gamble have to compete in a data analytics arms race with companies like Walmart and Amazon, both of which are trying to capture as much data on customers as they can in the retail ecosystem. In order to be able to win the packaged good companies like P&G are employing such measures as tagging individuals on the websites in which they are currently advertising and building huge databases with the profiles of people who are interested in their products. They are also hiring teams of advanced analysts to analyze all these digital footprints. In addition to the digital footprint world P&G is also participating in the internet of things, better known as the IoT. I was recently involved in a smart toothbrush project in which an Oral-B electric toothbrush collects data while the customer is brushing their teeth which is used to measure and improve oral health. Bhaduri and Fogarty (2016) discussed the use of analytics in business to gain a competitive advantage. The P&G example above demonstrates that for many firms advanced analytics is no longer being used to get ahead of the competition but is instead becoming table stakes for any firm wanting to remain competitive within an established marketplace.

The implications of all of this for managing at a distance in the workplace are significant. For example, when I started as an entry-level analytics professional in the early 1990s as a risk management analyst for the credit card business at GE Capital getting data extracted from the legacy systems, in particular the IBM or Digital Equipment Corporation mainframes, was extremely challenging. Therefore, the use of analytics was only for a single purpose which was to assess credit risk on an unsecured loan portfolio. Moreover, there was only one department in the firm doing analytics and only a few analysts across the entire business. It was only after data started coming down off the mainframe computers, initially to IBM OS/2 applications and then finally to RDBMS or relational database management systems which eventually led the ubiquitous "data warehouse," did other functions start developing their own analytics applications. While I was working as a risk analyst at GE I was able to start a marketing analytics function (see below).

Barrero et al. (2023) point out that working from home has been rising in the US for many decades, driven by the continuing improvements in technology that enables remote working. They also note that in the 1960s around 0.4% of full paid days in the US were worked from home. By the 1990s the work-from-home share had more than doubled to 1% as the personal computer started to become available. The use of a modem to connect to the workplace technology was also a contributing factor. Remote work quadrupled again, to 4.0%, by 2016 as the internet became widely available. The authors made an interesting finding that even pre-pandemic working from home rates were growing rapidly, doubling roughly every 15 years. They attribute the driving force behind this pre-pandemic growth in working from home was improving technology culminating to those developed after 2000 including video-call software like Teams, WebEx and Zoom, cloud file-sharing packages like Box, Drive, and Dropbox, and connectivity software like Asana, Gmail and Slack were widely available and facilitated remote work. These technologies are essential for remote work as we know it today, but none of them existed in 2000. Instead, remote work relied on telephone calls and file sharing by email or FTP. Earlier, in the 1980s, telecommunications were even more rudimentary, so remote work typically involving driving or mailing paperwork between home and office locations. The authors purport that another key driver of the growth of remote work in addition to technology is analytics. At a high level analytics takes the human element out of decision-making and therefore reduces the need for face-to-face collaboration and integration.

The following sections across the various business functional areas make this case clear:

Analytics and AI for Marketing

Nineteenth-century Philadelphia retailer John Wanamaker is quoted as saying, "Half the money I spend on advertising is wasted; the trouble is I don't know which half." The goal of marketing analytics sprang from the desire to measure, manage, and analyze marketing performance and optimize return on investment (ROI). The overall goal is to use data science to better perform the traditional marketing function activities such as customer and client acquisition, retention, and loyalty. Understanding marketing analytics allows marketers to be more effective and efficient at their jobs and maximize the ROI of marketing investments

As firms advance into the digital space the list of analytics activities that fall under marketing analytics will continue to grow. In fact, AI marketing as described by Alford (2017) uses techniques such as AI and machine learning to improve customer experiences by making individualized offers in real time. The organizational benefits of AI marketing come from automating large-scale, repetitive tasks, thus allowing leaders to refocus resources toward areas which require fewer creative skills but which are just as critical to marketing such as creative messaging and strategic planning. However, the irony of all this that is that society is in effect using machines (represented by automated algorithms and not physical machines like robots as the mind tends to conjure up) to shift brands away from marketing automation toward more one-to-one personalized experience. Halper and Stodder (2016) discuss AI marketing and confirm that marketing is often one of the first departments in an organization to use advanced analytics to make marketing investments more efficient and effective around customer churn. In order to accomplish this, cross-selling and acquisition are used along with additional investments related to customer experience. In this context, it would only seem logical that more advanced machine learning AI tools used for marketing would also be among the first to be implemented in the firm. Having marketing technology and analytics make the campaign decisions, a concept which was pioneered by companies like Capital One, is an excellent use of analytics and one that enables employees to work remotely.

Analytics and AI for Sales

After marketing analytics the next logical area to apply analytics in the firm is in sales. In direct-to-consumer organizations the lines between marketing and sales are more fuzzy since many marketing activities can be linked to direct sales. However, in a B2B company, this is not usually the case. The sales cycle can be rather long and there are activities such as client events which are not usually considered to be traditional marketing activities. It is here where analytics and AI can really add value and enhance the sales process through prospect targeting and client retention. B2B analytics for sales has always been challenging since it is difficult to attribute the analytics and targeting activities to actual sales. Moreover, this could challenge sales commissions so one is likely to see resistance from sales. However, sometimes analytics can be used with great results. For instance, GE Commercial Finance conducted client surveys whereby the client was able to communicate how much they valued the product and/or services and whether there were any areas for improvement. The process was a function of the Six Sigma "Voice of the Customer" methodology. However, GE was able to develop custom questionnaires for each client which enabled the sales organization to determine exactly which products the client was eligible to be cross-sold or upsold. This B2B analytics technique significantly increased the number of products and revenue per client at GE Commercial Finance and became a global best practice across sales departments at GE. Lead generation is another example of where analytics can come into play. For instance, in an auto finance business in Europe, an analytically driven lead generation process brought leads to auto dealers of customers who would keep their cars long enough to break even with the commissions paid to auto dealers. This enabled the firm to negotiate new commission rates with the dealers and also work on retention campaigns directly with the customers. These campaigns would inevitably involve enticing the customer to visit the dealer again to trade in the existing vehicle and therefore the dealers would be happy to receive the fresh leads. This process was eventually patented by GE. The COVID-19 pandemic accelerated B2B analytics since sales associates were unable to meet their current and prospective clients face-to-face. Therefore, greater emphasis was placed on lead nurturing through digital channels. One of the interesting techniques was individual models where prospects were profiled and modeled based on their internet and social media data and compiled into a profile report for sales to study before an engagement. This reduces the need to take clients to sporting events or dinners in order to get to know them better. We call this remote CRM (customer relationship management). Although we are back to meeting face-to-face some of the techniques developed for sales during the pandemic have stuck and now this facilitates more remote work for sales.

Analytics and AI for International Business

Another area where technology is entering the workplace is via electronic messaging and making global teams cohesive despite the wide geographies from which these teams are dispersed. Failed expatriate assignments can be extremely costly for businesses wanting to send employees overseas for either specific skill transfers or leadership development.

There are many stresses to expatriates moving overseas and also in returning which have been well documented. Fogarty and Coughlan (2016) demonstrated that the existence of virtual proximity, or the use of computer and IT, reduces the psychic distance and serves to compress the perceived distance of expatriates to their home countries, thereby alleviating some of the challenges of dealing with adjustment. It also proposes the use of virtual proximity training tools to prepare expatriates and their families for international assignments. The importance of this research served to improve the effectiveness of international business via technology by fueling innovation and improving the quality and effectiveness of international expatriate assignments and the creation of a new generation of expatriates who are well-adjusted to a global lifestyle.

The next phase in virtual proximity is to also have AI technology like Alexa or Google Home not only facilitate regular communications with the teams but also keep people informed as to what is going on with the various units. This could occur across all communication channels including verbal, video, and written and make it easy for parties separated across vast distances to communicate better. While one might think that the COVID-19 pandemic would have forced businesses to manage their international subsidiaries without expatriates the trends continue to show increases in expatriate assignments in tandem with increased globalization. However, this does not negate the need for analytics to facilitate the managing of expatriates at a distance.

A study by Hsieh et al. (1999) shows that 70% of expatriate assignments fail, meaning that the position gets vacated, and companies have to spend extra money to replace and train personnel, meaning slower growth. Therefore, contingent upon a firm to invest to see that these relationships continue to succeed.

DavidsonMorris (2020) points out that advanced analytical software is increasingly being utilized in expatriate talent searches, making it easier to choose the best employee for an international role based on their skills, experience, willingness to relocate, and other data points. This allows for greater accuracy in relocation cost forecasts, and faster deployment of the employee. With sufficient data firms are also able to build expatriate success models to predict the success of expatriate assignments based on individual and family characteristics. When I did my first expatriate assignment 25 years ago my family and I faced a day-long evaluation by a psychologist. Now there is the ability to get this done remotely via analytics.

DavidsonMorris (2020) also observe that there is scope for virtual reality technology to be utilized during the planning and training phase of an international relocation. The company could save money, time, and resources by giving the employee a virtual tour of their new city and workplace, as opposed to sending them on a pre-relocation visit with first-class tickets and lodgings for the employee and their entire family.

Finally, DavidsonMorris (2020) discuss the use of AI and machine learning for managing at a distance in expatriate assignments. For example, AI chat bots can make it easier to touch base with expatriate employees and monitor their experiences abroad. This allows for hands-off data collection which frees up more time for global mobility professionals to manage other tasks. As a scheduled chat bot survey is a fast and efficient way for the employee to report their experience to human resources, problems will be picked up sooner and expatriate failure becomes less likely of an occurrence. Machine learning and robotic process automation can be used to enhance practically every system associated with expatriate management. Firms are increasingly using smart or expert learning systems which learn real-time from the data they receive, providing ever more accurate predictions on success rates, cost, and other important factors.

Analytics and AI for Business Operations Management

The growth of IOT is nothing less than spectacular. Statista (2019) estimates that there will be over 30 billion connected devices by 2030. IOT is also showing much promise in terms of delivering data to operations managers. IoT deploys the use of software or sensors to allow physical objects to actually create new information which can then be collected on the web. One of the first implementations of this that I was involved with was at GE and real-time data coming from its aircraft engines in flight and on the tarmac. GE was able to sell this information to its airline clients who viewed it as important for safety concerns. However, in addition to being able to monetize this information it also had an important other use in that it reduced the cycle time to get the engines overhauled. Prior to having this information, the overhauls would run on a fixed schedule. However, this information was able to allow the maintenance crew to evaluate an individual engine and determine the optimal time to obtain an overhaul in order to reduce failures. Failures in aircraft engines are both costly and can represent safety concerns. GE then took this initial foray into the IoT and created an entire initiative known as the industrial internet. The IOT and data analytics coming from the streaming data enables employees to manage processes and machines at a distance (even from a mile in the air) and thus are facilitating managing at a distance.

Analytics and AI for Accounting and Finance

Analytics has many innovative and helpful uses which are changing how work in the area of Finance and Accounting is being done. EY (2016) claims that one of the most promising areas for the application of analytics and AI in the world of finance and accounting is in the discipline of auditing. In the past one of the most difficult jobs of the internal audit staff of corporations was the arduous travel schedules required of the auditors to be on the ground auditing the books and processes of internal subsidiaries. Today, in the area of forensic accounting analytics, especially automated algorithms, can be trained to search for anomalies on financial statements and spreadsheets and report back to auditors when an audit is necessary is helping to modernize and make the entire auditing function more efficient. We call these analytics-driven audits "virtual audits" and instead of auditors going on-site the data comes to them and analytics can then help to perform the audit. Thus, analytics facilitates managing at a distance with finance and accounting.

Chapter 10 Takeaways

This chapter has reflected on how analytics has changed the workplace in recent years. The overall implications of this is that analytics is no longer a specialized field in a firm; instead, all employees now have analytics as a part of their job function and the collective impact of analytics and the unique data that firms are gathering is creating a core competence which cannot easily be duplicated by the competition. Corporations which hire the brightest people can collectively deal with challenges and come up with better ways to do business which often end up improving the lives of their customers. They have done this throughout history. The use of analytics in the workplace means that fewer individuals are needed to provide expertise and this facilitates the remote work for those who remain in the firm as decisions based on analytics do not require the level of collaboration that other types of decisions require. Not only does analytics facilitate remote work but it also allows managers and employees to make their jobs more efficient and effective. However, managers need to refrain from coming across as "big brothers" as research has demonstrated that employees are then more likely to break the rules.

References

Agarwal, D., Bersin, J., Lahiri, G., Schwartz, J., & Volini, E. (2018). *Human Capital Trends: People, Data, Analytics, Risks and Opportunities.* https://www2. deloitte.com/insights/us/en/focus/human-capital-trends/2018/people-data-analyt ics-risks-opportunities.html?id=us:2ps:3gl:confidence:eng:cons:031616:em:dup1 179:EpqfrB65:1100004719:268089541421:b:Human_Capital_Trends:People_Da ta_BMM:nb.

Alford, J. (2017). *AI Marketing: What Does the Future Hold?* https://www.sas.com/ en_us/insights/articles/marketing/ai-marketing-what-does-the-future-hold.html.

Barrero, J., Bloom, N., & Davis, S. (2023). *The Evolution of Working from Home.* https://wfhresearch.com/wp-content/uploads/2023/07/SIEPR1.pdf.

Bell, P. C., Anderson, C. K., and Kaiser, S. P. (2003). Strategic Operations Research and the Edelman Prize Finalist Applications 1989–1998, *Operations Research*, 51(1), 17–31.

Bell, P. C., and Zaric, G. S. (2012). *Analytics for Managers*. Routledge.

Bernstein, P. L. (1998) *Against the Gods: The Remarkable Story of Risk*. John Wiley & Sons.

Beverakis, G., Dick, G., & Cecez-Kecmanovic, D. (2008). Taking Information Systems Business Process Outsourcing Offshore: The Conflict of Competition and Risk. *Journal of global Information Management*, 17(1), 34–46.

Bhaduri, S. N., & Fogarty, D. J. (2016). *Advanced Business Analytics: Essentials for Developing a Competitive Advantage*. Springer.

Cokins, G. (2015). *Trends and Visions of Analytics in the CFO and Accounting Functions*. International Institute for Analytics Enterprise Research Services. https://www.sas.com/content/dam/SAS/en_us/doc/research2/iia-trends-and-visio ns-of-analytics-cfo-accounting-108089.pdf.

Dans, E. (2018, May 27). How Analytics Has Given Netflix the Edge over Hollywood. *Forbes*. https://www.forbes.com/sites/enriquedans/2018/05/27/how-ana lytics-has-given-netflix-the-edge-over-hollywood/#6920f7496b23.

Davenport, T. H., & Harris, J. G. (2007). *Competing on Analytics: The New Science of Winning*. Harvard Business School Press.

DavidsonMorris (2020, January 2). *Global Mobility Trends: 2020 & Beyond*. http s://www.davidsonmorris.com/global-mobility-trends/.

Devata, A. C., Kumar, R., & Stratopoulos, T. (2005). Business Process Outsourcing: A Manager's Guide to Understanding the Market Phenomenon. In P. Brudenall (Ed.), *Technology and Offshore Outsourcing Strategies* (pp. 97–115). Palgrave Macmillan.

Dibbern, J., Goles, T., Hirschheim, R., & Jayatilaka, B. (2004). Information Systems Outsourcing: A Survey and Analysis of the Literature. *The DATA BASE for Advances in Information Systems*, 35(4), 6–102.

EY (2016). How Can Your Finance Function Benefit From Data Analytics?http s://www.ey.com/Publication/vwLUAssets/ey-how-can-your-finance-function-ben efit-from-data-analytics/%24File/ey-how-can-your-finance-function-benefit-fro m-data-analytics.pdf.

Fogarty, D. J. (2012). Using Genetic Algorithms for Credit Scoring Maintenance Functions, *International Journal of Artificial Intelligence and Applications*, 3(6), 1–8.

Fogarty, D. J. (2014). How Health Consumers Can Get Closer to Consumers. *Knowledge at Wharton*. http://knowledge.wharton.upenn.edu/article/health-in surers-can-get-closer-consumers/.

Fogarty, D. J. (2015). Lean Six Sigma and Big Data: Continuing to Innovate and Optimize Business Processes. *Journal of Management and Innovation*, 1(2), 6–10.

Fogarty, D. J. (2015). Lean Six Sigma and Data Analytics: Implementing Complementary Activities. *Global Journal of Advanced Research*, 2(2), 28–33.

Fogarty, D. J. (2017). *From Beer to Derivatives: The History of Analytics in Business*. Sara Book Publication.

Fogarty, D., & Bell, P. (2013, December 19). Should You Outsource Your Analytics? *MIT Sloane Management Review*.

Fogarty, D., & Bell, P. (2021, July 28). *Analytic Business Process Organizations and their Clients: A Dual Perspective*. Proceedings of the Global Conference on Innovation in Management and Business.

Fogarty, D. J., & Coughlan, T. (2016). Using Virtual Proximity to Promote Expatriate Cultural Adjustment and Innovation. Proceedings from the 2016 ISPIM Forum, Boston, MA.

Gent, E. (2019). *The Armies of Invisible Workers Who Help Technology Run*. BBC Worklife.

Gilliland, D., & Ramamoorthi, R. V. (2010). A Conversation with James Hannan. *Statistical Science*, 25(1), 126–144.

Halper, F., & Stodder, D. (2016). Marketing Analytics Meets Artificial Intelligence. *TDWI Checklist Report*.

Hsieh, T., Lavoie, J., & Samek, R. (1999). Are You Taking Your Expatriate Talent Seriously? *The McKinsey Quarterly*. https://www.questia.com/library/journal/1G1-63725939/are-you-taking-your-expatriate-talent-seriously.

Klein, H., & Myers, M. (1999). A Set of Principles for Conducting and Evaluating Interpretive Field Studies in Information Systems. *MIS Quarterly*, 23(1), 67–88.

Maloney, P. (2016). Original Story: The Founding of Pandora Radio. *Startup Grind*. https://www.startupgrind.com/blog/origin-story-the-founding-of-pandora-radio/.

Matthews, H. (2016). *eHarmony Success Rate (7 Surprising Stats)*. http://www.datingadvice.com/online-dating/eharmony-success-rate.

Patnaik, M., Lamorgese, A., Linarello, A., & Schivadi, F. (2021). Management Practices Boosted Firm Performance in COVID-19 by Facilitating Remote Work: Evidence from Italy. *VoxEU*.

Pemberton, C. (2016). *What Makes a Marketing Center of Excellence?* https://www.gartner.com/en/marketing/insights/articles/what-makes-a-marketing-center-of-excellence.

Sangari, M. S., & Razmi, J. (2015). Business Intelligence Competence, Agile Capabilities, and Agile Performance in Supply Chain: An Empirical Study. *The International Journal of Logistics Management*, 26(2), 356–380. https://doi-org.contentproxy.phoenix.edu/10.1.108/IJLM-01-2013-0012.

Scur, D., Sadun, R., Van Reenen, J. M., Lemos, R., & Bloom, N. (2021). World Management Survey at 18: Lessons and the Way Forward. *SSRN Electronic Journal*. https://doi.org/10.2139/ssrn.3794092.

Statista (2019). *IoT Connected Devices Worldwide 2019–2030*. https://www.statista.com/statistics/1183457/iot-connected-devices-worldwide/.

Thiel, C. E., Bonner, J., Bush, J. T., Welsh, D. T., & Garud, N. (2023). Stripped of Agency: The Paradoxical Effect of Employee Monitoring on Deviance. *Journal of Management*, 49(2), 709–740. https://doi.org/10.1177/01492063211053224.

Tukey, J. W. (1954). Unsolved Problems of Experimental Statistics. *Journal of the American Statistical Association*, 49(268), 706–731. https://doi.org/10.2307/2281535.

Walsham, G. (1995). The Emergence of Interpretivism in IS Research. *Information Systems Research*, 6(4), 376–394.

Willcocks, L., Hindle, J., Feeny, D., & Lacity, M. (2004). IT and Business Process Outsourcing: The Knowledge Potential. *Information Systems Management*, 7–15.

Yang, L., Holtz, D., Jaffe, S.et al. (2021). The Effects of Remote Work on Collaboration Among Information Workers. *Nat Hum Behav*. https://doi.org/10.
1038/s41562-021-01196-4.

Zainal, Z. (2007). Case Study as a Research Method. *Jurnal Kemanusiaan*,
6–9.

Centers of Excellence

What Is a Global COE (Center of Excellence)?

Foreword

The primary goal of this book is to serve as a strategic guide for managers during a time of significant change in the management environment – and the factors that have led to the expansion of hybrid/remote work certainly constitute such a change. Therefore, the book up until this point has focused on building a theoretical framework to support decisions on how and when to implement hybrid/remote work strategies and policies.

However, there are situations where hybrid and remote work may be less than optimal, could affect the effectiveness of a work process, or would simply be impossible. For example, much of the patient care in a hospital requires physical presence, and given the current state of technology most factory work or transportation business requires a physical presence.

Therefore, when co-authors David Fogarty and Tom Coughlan first discussed the development of this book, they felt that it would be appropriate to include a chapter on global centers of excellence (COEs) – and that there is no one better to explore this topic than Gary Bernstein. Currently these centers typically benefit tremendously from the co-location of their team members.

In this chapter Gary explores some of the critical success factors in COEs, and even touches on how we may soon see pressure to include hybrid and remote elements in operating models that focus on this strategy.

Introduction

It is important to think of a center of excellence (COE) as having two primary approaches. The most common, often most effective, and

DOI: 10.4324/9781032646657-11

typically most cost-efficient approach is the physical COE. An alternative model could loosely be described as a virtual COE. The key is that while the models and mode of operation may be different, the COE is run by a common management, operates under common practices, standards, and processes, and should drive towards the use of common operating tools such as IT systems. Our focus will be on the physical and primarily global COE in the discussion on this topic. It should be noted that a COE is not always the right approach to all an enterprise's needs, but it has a very important place in the overall suite of operations.

It would, however, be remiss to avoid the pivot that has taken place during and after the COVID-19 pandemic in relation to COEs. Traditionally, a physical COE was typically structured to require employees to work together in one physical location. This enabled the attributes that will be discussed later in terms of optimizing labor costs, productivity, innovation, and skills development. The pandemic has likely had a lasting impact on the office-based workplace and COEs are not immune to that change. During the pandemic, while often not optimal, business continuity required significant remote work arrangements. While there has been a move back to office environments, employees have learned to work remotely and are demanding some level of remote work. While offering remote work is not an employer requirement, gaining and retaining top skills will require some degree of at least what is commonly referred to as a hybrid work arrangement, usually involving three days in the office and two days working remotely. Although this goes against the traditional grain of a COE, as discussed earlier the notion of cumulative proximity does and will continue to some extent to apply to COE environments. Exactly how this notion will play out is in its early stages, but it appears to be an inevitable trend. While this shift towards an effective cumulative proximity model will create leadership challenges, one area that the pandemic has actually created is a more robust business model is improvement in business continuity options that will be addressed in detail later in this discussion on the COE model.

Recall the business world before the advent of technology that made the movement of data, communications, and organizational effectiveness require a physical proximity for almost all tasks. I emphasize the notion of almost all tasks, as even with the current state of technology enabling the ability to operate seamlessly, overcoming distance and physical barriers, it is important that one does not broad brush the issue and suggest that a COE is the most effective mode of operations for all tasks. It can be extremely cost-efficient and effective for many operations of an enterprise, particularly those that respond well to standardization and centralization of processes. However, it is not an elixir for all operations, particularly those where physical proximity to multiple functions is a key requirement.

While it is important to be extremely circumspect about the tasks that respond well to centralization, there is a tendency for management to resist change and assign too much need for the local proximity and not embrace the transformation to COEs. It is critical that the COE concept is embraced by the most senior leadership to ensure enterprise-wide acceptance.

What Exactly Is a COE?

A COE is an organization with a common mission to support one or more aspects of operating a business. Typically, it is centralized under a common management and operates in a matrixed manner to support its constituent organizations throughout the business.

A COE yields its optimization by common leadership, standardized processes, common IT tools, and a relentless demand for process transformation that is greatly enhanced by having a common leadership. The labor model is crafted to be highly efficient, and there must be a strong set of operational controls. Later in this chapter we will explore the details of a COE model, its benefits, the costs, and impact on a business.

A COE can serve a very wide variety of missions or processes depending on the mandate by the business. The level of COE complexity can vary greatly. For example, it is very efficient to set up a COE for a lower skill call center. The premium is on precisely standard processes, well-defined scripts, escalation points, and managing labor globally with the utmost efficiency while ensuring a quality customer experience. On the other hand, at the far extreme, a COE may have a mission of complex decision-making support for senior line management that requires a more flexible work model that is not based time efficiency, but rather on delivering effective results.

Globalization of a COE

A COE does not have to be operating in a global model to garner many of the benefits of a centralized operation. In fact, there are many reasons why an enterprise may choose to seek out the benefits to be achieved through COE operations, but decide to stay local in their home country or in proximity to their primary operations.

First, culture must always be considered. Not only the culture of the enterprise, but also of its customers. If cultural attributes are a premium, often a global model may not be the best choice for a COE location. Furthermore, if the service is considered a premium one and the customer demands a high level of service a location more proximate or co-located with senior-level decision-makers may be desired.

Accordingly, many companies are repatriating COE operations to their home countries, realizing that the higher costs will provide a higher level of customer satisfaction and fewer escalations. Customer support centers can be viewed not just as costs, but as potential profit generators that will often improve enterprise return on investment (Conejo, 2021). Another key consideration in the decision to globalize a COE is scale of operations. While in most cases the financial implications of a global COE are positive, initiating one does not come without cost or operational challenges. A company must have a reasonable level of scale to accrete the value from a global COE. There are startup costs to consider, training, IT, telecommunications, safety, security, facilities, and other infrastructure costs that must be evaluated. While there is no textbook to establish the optimal level of scale, a global COE must operate at a level such that all incremental operational costs are significantly more than offset by the operational efficiencies and labor cost savings of a COE.

Alternative models exist if the business case determines that the needed level of scale cannot be achieved. Sometimes the best answer is to outsource an operation with a business partner that runs global centers with similar operations for multiple customer enterprises and that has deep subject matter expertise. This option, while often a good one, is not always the right choice. If the process was extremely sensitive to the company's operations or extremely proprietary in nature, it could be a poor choice. In addition, the business partner will be adding their margin on to the costs. But without an adequate internal scale, the added margin to be absorbed may still be more cost efficient.

Once a business crosses the threshold that makes a global COE attractive economically and process-wise, it can be a very powerful way to gain operational leverage. An ideal option if scale can be achieved is to operate a global COE in multiple locations and countries while maintaining the common management concept. Multiple country locations will balance skills, labor costs and currency exchange rate risks, but of enormous importance is business continuity.

As an enterprise moves more and more processes to global COEs and in turn higher value processes, the attendant business continuity risk of being in one location becomes significant. The risks run the gamut from political stability to natural disasters, such as something as mundane as a fire impairing the operation's infrastructure. The concept and execution of business continuity planning will be examined in detail later in this discussion of COE operating models.

Why Do Companies Need Global COEs?

Once it has been established that a global COE makes good business sense for an enterprise, why is it then so slow to establish one? Although the effects of the COVID-19 pandemic and other geopolitical tensions may slow and, in some instances, reverse the globalization of businesses, it is a safe bet to assume that globalization will remain an inevitable path. The argument in favor of globalization is simply too compelling. Establishing efficient and resilient supply chains, operating closer to customers, building cultural diversity and leveraging the innovation that it can provide and balancing cost structures to be optimally competitive will drive the globalization of businesses, including utilizing global COEs.

A Global or Localized COE is Far More Than Just About Cost Savings

It would be a great mistake for a company to look at a COE merely as a means of making cost savings by developing a lower cost labor model. Certainly, that is an important feature, but as businesses tend to measure themselves on a year-over-year basis, the labor cost savings will continue but the year-over-year boost to profit is a one-time event. The power of the COE is ultimately in driving new and better processes, as well as driving commonality in the use of technology. The DNA of a great COE should be rooted in perpetual process and productivity improvements. That is the benefit that will roll over perpetually to the businesses operating results.

Finally, one should never overlook the value of process standardization. Certainly, it is a key attribute of continual productivity. But it is key to optimizing labor costs and common levels of customer support for internal and external customers, as well as minimizing the need for redundant IT systems. Standardization is often confused with a lack of flexibility in business processes. If managed correctly, this is just not true. Standardization does not mean that there is no room for exceptions or escalations in processes; instead, most aspects are handled in a standardized manner (Conejo, 2021).

The challenge for COE development will be resistance from middle management who may not have the same level of buy-in to change as senior management. Budgetary management can be a very powerful tool to get middle management buy-in. If management can see how a COE can help them to achieve budgetary challenges, it will greatly enhance the needed buy-in. While senior leadership may have to be heavy-handed and declare a COE approach for all impacted processes with no option for units to opt out, that level of support is usually critical to a COE's success.

It should be noted that the COE concept is not in conflict with an enterprise that operates on a centralized or decentralized model. The COE is about taking processes that are not core to line management's key focus areas and centralizing those operations. However, the ownership of the results should never shift from the various line organization structures. Accordingly, the COE model can be consistent with almost any variation of management systems a business has in place.

What Type of Companies Develop Global COEs?

Of course, there are no absolute rules or criteria as to what type of companies develop global COEs, but we can form some key attributes and generalizations.

First, based on the discussion surrounding scale, generally larger companies have the greatest propensity to gain the most benefits from a global COE. Second, consideration clearly must be given to the complexity and business impact of the processes under study. Due to their sensitive or high-risk nature to the enterprise some processes should not be considered for centralizing in a COE. However, close evaluation is needed as these situations should be the exception not the rule to ensure that they are not just related to common leadership resistance to change.

An example will amplify the point on the benefit to a global enterprise. Consider the accounts receivable process of a company. Receivables initiate with sales and are local to a country. Even where the sales occur in a high-cost locale, the sale execution generally needs to be localized. Customer facing issues that are sensitive may need to remain local with a small team of experts. However, as noted below, while it may be convenient to management to have all the administrative tasks in the back office for receivables done locally, the value proposition simply cannot justify the high costs. Moving these back-office processes to a COE cannot only yield material savings, if managed properly they can provide a better customer experience through totally focused process expertise.

It is important to keep in mind that business line process owners will delegate activities to the COE, but they should never be absolved of maintaining process ownership. The relationship between a COE must remain integrated and not be allowed to silo from the process owners in line management. Put another way, the COE owns the process expertise and constant drive for productivity, while line managers' time is freed up from operational tasks so that they can focus on the products or services, customer relationships, delivering revenue and profit growth.

A COE Should Never Be Allowed to Remain Static

It would be very misguided to view COE operations as ever-growing static. Success in developing and managing a COE requires that it is treated as a live and growing organism. For this very reason it would be unreasonable to assume that COEs will always primarily be co-located operations – even though today in most cases they generally are for the reasons already discussed.

To yield the optimal benefit from a COE model, the COE should continually expand its scope as skills in the COE mature. Allowing the enterprise to benefit from utilizing these maturing skills to take on increasingly complex tasks. This may require being open to hiring talent outside of a commutable distance of a particular location.

This is important to drive continual productivity and savings, but also COE staff want to see a career path. Even with strong career pathways, the COE organization will usually have attrition rates that are higher than the legacy organizations, but standardization, strong controls, scale and leveraging a small group of subject matter experts across a large organization performing similar tasks, allow the COE to operate in a higher attrition mode. It may seem counterintuitive to view a manageable but high level of attrition as a positive COE attribute, but it is actually necessary. Keeping the high potential and skilled employees with career pathways allows for ever-evolving growth in task complexity. At the same time a steady evergreening of the staff keeps labor rates at the lower end of the scale attendant with newer and less experienced employees. Essentially an up or out model is ideal, but should be closely managed to stay within a targeted attrition range.

Principles of Governance

Five Key Operating Principles

Just as there is a wide spectrum of local versus global structures, there would naturally be a spectrum of options for governing a global or even a regional COE. These principles should apply equally to either structure.

1   It is critical that the global COE approach has unwavering support within the business on a top-down basis. The reality is that if top management does not advocate the COE approach and in fact in many instances dictate the approach, success will be suboptimized. Establishing a single management structure to lead the global COE should be a cornerstone requirement.
2   The transition from a local to a global process must be carefully managed. The investment in transition management must be well thought out and adequately funded.
3   While a COE is managed centrally by definition, as mentioned earlier, it is important that the COE does not silo itself from line business process ownership. The COE must drive standard processes enterprise-wide. This will require compromise to transform the processes, but ultimately will yield the desired efficiencies and the necessary robustness of business continuity.
4   In business, leaders tend to get what they measure. A COE should have clear and concise target objectives for cost, controls, effectiveness, productivity, continuous employee training and growth. Key metrics measuring these and other established objectives should be strenuously established and regularly assessed.

5   The COE must fully embrace the notion that its job is to drive end-less process improvement and the attendant year-over-year productivity targets as established by senior leadership (Jones, 2013).

Key Operational Attributes

Beyond the broad governing principles there are a number of key attri-butes for management to consider when establishing the governance of a global COE. It should be noted that the number of varying COE struc-tures is virtually limitless, so this discussion should be viewed as options for best practices, but in all circumstances the exact governance of a COE will be dependent on the specific facts and circumstances at hand.

1 *Is the global COE operating out of one location proximate to the enterprise headquarters or other material divisional operations?*

If the COE is operating out of one location, the enterprise will elim-inate many areas of complexity, but will at the same time amplify other areas of complexity. A single site location will simplify the leadership construct in that the center will likely have one overall leader who will likely report to either a functional management head or to a corporate shared services leader, thereby making the chain of command shorter and reducing complexity.

A single location COE, be that in the home country or not, will sim-plify training, increase the concentration of subject matter experts, foster fewer cultural obstacles, enhance the ability to achieve a high level of operating scale, and reduce costs.

However, there are multiple issues to be considered when operating out of a single location center. First, there is a risk to business continuity. A single location provides fewer options in the case of a man-made or nat-ural disaster. Certainly IT systems and data can be backed up in a sepa-rate location, but the enterprise is still fully dependent on just one or a concentrated set of physical facilities as well as a single workforce, and lacks a sister location to pick up the impact should the COE have to shut down or is impaired in some manner.

While a single location has many advantages, one of the greatest risks is in managing labor costs. Enterprises tend to aggregate similar centers based on existing skills, robustness of educational opportunities and attractive operating costs. As more multi-company operations evolve in a geographic area, the scarcity of skills and labor will drive up competitive wages. This phenomenon is more severe in smaller scale labor markets, but also in large markets, such as those found in centers throughout India. While the workforce in India is certainly large, it is also inviting for many companies to tap into that same workforce and for them all to be chasing similar skills, which ultimately leads to higher attrition and increasing wages.

It should also not be lost in the calculation when considering a location of other operating costs, such as rents, communications, IT, and other infrastructure. These should not only be considered in a location selection, but would also argue for having a diverse location strategy to mitigate against local conditions and optimize total cost over time.

2 *Is the global COE located in the home country of the enterprise as opposed to operating out of a country that is not part of the company's normal operational structure?*

There are clear operational advantages to operating a global COE out of the enterprise's home country. Considerations that can be optimized include the benefit of culture affinity towards the enterprise's head-quarters, knowledge of labor and skills markets, training, and travel. Furthermore, the timeline from startup to delivering on productivity goals is typically shortened due to the proximity to leadership and subject matter expertise. If the home country is in a stable and mature location, rather than in an emerging location, it does not eliminate business continuity concerns, but will lower the risk level.

However, the normal tendency is that when a global enterprise is operating out of a relatively high-cost location and is contemplating shifting operations to global COEs, one of the major driving factors is to obtain a materially lower labor cost that will more than offset the startup, and other operational issues noted above. This argument tends to be an overwhelming one for shifting work to lower cost locations outside of the home country, particularly if highly specialized skills are not required.

In the future, as we find ourselves moving towards more hybrid/remote models of operation, we may find when recruiting that these models allow for a broader pool of candidates and low salary requirements. A number of recent studies have suggested that many candidates in high-cost locations would be willing to accept lower compensation for greater flexibility in location and work hours.

3 *Is the global COE focused on one function of operations and independently located or is it co-located with other global COE functions?*

At first glance one may not appreciate the complexity of this attribute. However, it can have a material impact on the cost and effectiveness of a global COE.

I believe that there should be a strong bias towards co-locating multiple different COE functions into one and preferably more than one location. Co-location has the benefit of allowing for shared infrastructure, such as security, IT, cafeterias and recreation, human resources, and real estate, to name just a few. This potential to share infrastructure will lower the average cost attributed to each of the different COE functions, making them more competitive and allowing the center's leadership to focus solely on their processes while allowing others to be assigned to manage the infrastructure.

4 *How will the management structure of the COE be established? Will it be managed independently as a true shared service or integrated into a divisional or other management structure?*

As one would expect, there are no absolutes of right or wrong with structural decisions in business, but the structure would tend to depend on the circumstances and objectives of the business.

The traditional approach to a true shared service in a COE would be a separate leadership structure that ultimately reports to an overall shared services leader, typically at corporate headquarters. At the same time, the COE leadership must have some level of matrix accountability to the various division executives supported. The degree of accountability between a COE leader and the division heads supported can vary greatly. If the process is extremely integral and is at a higher level involving decision support activities a truly matrixed approach may be optimal. In this instance, the division heads would be highly integrated into the COE activities, training, maintaining responsibility for the process and key metrics, controls, outcomes and shared cost management responsibility. While maintaining the matrixed responsibility, the divisional leadership would be relieved of many daily responsibilities, such as managing the work environment, hiring and firing, detailed training, general workflow and other personnel issues, with the big prize being that their focus would be where it should be and that is on the business strategy, clients, innovation, growth, quality and profitability. Operational leaders cannot ignore the COE's operations and must maintain some level of ownership for them, but they do not need to be distracted by the day-to-day activities.

Conversely, if the operations in the COE tend to be more process and procedural in nature, this would facilitate a more independently run COE, with the COE leadership managed by hard metrics and established inter-company billings., while cost management would remain the responsibility of a COE rather than being shared. Let us use an accounts payable operation as an illustration. Without doubt a well-managed accounts payable process is critical to any business, but should a divisional leader care about the billing process and normal collections? Their time is better spent on managing other business issues so long as the COE delivers on agreed upon cost and productivity metrics and meets all the material control and audit requirements. Naturally, the division cannot walk away entirely from total process ownership in virtually any example. Using this particular example, the divisional ownership would need to have a well-defined collection escalation process for delinquencies and client relationship management, but that should be the exception.

These are two extreme examples of leadership approach. The circumstances could dictate any level of variation and structure in between these extremes. However, regardless of the structure put in place, the most important aspect is that the COE and the division leadership have firm, documented and agreed upon ownership of control processes. As is often said, few leaders get fired for a reasonable miss to a budget or profit level, but a lapse in control can often result in a quick exit and will certainly be career limiting. There is a great risk that control falls through the cracks if both the COE and division leadership do not give them a great deal of attention on set up and when any material changes occur.

There is a variation to the traditional global COE structure that can yield many of the benefits through the management structure while providing a greater level of flexibility. This is particularly true for operations that require a very high level of intellectual experience and skills. This concept is often described as a virtual global COE. In most aspects a virtual global COE model will be managed and operated in a manner that is similar to the traditional notion of a COE where there is a co-location of people. But in the case of a virtual COE, while the organization yields most of the COE benefits, co-location is not a prime requirement. In this instance, using technology tools the staff may be physically anywhere, but they operate as a single organization under a defined leadership structure. This option would tend to be oriented towards highly specialized work, rather than to activities that are core to line management's daily responsibilities.

There is, however, one major downside to the virtual concept. It makes the issue of training new staff due to attrition, retirement, or simply growth much more difficult with a staffing model that is far flung and often works remotely from home. A hybrid to this model that will help to mitigate this complexity is to have the virtual COE work in clusters that are smaller than the whole organization, but large enough in scale to facilitate personnel changes and utilize existing enterprise locations which would not add any material cost to enterprise overheads. As technology continues to evolve, this should become less of an issue.

5 *What is the nature of the tasks assigned to the COE? Are they lower end transactional activities or are they decision support in nature?*

The decisions surrounding this attribute follow very closely from the one above (4), but require further examination. As noted earlier, the level of divisional direct ownership will vary according to the nature of the work being assigned to the global or any COE function.

By its very nature, as a COE orients towards decision support activities, successively greater integration between the COE and the divisional/line leadership is required. In extreme cases, if integration is of such great necessity to operational outcomes, the COE can literally become a lower cost and remote operation, while remaining a direct arm of the divisional leadership. The divisional leadership retains full responsibility for managing the daily COE staff operations and the local COE management is essentially relegated to coordinating selected activities, staffing and managing human resources conditions on the ground. While this structure can ensure a very effective COE operation, it could serve as a distraction for line management's focus on higher value activities by limiting the role and benefits of the COE.

On the other hand, in the case of transactional activities the argument could be made, as building some level of operating firewall between the COE and the division can be productive. A key area that is facilitated by some degree of separation is that of the standardization of operations enterprise-wide, which is critical to driving continual productivity. It is natural for humans to enjoy the status quo of processes that they have become comfortable with and change is not always embraced. The risk of bifurcating the leadership of the COE too greatly is that divisional processes will be maintained along historical lines and will not be integrated into a standard approach. It is true that standardization often requires business operations to accept process changes that may need to compromise to achieve enterprise-wide consistency.

There is one hard rule that any COE should live by. It is acceptable to make independent process changes when it is purely productivity driven and the change has no impact on outcomes or controls. But it can never be acceptable for a process change to be implemented that does impact outcomes or controls on a fully independent basis by the COE without line leadership concurrence. This principle would apply equally, if not assuming even greater importance, when a process is outsourced to a third party.

6 *How will the financial responsibility for the global COE be assigned? How much interdependence does the global COE need with the business units it supports, or is it operating independently of established operational and cost metrics?*

This attribute adheres very closely to the structures and approaches discussed above, but there are considerations that can have a material impact on the economic success of the global COE.

Specifically, the way in which an enterprise's division or business unit "pays" for the COE's operations should be interdependent and flow directly from how the organization is structured and run. If the structure is following along the lines of the previously used accounts payable example, the operation is run by hard metrics and agreed upon cost targets, it may be logical for the cost to be retained at a corporate level or assigned via an allocation process. In this instance new or incremental work needs to be negotiated separately or as an addendum to the primary operating agreement.

Conversely, where the divisional structure is more directly involved in driving the staffing levels, infrastructure, IT, and other investments a direct billing of actual costs to the division would tend to be a preferable method to optimize enterprise-wide spending. The fact is that spending on operations can happen in either the divisional or COE structure, but should not be allowed to become redundant. The direct billing approach will force the optimal spending trade-offs and minimize enterprise spending in total. While this approach has inherent additional complexities and may lead to more debate, ultimately this scrutiny and debate will provide the best enterprise outcome and be a healthy process in the long run.

7 *How critical to the enterprise's operations are the COE's activities, and how much needs to be invested in business continuity planning?*

It is literally impossible to understate the burning need for a comprehensive level of business continuity planning (BCP) for operating a COE and even more so for a global operation. By definition, a COE involves a material concentration in one or more places of a workforce performing required business functions.

It is easy to point to recent geopolitical unrest and the massive impact of the COVID-19 pandemic to interrupt a center's operations. While these risks certainly get an amplified amount of attention, there is the constant threat of more mundane one-off risks that can interrupt a center's ability to accomplish its mission at any moment, such as building fires, cyber-attacks, labor strikes, natural disasters, or other infrastructure failures. It is certainly a prudent business decision to have BCP in general, but the premium can increase greatly in a global COE environment where operations tend to be in higher risk emerging market countries that offer significant labor cost advantages. At the same time as centralizing operations will increase the risk, an enterprise that has strong BCP can leverage its scale in a COE to actually increase its resiliency.

Regardless of the cause, prudent planning would dictate that a COE should have options in place to handle as many of the possible business interruption scenarios as is economically possible. I stress economically possible since short of complete redundancy, no level of planning can completely mitigate the myriad of potential impacts that could happen. Accordingly, there must be some level of a balance point between cost and risk. Just how critical the COE mission is to the business will strongly dictate that balance point trade-off.

There are varying terminologies that describe severity levels when considering BCP. For simplicity four levels of severity will be explored in depth as BCP is so critical. Furthermore, consideration will be given to the scenario where an enterprise has multiple locations, rather than just one, for a COE making the risks and options to mitigate those risks exponentially higher.

Business Continuity Planning Guiding Principles

Before addressing severity level scenarios, there are a number of guiding principles that are important.

1   Operating or desk procedures should be very well documented and sufficient detail provided so that with the help of a subject matter expert a new or different staff member could be trained and at least have acceptable capabilities relatively quickly. Furthermore, those desk procedures should be stored off-site or preferably in a cloud environment with selected staff from within the COE and outside of the COE being entrusted to have access to them.

2   There should be a well-defined and -documented communication plan for management and staff to follow to receive instructions in the case of an emergency.

3   There should be normal IT resiliency for common systems, but we live in a world where so much information is held on a personal computer and often in Excel worksheets, so the cloud or other backup options should be used and regularly tested. Like desk procedures, trusted staff outside the COE should have access to these critical files.

4   In knowledge-based roles, virtually every employee uses a computing device to perform their tasks. If these devices were lost to a fire, for example, plans for their rapid replacement and deployment, including sharing devices across shifts, should be in place.

5   The enterprise must establish which truly critical processes must happen in a disaster. There are many nice things to have and that are necessary in the long run, but in the short run an enterprise can survive without many of them. Measurements, budgets, utilization reports, HR measurements, etc., are all very important, but are not immediately critical needs. On the other hand, the ability to manage and move cash, meet statutory requirements, pay employees and suppliers and manage a supply chain to satisfy customers are critical.

6   In the case that an enterprise has multiple locations of global COEs, process and IT standardization are of particular importance. Process standardization can allow for sister operations to pick up some if not all tasks, particularly those deemed as critical. However, certainly focus first on those deemed critical. IT standardization will ensure that all COEs receive common upstream data feeds and downstream outputs.

7   Practice, practice, test and test some paper procedures for a disaster. This is a nice start, but in the absence of actual testing and practicing based on multiple scenarios to ensure they will work, the enterprise remains very exposed. There is no way to prepare for all the potential scenarios, but the more testing that is done, the greater the robustness that plans will have.

8   The enterprise must accept the fact that along with the benefits of a global COE, there is a heightened cost to have a strong level of BCP. As noted earlier, the level and robustness of a BCP is an economic

trade-off of cost versus risk and needs to be very closely examined by and accepted at the most senior level in the business.

Examining Business Continuity Planning and Severity Levels of Events

Business continuity interruptions may manifest themselves in a wide variety of ways and levels of severity. Depending on the level of severity and attendant degree of business operations interruption, different actions will be required.

Regardless of the degree of severity, as previously noted it cannot be emphasized enough that it is essential to have not only well-documented and detailed plans, but to actively and regularly test these plans using realistic scenarios and simulated events. Paper plans without any significant testing and regular updates simply put an enterprise at an excessively high level of risk.

When developing plans consideration should be given to the level of infrastructure and employee concentration. How critical are the tasks to the business in terms of creating downstream bottlenecks or incurring customer dissatisfaction? As noted above, not all business processes are critical in the short run. For example, a business can manage with delayed internal reporting of budget performance or other operating reports. However, it must be stressed that some processes are not considered optional and must be able to continue. Typically they include key supply chain steps, the movement and management of cash, statutory reporting requirements, the payment of employees and suppliers, and customer delivery commitments.

There are many mitigating factors that should be considered in the BCP process. For example, are there sister COE locations that are trained and can seamlessly pick up the work? This may require the sister locations to only focus on the critical tasks performed by all the related centers. Do any of the remaining staff in divisional or corporate headquarters have the necessary training and skills to pick up tasks?

One thing that must not be forgotten is the timing of the operations outage and the timing of when tasks are required as most businesses operate in monthly or quarterly cycles with some time periods being more critical than others. A short term or low severity outage may prove to be an inconvenience but if it occurs during a relatively slow period in the business cycle it may be more easily manageable.

Business continuity is more complex than simply putting plans in place once a COE is in operation. It should be considered during the planning phase for a location. Concentration was already mentioned as a key consideration. Other considerations include political stability, infrastructure reliability, natural disaster history, and labor stability in the locations considered. The importance of a robust planning stage and consideration of the process criticality cannot be overstated. First, it is impossible to plan for all possible contingencies. The pandemic certainly made that painfully clear. But also the level of BCP needed comes with a cost well beyond documentation and planning. Is redundancy covered, and to what level is it required in a sister operation? Is the hardening of IT and location infrastructure among the many cost considerations? Accordingly, the cost of effective BCP must be considered in the business plan when initiating and executing a COE model. While there are many nomenclatures for labeling severity levels, for the purposes of this discussion we will consider severity levels one to 4 at a highly summarized level, as there are numerous possible scenarios.

A severity level one business continuity event would be the least severe and would typically entail a short-term disruption of either staff availability, IT, or facilities. In this scenario, prudent planning would entail a well-defined communications plan, backup IT operations, and the ability to utilize a limited percentage of staff either from an available facility or remotely to on a short-term basis focus on the critical level tasks. Typically this type of event would not have a material impact on operations.

A severity level two scenario would entail a more extended loss of facilities, IT, or staffing. In this scenario there are endless permutations, but similarly to a severity level one event communication plans remain paramount. Work would typically be shifted to a sister COE or back to headquarters staff to execute critical activities on a temporary basis. While disruptive, a well-planned and -tested set of action plans would generally not significantly impair operations.

A severity level three scenario can also occur in an endless number of ways, but would typically entail an extended loss of either facilities, IT, or employees. In such circumstances, a well-defined business continuity plan would allow for the utilization of any existing staff available on either a remote or on-site basis, with the remaining critical tasks transferred to a sister COE or to headquarters staff. This scenario is highly complex and given its extended anticipated time frame, extreme attention must be given to executing only the key critical tasks. Preparing for such an event is expensive in terms of testing as well as having some level of redundancy. The level of redundancy is an economic decision the enterprise must make based on the sensitivity to the impact of the business tasks that are impaired.

In a severity level four scenario, a business must be ready to enter into a crisis mode. There is a complete and extended loss of the COE operations and the work must be transferred to a sister COE or headquarters staff for an extended time frame. It is of paramount importance to focus only on truly critical tasks.

In sum, there are endless scenarios within each level of severity. Particularly beyond a severity level one event, there are no easy answers and all scenarios cannot possibly be planned for. However, well-documented procedures, communications and business continuity actions plans should always remain as a top priority for COE leadership.

Examples of a Global COE

The possibilities for varying different global COE missions are endless. Typically they tend to be oriented towards services operations, since a production facility would usually be considered an integral part of a supply chain operation versus a COE, but it is not an absolute distinction. That is not to say that technically a segment of a supply chain could not be operating along the lines of a global COE; however, our focus will be oriented towards services missions.

Global COEs can range in mission from very low end processing to complex decision support activities and virtually anything in between. The considerations of the where and how are very dependent on the "what" of activity.

At the lower end of the complexity range, it could be simply order processing, reconciliation work of some type, mail or document handling, simple control testing processes, etc. The point is that these types of operations are all traditional back-office activities and are internally oriented rather than customer interfacing. They tend to be very repetitive in nature, follow a strict and standard set of procedures, and or entry into a standardized system. The skill level is relatively low and finding a low labor cost location within the level of BCP risk tolerance, as noted above, is typically a primary consideration. A modest level of experienced leadership and supervision is required for interaction with the enterprise process owner and human resources activities. Typically a high level of attrition that comes with lower end roles in a low cost location can be mitigated by procedures, simplicity, standardization, and is tolerated in consideration of the other cost savings and operational efficiencies. As previously noted, the value of taking mundane tasks away from more senior leadership so that they can focus exclusively on higher value activities such as customer delivery, satisfaction, innovation and revenue growth should never be underestimated.

However, before an internally managed COE operation is established, careful consideration should be given to simply outsourcing low end tasks if the cost points, controls and results can be achieved, as well as avoiding other limiting factors such as a government contract that may limit outsourcing.

Moving up the complexity chain are global COEs that are customer facing, such as a business-to-business support technical support center or financial operations. While these operations still tend to operate to a standard set of procedures and even to a predetermined script, they are inherently more complex from a skill level point of view and sensitivity to customer satisfaction. While the labor cost of the location will be a strong consideration, there are many other considerations. For example, language skills become a premium issue and often a higher level of education is required. If different time zones are significant, finding the appropriate skills willing to work second or and third shift operations is an additional challenge and often comes at an incremental cost. While the global COE by nature is established or built to manage a higher than traditional level of attrition, the very nature of greater complexity and customer facing activities make managing attrition to an acceptable target an imperative. While skills for higher level tasks in particular tend to agglomerate in locations where global COEs are developed, this can be a double-edged sword when managing operations. On the positive side of the equation, the location offers attractive skills sets within the hiring pool. The negative side is that there will be more competition for similar skills which over time can drive up labor costs and attrition, particularly in a smaller market location. As a COE moves up the complexity chain and there is a higher level of business impact to the operations involved as the scale of operations allow having multiple locations should be a strategic imperative, and not only from a BCP point of view, which is, of course, very important. Multiple locations allow for labor cost management if one location is seen as too great a trend upward, allowing for a relatively seamless shifting of activities.

At the higher end of complexity, when the global COE is responsible for true decision support activities that support senior management directly, or have a high level of impact on relationships with customers, the strategic decisions surrounding the COE becomes increasingly more complex and the premium shifts from labor cost to skills and continuity of staffing, while labor cost remains a consideration, it may not be the highest order of criterion in the location decision-making strategy. Examples of activities include treasury operations, procurement, key controls management, financial planning, pricing, receivables management, customer relationship management, and higher level technical support. In these types of operations, access to skills, a stable workforce, and the ability to more seamlessly integrate with broader business operations becomes a stronger decision-making factor.

In the best scenarios for higher value roles, employee attrition is still likely to be a challenge facing leadership. Mitigation factors in some cases mirror BCP, such as extremely detailed operating and training procedures, as well as a core of subject matter experts who can manage a constant level of training as well as filling in the gaps when unexpected holes develop in the overall staffing balance.

A key strategic decision that an enterprise must make is how to staff the most senior COE leadership. Should the leadership be filled locally or by expatriate assignees with a deeper knowledge of the enterprise? If a high level of enterprise-wide interaction is required and there is a need to avoid allowing the COE to silo and operate very narrowly, the expatriate assignee option should be strongly considered, albeit that it is more expensive, certainly at least until the leadership at the COE level matures significantly in their business experience specific to the enterprise.

How to Get a Global COE Initiated

Above all, there is no textbook formula for the creation of a global COE or any COE for that matter. The answer is entirely dependent on all the factors addressed above: complexity, risk tolerance, labor cost requirements, BCP, skills and language requirements. In addition, a number of other factors should be considered, including a strategic evaluation of labor cost trends, the future needs for growth, and whether the location can support these needs. Furthermore, a key consideration should be synergies with other existing operations in the enterprise and co-location opportunities. Cost and speed to operational status is much faster when leveraging an existing location with other operations versus a greenfield startup. However, in all cases the guiding principle of top-down support should never be violated.

Another consideration is timing from investment to how fast the enterprise can accrete that up-front investment. The up-front costs to start a global center can be material. Once you get past the initial costs of establishing your strategy and determining the desired location, there are real estate and other infrastructure costs, IT and telecommunication investments, that are of course going to be dependent on the type of operation in terms of its complexity. Typically a global COE will start with a small group of expatriate leadership on assignment in the location as well as other subject matter experts. While invaluable to startups expatriate assignees tend to be very expensive.

After establishing human resources practices, including compensation ranges, the hiring and onboarding process can be a material investment.

A prudent enterprise would establish a very disciplined approach to transfer work to the center. The implications range from modest to very costly. At a minimum all processes must be thoroughly documented. Depending on the complexity of the work, there is usually a period that can range from as little as a month, to many monthly cycles while the company is incurring duplicate staffing costs in the task sending location and the COE. The legacy costs of the sending employees and operations remain in place until the receiving global COE is fully staffed, trained, and in a position to "go live" and replace the sending locations staff. There is typically a test period involved to ensure that the COE is truly operational, effective and in an appropriate control posture. It cannot be emphasized enough that the process of handing over work to a global COE requires that there is a very well-defined and disciplined process. Deviating or rushing the process will frequently extend the time frame of the ability of the COE to operate effectively and will ultimately lead to errors and likely additional costs to remediate the situation.

While the long-term goal of the global COE is to standardize processes, make them more rigorous, and drive constant productivity, the fact is that in most cases the work is moving from a higher labor cost to a lower labor cost jurisdiction. This can lead to unintended impacts if they are not managed in a thoughtful and strategic manner. Specifically, the costs of execution as noted above are going to be roughly the same regardless of when during the enterprise's fiscal year startup happens. However, a strategic approach would be to plan the execution, all other factors being equal, early in the fiscal year, such that the labor cost savings will fully or at least partially accrete against the startup costs during that same fiscal year.

Stepping back, during the strategic planning phase there are two basic approaches that can be taken to moving work tasks into a global COE. One option is to reengineer the work before the transfer and execute a transfer of an efficiently reengineered process. While this is certainly a common approach, it tends to have two major flaws. First, it can greatly expand the time window until the work is moved to the COE and in turn the time for the initial labor cost savings to be achieved. Second, the business misses the "fresh set of eyes" approach to process changes.

The alternative approach is to "lift and shift" the work as is and let the reengineering happen over time in the COE. The advantage of this is the quicker labor cost savings, but a new and inexperienced staff in the COE is going to need time to master the basics before they are in a position to truly reengineer the processes and drive productivity.

The more practical approach is a hybrid of the two, involving a lift and shift approach to gain the speed of labor cost savings, but sacrificing some of that speed to do an initial reengineering of the lower lying fruit for transformation during the transfer, leaving the ultimate reengineering to the COE.

As complex as the startup and transfer phase is, the real heavy lifting begins once the work is effectively running in the global COE. Following the guiding principle of literally building the notion of continuous improvement and productivity into the DNA of the COE organization, literally every step and process must be evaluated for the potential to reengineer. While there are endless approaches, a very effective approach is to train the staff in Lean Six Sigma (LSS) techniques. It is worth repeating that while the transformation of processes is paramount, ensuring that the impacted receiving organizations are involved in the processes and that no controls lapse is also essential.

Some companies take a process-by-process transfer approach as opposed to transferring multiple partial processes and building up towards complete COE process ownership more slowly. There is no right answer, as each transfer needs to be evaluated to find the optimal approach.

To wrap up this section of the chapter, it would be remiss of me not to address the subject of leadership and staffing. With regard to leadership, there are two key considerations. The obvious one is local skills availability. But the less obvious one is the issue of culture, which is a critical success factor and cannot be ignored strategically.

If local leadership skills are available in the market and culture is not a key issue, then the speed at which assignee or expatriate leadership can be replaced with locally sourced leaders will yield a significant financial saving. It will also boost the COE staff morale in terms of commitment to the location. Cultural integration is a critical element. However, it is often misunderstood to be all about culture in the global COE; in fact, culture is a two-way street. The global COE must also adapt to the cultural norms of the organizations that they support. This would often imply a longer timeline of expatriate leadership.

In all cases the startup of a global COE should be a very strategically evaluated endeavor with location planning, roles to be transferred, and organizational decisions being as important as the actual execution of starting up. At the same time any enterprise embarking on this path is bound to make some mistakes. It is critical to remain agile and constantly reevaluate the strategy and not be blindly wed to approaches that may turn out to have a different result in execution than on paper.

Ultimately, a COE can be structured in an almost endless number of ways and can be deployed to execute an almost endless number of different work missions. But the common theme should always remain that the process of continuous improvement never ends. The final punch line is if a global COE leader ever asks when they might achieve a level of status quo, the answer is simple – never.

Chapter 11 Takeaways

The success of a COE strategy is best accomplished with unwavering senior management commitment.

Centralized leadership of the COE's operations is a key driver of achieving objectives.

Leveraging operating scale by large teams working on standardization of enterprise-wide processes along with lower cost operating locations yields both operating excellence and material cost savings.

Utilizing subject matter experts to supervise large operating teams leads to consistent processes, higher levels of customer satisfaction, and productivity gains.

COEs must remain open to operating changes and always stay integral and in lockstep with the organizations supported.

You get the results that you measure and hard metrics are critical.

The drive for operational excellence and productivity improvement by a COE is an objective that never ends.

References

Cavalier, J. (2019, July 7). *Using Centers of Excellence to Change the Game.* Cohen & Co. https://www.cohencpa.com/knowledge-center/insights/june-2019/using-centers-of-excellence-to-change-the-game.

Conejo, G. (2021, July 2). *Why Organizations Need a Center of Excellence.* Globant. https://medium.com/globant/why-organizations-need-a-center-of-excellence-345969f54f84.

Jones, C. (2013). *Five Guiding Principles of a Successful Center of Excellence.* Perficient. https://www.perficient.com/-/media/files/guide-pdf-links/five-guiding-principles-of-a-successful-center-of-excellence.pdf.

Chapter 12

Implementation

Introduction

If you have made this far in the book, or if you follow management closely, you can identify several trends in the workplace that affect the decisions and actions of an effective manager. However, it is probably also clear by now that management success is also highly contextual.

The core processes of management were identified by Henri Fayol about century ago, namely planning, organizing, staffing, leading, and controlling. These processes are still relevant; however, the environment (context) in which these processes are being implemented has significantly changed, and therefore our implementation strategies and tactics must change too.

Here Be Dragons

In this chapter we will look at the challenges of identifying and implementing the changes necessary for management moving into a remote or hybrid work environment. As we progress into somewhat uncharted territories, one metaphor that might be useful is the annotation "here be dragons" used by ancient cartographers to fill uncharted spaces on their maps. Like those ancient cartographers, we might point to the blank spots on our maps – the ones we use to help us to plot our businesses, industries, and professional environments – pointing out that certain areas are uncharted territories, and there may be dangers lurking beneath the surface.

If we continue with our metaphor, we might view ourselves as explorers and captains of the ships that must navigate these uncharted waters. We should rely on the seamanship (management skills) we have developed in the past to move us forward, but recognize that as Abraham Lincoln said: "The dogmas of the quiet past are inadequate to the stormy present. The occasion is piled high with difficulty, and we must rise with the occasion. As our case is new, we must think anew and act anew."

DOI: 10.4324/9781032646657-12

Therefore, we must be willing to modify the practices of the past where necessary, and possibly develop an entirely new set of skills due to the radical changes in the environment that we find ourselves operating in.

Changes in How We Manage

Significant work has been done to identify the changes that are on the horizon; however, this area is still developing. Therefore, there are no firm rules or universal best practices to implement. The best managers can do is to take a measured approach and maintain awareness of their progress and the how the environment may still be changing.

It is also important to remember that many of the trends we are now experiencing had already begun before the outbreak of the COVID-19 pandemic, and the resulting spike in remote and hybrid work it fostered. Pistrui and Dimov (2018) had identified how the role of a manager had already begun to change almost a year and a half before the pandemic appeared on the radar of most management professionals. They suggested there are five key areas of change:

Directive to instructive: Managers need to help others to extend their own frontiers of knowledge and learning through experimentation to develop new practices.

Exclusive to inclusive: Too many managers believe that they are smart enough to make all the decisions without anyone else's help. Managers need to bring a diverse set of thinking styles to bear on the challenges they face.

Repetitive to innovative: Managers often encourage predictability. The problem with this is that it leads managers to focus only on what they know – on perpetuating the status quo – at the expense of what is possible.

Problem solver to challenger: Solving problems is never a substitute for growing a business. Rather, the role calls for finding better ways to operate the firm – by challenging people to discover new and better ways to grow, and by reimagining the best of what has been done before.

Employer to entrepreneur: The emphasis on customers, competitors, innovations, marketplace trends, and organizational performance morphs too easily into what the manager wants done today – and how he or she wants it done. Thinking like an entrepreneur simply means to expand your perceptions and increase your actions – both of which are important for finding new gateways for development.

This list is far from a compendium of all the changes in the way managers should now be operating, but a glimpse shows that the vast majority of managers will have to rethink many of their core practices in this environment. As mentioned earlier in the book, this is also where developing the mindset of authentic leadership can be extremely helpful to setting managers in the right direction on their journey of discovery – discovering what is the right approach for their team, department, company, industry.

Leading Change

Although it is important to maintain flexibility in our approach, Hunsaker and Knowles (2022) are quick to point out that the most important attribute we can work toward is being *contextually effective*, i.e., being effective in the situation and business environment that we face. They suggest that there are three imperatives to being contextually effective:

Drawing the map: Great leaders consistently map the changing dynamics of the company's environment and create a clear, prioritized vision for where the business should be headed.
Establishing the mindset: The leader's mindset drives a shared conviction about the need for change and an enthusiasm for the improvements that successful change will bring about.
Communicating the message: If the map credibly identifies the needed change, and the mindset creates the appetite for change, the message is the key tool for activating that change among the broader population of employees.

I suggest that the core concepts here are not really new. For decades business schools have touted a number of tools that will help managers to begin the process of environmental assessment (drawing the map), including the ubiquitous SWOT (Strengths, Weaknesses, Opportunities, Threats) or PESTEL (Political, Economic, Social, Technical, and Legal) models

Many have focused on helping employees to properly frame the inputs they are receiving by developing a strong culture (establish the mindset), or by promoting the popular growth mindset.

Organizations use all-hands meetings, training sessions, and internal communications campaigns to promote company values, initiatives, and culture. These are still necessary, even if we have only slightly reshaped them and put a new name to it. The principles behind these efforts are still sound – and in turbulent times they become more important than ever.

The Holy Trinity of Mapping Direction: Mission, Vision, Values

When attempting to navigate this new business landscape we will need a compass to provide a core direction to the organization. For many firms this will be the holy trinity of mission, vision, values.

The mantra of mission, vision, values has been taught since time immemorial in business schools around the world. Unfortunately too often this trinity is developed to satisfy what managers see as a requirement. These represent boxes to check – ones that make many managers uncomfortable due to their soft skills nature. These are the squishy things that hardnosed management types often have a difficult time wrapping their head around. So, they are avoided at all cost, and there is little thought or time allotted for them, often resulting in a series of platitudes that accomplish checking the boxes on the task list and little else.

The process is often poorly structured – almost as an afterthought. For example, this task might be done as part of an off-site meeting. It might be slotted in after the final department report and before the cocktail hour. A collection of platitudes is written on a whiteboard and manipulated until a popular combination emerges. All the team tasked with these jobs wants is to check the box and move on.

Before sitting down and working on any of these tasks there needs to be an honest assessment of the environment, an assessment of the company's current ability to compete, trends and their current direction, and a forecast of where the company could find itself given the current direction. The point of these tasks is not only to evaluate the business as it stands, but to evaluate it in the context of the current environment, and the environment we can reasonably assume will exist in the future. This is where the Managing at a Distance framework discussed in Chapter 4 can help. Like other environmental assessment frameworks, such as SWOT or PESTEL, it gives us a starting point from which to begin our assessment – and like these other frameworks it can be done well or poorly depending on the resources and effort we bring to bear on the effort.

However, if we apply the MAAD framework properly, many if not most companies will find that the business environment they experienced in 2019 is not the same as the one they find themselves in today. Therefore, the map that they are using to navigate the future should also be updated to match what is happening. (We will include some tips on the use of the MAAD framework later in the chapter.)

Mission

The mission is a rallying point – one that should allow us to understand how our organization creates value. When environments change it might be time to reassess our mission. We might realize that the value we were creating is no longer relevant or compelling. We might begin to question what the business is really all about. It should be value-focused – not product-focused – and it is about the customer and not the company. In addition, it should be short and memorable so that employees understand it and use it.

This is why I like Google's mission statement: *Our mission is to organize the world's information and make it universally accessible and useful.*

It is clear, concise, value-focused, short, and memorable. This can help a manager to decide if a new opportunity could possibly fit in to the company's core value creation strategy.

In addition, when developing a mission, it is important to focus on the larger strategic direction (the big M mission), rather than a specific goal (the little m mission). Specific goals can often be accomplished in the short-term leaving the organization without direction, whereas a strong strategic direction often allows the organization to work in a specific direction for an extended period – sometimes even decades.

For example, President Kennedy wanted NASA to make landing on the moon its top priority (a little m mission), whereas NASA's chief James Webb wanted the mission to be "preeminence in space." Of course, since Kennedy was the president of the US he won the argument, and the results were predictable. After achieving the moon landing in 1969, there was little direction or purpose for NASA, which went through a series of budget cuts and became a shadow of what it once was (Kinni, 2023).

Vision

Your vision is your aspiration for what the world will be like if you are successful. Again, this should be aspirational. If God smiles, and the stars align, what will your world look like at some distant point in time – let's say 10 or 20 years from now.

An example of this was the vision Bill Gates set for Microsoft in the early 1980s: "A computer on every desk, in every home – and Microsoft software on them all." As I write this four decades later this does not sound particularly aspirational. If I look around my home, I have a lot of computers – but Gates said this in the early 1980s.

IBM released the IBM personal computer in August 1981. Not only was the device anemic by today's standards, it was also very expensive. It was common for a department to share a computer. Even then they were difficult to use and limited in their capabilities, so this was not a common item in the average American or European home. So yes, this was an aspirational vision at the time.

For decades Microsoft's vision provided clear direction and guidance when making tough business decisions. However, over time the vision became less relevant to the business environment Microsoft found themselves facing, and it needed an update.

As we develop our vision for the future, some suggest the format used to create it needs an update too. They feel that the standard vision is too short and vague. They feel more comfortable with a longer narrative that creates a day in the life view, or extended profile view, of what they are working toward. This technique is sometimes described as a vivid vision (Herold, 2018).

In this extended vision, you might have an integrated vision for each discipline or department. This vision might need regular updates to be valid, because more areas are at risk of becoming dated or irrelevant.

Values

Even though all the elements can fall victim to platitudes, values seem to be where the company's statement of what it believes in, and what the reality of its values in practice might be, can see significant divergence. Thus, this section might be the hardest to get right out of the gate.

One doesn't have to go far to find a value statement that does not seem to match practice. For example, Theranos, the company founded by Elizabeth Holmes, whose claims, if true, would have changed the entire landscape of medical testing. Unfortunately, the company's claims were fraudulent, and in 2016 the company lost billions of investors' money.

In its value statement, Theranos claimed that integrity was one of its core values. Similarly, integrity was also claimed as one of the core values of Enron (the company responsible for the largest corporate scandal of first decade of the 21st century), and of Volkswagen just before it was caught cheating in the emissions tests of its diesel engines.

When coming up with a list of your core values, you might consider what it looks like when you are living these values, and what it looks like when you are not. This could be matched with a cultural assessment to uncover what you aspire to, and what your reality is currently.

There is nothing wrong with some aspirational values. I would encourage the practice – so long as you are not deluding yourself into believing that you currently possess them.

Applying the MAAD Framework

We introduced the Managing at a Distance framework in Chapter 1 and developed some of its concepts in Chapter 4. Here I wish to revisit elements of the framework. We will begin to identify some factors to consider when applying it in the field.

Business Outcomes

Stephen Covey popularized the phrase "begin with the end in mind." We should know the outcomes we are looking for. However, this list of desired outcomes should not be developed in a void. Context is important, and our context is fluid, so our first step should be to develop a process for assessing our environment to enable us to set reasonable objectives.

The outcome we are looking for is in a sense a forecast of what we believe could be – or a prediction of the future based on our environment and our plans. Paul Saffo, who describes himself as "a Silicon Valley-based forecaster exploring long-term technology trends and their impact on society," is also a professor of engineering at Stanford University (Saffo, n.d.). He has popularized a forecasting technique he describes as "strong opinions, weakly held."

This process starts with an assessment of the environment and the rapid formation of an opinion. Next the forecaster develops an argument to support the new opinion. However, even though you are initially arguing for the opinion you soon switch roles to argue against it while attempting to discover the truth. Once you have fully developed both sides of the argument, you reassess what you have discovered and begin the process all over again – until you come to what you believe is the truth, or at least a strongly defensible position.

It would also be helpful if you could make this a team process – invoking the collective wisdom of the crowd. One way to do this would be to allow your team to pull apart your arguments, and you might even participate in discounting your own arguments. The point is to argue for the position, and then against it, and iterate until you are really the best possible position.

The true goal list should be limited to not overwhelm the team with too many competing objectives. The number will depend on the complexity and size of the organization; however, rule of thumb recommendation varies between three to five and five to seven quarterly goals that feed back to a strategic direction.

Objectives/Environment

When you are developing your list of objectives, and arguing for an objective, it is important to put that objective in context with the environment in which you find yourself. Earlier we suggested that a place to start was with an assessment tool such as SWOT or PESTEL. As we discussed in Chapter 4, there are several limitations to these tools:

- These tools are primarily subjective, often leading to less than a complete picture of reality.
- They are only as good as the input provided in their defined categories, and there are categories missing from all environmental models.
- George Box famously quipped, "all models are broken, but some are useful." These models are inherently flawed and useful at the same

time. We should be looking to supplement the models with other content to develop more realistic pictures of environment.

Therefore, in order to compensate for these limitations, it is incumbent on the strategic planner to have a plan on how to collect additional information on the state and direction of the environment. These could include:

- Reading broadly and regularly including:
    - Business and economic news;
    - Business and economic journals;
    - Books from thought leaders;
    - Reports from industry consulting firms.
- Developing a set of metrics and assessments on your firm's progress toward its goals, and its position relative to competitors;
- Attending (live or virtual) industry conferences and meetings;
- Joining industry associations;
- Communicating with customers and interviewing them about their current concerns and where they see the industry going;
- Identifying who is undeserved in the current market, and their potential relative importance in the future, before communicating with them on their needs;
- Constantly communicating with your team to understand their successes and challenges.

People/Talent

If you understand your objectives, and your environment, and have aligned them, then you can begin the process of mapping your talent pool to those objectives – both now and in the foreseeable future. It will not surprise most seasoned managers when gaps in the alignment occur.

The next step will be to develop a strategy to fill those gaps. This can be done organically by creating policies and training programs to develop the talent internally, or it might require finding the talent outside the firm. This access to outside talent could be obtained in several different ways:

- Hire to fill the talent gaps;
- Outsource to a series of contractors;
- Or partner with other firms which could take on several flavors:
    - loose affiliation;
    - project based cooperation;
    - joint venture.

Of course, in the remote and hybrid world of work the next question is where are these pockets of talent located, how do we access them, and finally how do we keep them?

- Do hire talent in your local community. This is where companies have traditionally hired. This has two strategic issues: it limits the total population which you can draw on and could result in inflating the price of the talent being acquired.
- Or do you hire remote talent? This can open your potential pool to a much larger number of potential candidates; however, you might find communication, coordinating of efforts, and the development of culture and engagement more difficult.
- The changes in the remote and hybrid environment have also driven employees to question their relationship with work. This has manifested in the Great Resignation or the Great Reassessment. However, you define this trend its result has been that employees have been making remote policies an integral part of their decision process when deciding to stay with a company (or even accept a job offer to begin with).

Culture/Context

As we discussed in Chapter 3, culture is a living, breathing thing, and it must be assessed and cared for. If we don't, it can turn in a direction we don't care for, or one that proves to be less productive than we need. The hardest part of being remote is that many of the tools we have used in the past to help to measure and maintain our culture are no longer effective.

Managers and leaders need to ask some basic questions about culture:

- What is it?
- Has it changed significantly?
- What trends do we see on the horizon that will affect the culture?
- What do we need to look like in order to create the environment we need? We need an environment that is:
  - productive;
  - in line with our values;
  - and will create a feeling and sense of being which will attract the retain the type of people we want and need.

Therefore, we need to do some sort of cultural audit. This audit's shape and structure will change for each company, but there are some good templates available from groups such as the Society of Human Resource

Management (SHRM), as well as several HR-focused consulting practices.

With a successful audit, we can develop a plan on how to create and maintain the culture we need. This plan should include:

- How will we communicate (more on this in communications and proximity)?
- What are the values we wish to reinforce?
- How will we reinforce those values?

  - What must be communicated and how?
  - How will we demonstrate those values in action?
  - What are the rites and rituals we will need?
  - What are the artifacts that we will use to demonstrate our values?

Autonomy/Personal Responsibility

One could argue that the level of autonomy that an organization allows is part of its culture and the organizational design. However, in knowledge work or creative work this is so integral to the overall outcomes of the organization it is work calling out separately. Not only should there be an appropriate level of autonomy, but there should also be an appropriate level of personal responsibility.

As we discussed in Chapter 4, there are a number of factors driving a trend toward higher levels of both autonomy and personal responsibility. Too little autonomy stifles innovation and has generally poor effects on organizational culture, and has a negative effect on employee retention rates. Too much autonomy can create chaos and create environments where independent decisions are in direct conflict with each other.

In the past there were opportunities to make effective decisions in a centralized process. As organizations and environments become more complex, it becomes harder to make those decisions effectively in a centralized fashion. Some of the questions that might be considered could include:

- How time dependent are these decisions? Can there be detrimental effects which occur due to slowing down the decision process?
- What is the lowest level at which these decisions can be made without hampering the efforts of others in the organization?
- How can decisions be communicated so as to allow the decider and the stakeholders to coordinate their efforts?
- What are the decisions, if poorly restricted, that
- could affect organizational culture, employee morale, and employee retention?

In assessing the levels of personal responsibility, it would be helpful to understand what the effects are of taking responsibility and how mistakes were handled by both management and the culture. Things to consider might include:

- Are mistakes tolerated? Are mistakes punished? Or are they celebrated as part of the learning process?
- Is there a culture where employees are encouraged to stretch themselves, and encounter mistakes and mishaps along the way? Or is there a culture where mistakes and mishaps are punished?
- What do employees expect the result will be if they take responsibility for mistakes?
- What are the criteria that makes a mistake reasonable?
- What are the criteria that make a mistake reckless or unnecessary?
- What actions can be taken to adjust any negative effects of taking responsibility for reasonable mistakes?

Data/Analytics

Once we have our objectives, we should develop a process to ensure our success, and a process to constantly evaluate the effectiveness of our process. What should be included in the process are key performance indicators or metrics that allow us to know if we are on track. Of course, this principle is not new – it is as old as business itself. The difference is how the process changes as we become increasingly physically remote from each other, with the changes in where and how the decisions are being made, and the technology and data that can be used in the process.

The mistake that many managers make is in equating physical presence, or activity, with progress or results. The data is clearly in and tracking every activity is detrimental to organizational culture and employee retention – worse still it provides a way for employees to game a system in ways the hamper progress. Tracking should be focused on results, and progress toward organizational objectives. There is a place for activity tracking, but it should not be used as proof of results, or as a cudgel to punish employees. Its only role should be as supporting evidence, and only a small part of a broad set of data.

Proximity/Information Flow

The hardest part of proximity is understanding how much is enough. Organizations might consider undertaking an Organizational Network Analysis (ONA) to assess the types of relationships that exist, and the need for information exchange between the different roles.

The ONA should attempt to audit:

- The roles within the organization and how they interact with each other;
- The types of information necessary (both codified and tacit) for different roles and how that information might be exchanged;
- The level of cumulative proximity necessary to first achieve hygiene within these relationships, and how that can be (what is the metric/threshold?);
- What is the strategy to achieve and maintain these relationships?
  - What is the necessary mix of media and/or media richness?
  - What is the frequency of contact?
- Many senior management have the impression that the goal should be to have everyone on-site, and on the same work schedule. Certainly, the simplicity of this is attractive; however, this could put companies at a competitive disadvantage. Adam Grant, professor of organizational psychology at the Wharton School of the University of Pennsylvania, suggests that management should involve "just recognizing that every opinion you hold at work is a hypothesis waiting to be tested. And every decision you make is an experiment waiting to be run" (Chen, 2023). This is certainly true of our need for physical proximity to enable information flow.

Communication Infrastructure

According to the Canadian philosopher Marshall McLuhan, "First we shape our tools, thereafter they shape us." In Chapter 1 I spoke about how technology changes the way we think, our expectations, and even what we believe is possible. So, when deciding what our communication infrastructure should look like, there are a few decisions that need to be made, but they should be loosely held. What is possible can change quickly and competitiveness can change quickly. What we should not do is expect that our pre-remote infrastructure is adequate simply because it has been in the past.

In addition, this infrastructure is highly context-dependent on business processes, team norms, and the type of collaboration necessary. The more collaborative your team is the more richness you will need in your infrastructure.

Some key questions to consider include:

- How often do you expect the team to meet in-person? This can help you to set a base line on their natural interpersonal relationships and connectedness.
- What are the business processes that require communication?

- Do these need simple coordination, codified knowledge, or tacit knowledge? (see Chapter 5)?
- Can the communication tasks be batched or is real-time access necessary?
- Is it necessary, or indeed helpful, to share desktops or visual data in real time?
- Are drop-in, or ad hoc meetings, necessary or desired?
- Are visual clues as to availability necessary or helpful?

- What is the training process you will use, and who will be the product champions to encourage adoption by the masses? This is an area that is often overlooked. Without familiarity it is likely many, if not most, of your employees will avoid the time commitment to understand how to best use the infrastructure, and those who do may spend more time getting up to speed than necessary.
- How will you reinforce communication norms, and how often will they be assessed and modified to meet changing needs?

Organizational Structure

Our world is moving toward the increasing importance – especially for knowledge workers, but for other workers as well – of autonomy, flexibility, and agility. Therefore, we may find that the organizational structures that have served us well in the past are ill-suited to the current environment.

The questions we may ask ourselves might include:

- To maximize agility and efficiency, where should the decisions be made?
  - By whom should they be made?
  - What guidelines and information will they need?
  - How will these decisions be communicated and coordinated?
  - Is our current information infrastructure prepared for these changes? If not, what needs to be implemented?
- Decision-making is a skill – one that gets better with training and use. Do we have the level of skills necessary? Do we need to develop those skills?
- Is there a culture of psychological safety, and are people willing and able to take responsibility for their actions? Can they take responsibility for their actions?
- Does the structure support the culture we want for the organization? If not, why not?

Regulatory Challenges

Moving to an environment where a significant percentage of the work is performed remotely can present many regulatory challenges. In the past we had well-defined physical work sites that the company had control over and where workers would gather together. As workers have moved to remote locations (the home or elsewhere) we have lost control over the elements of the workspace – yet we may still be responsible for it – and we have increased the number of work locations, and typically the number of jurisdictions that the work in being done in.

Each of the jurisdictions will likely have their own work rules, health and safety regulations, and tax policies. Within the US states may have different rules on what expenses should be covered for remote workers, how work time is accounted for (and how over time might be calculated), as well as to whom has tax authority over the work being performed. For example, Connecticut, Delaware, Nebraska, New York, and Pennsylvania can tax income or wages earned from employers based in their state, even if the employees are located outside the state. However, this would not prevent the state where the employee is located from claiming tax authority as well.

If the company has workers outside the US things often become more complicated. These foreign remote workers fall broadly into three categories, two having to do with nationality (foreign nationals and US citizens traveling abroad) and one that is lifestyle-based (digital nomads). Typically, countries have employment rules covering their own citizens, and foreign nationals working within their borders. This is not typically a problem for short-term vacation or business travel; however, if these stays become extended (say several months) the company may find itself exposed to compliance with the rules of foreign regulators.

Common issues would include the right to disconnect, job-related expenses, what is considered a work-related accident, and liability insurance provided by the employer. A number of countries have some form of regulation to prevent around-the-clock work, thereby setting limits on the number of hours per day that an employee can be expected to work and requiring time for meals and other breaks. Others require employment contracts that outline the rights and responsibilities of both the employee and employer. These countries may also have rules on how work can, or should, be monitored. For example, recently a Dutch court ruled that an employee was wrongfully dismissed for refusing to leave his webcam on for several hours per day. Yet others require some form of formal tracking of work hours to avoid excessive work requirements. Still others have started to limit the type of information that can be collected from employees.

In addition, how work-related accidents are defined, and who is responsible, may be dramatically different based on the jurisdiction. Some jurisdictions require insurance covering employees while they are working at home. In many cases the courts have found in favor of the employee when deciding what qualifies as a work-related accident. Recently a German court ruled that a remote worker who fell on his way from his bed to his home office was covered under workplace accident rules (Chávarro, 2023).

Complicating the compliance challenges is the trend toward digital nomads. These are employees who are either fully remote, or spend a significant amount of time working remotely, and who while working remotely regularly move from place to place as part of a semi-nomadic lifestyle. According to the *Wall Street Journal*, the ranks of digital nomads grew by 49% in 2020 and by 2021 it had reached 16.9 million people in the US (Borchers, 2022).

Part of the challenge here is not only where these employees are, and how often they move, but how forthcoming they are about their lifestyle and locations. Not only are there data security issues, but there are issues of registrations and entitlement. There are some jurisdictions that are extremely welcoming and have gone so far as to create special digital nomad visas. However, others require registration, taxes, and fees. Failing to fully comply can cost tens of thousands of dollars in fines and penalties – if not more.

Chapter 12 Takeaways

As we begin to implement changes to meet our current challenges there are a few things to keep in mind:

- *Here be dragons*: This is uncharted territory. Whatever our assumptions of what the future will bring they will likely be less than 100% correct. Therefore, proceed with the mindset that our strategy should be emergent, and will likely change over time.
- *Changes in how we manage*: We will need to be more instructive, inclusive, and innovative as we move forward and adopt the mindset of an entrepreneur.
- *Mission, vision, values*: This trinity has been a staple of management for a while; however, as we shift to a world of greater autonomy these act as touchstones which will help to keep our teams on track.
- *MAAD framework*: The MAAD framework helps us to align our strategy and implementation processes in a dynamic environment.
- New rules may apply: Changes in how, where, and when our teams will be working can expose us to new regulatory challenges.

References

Borchers, C. (2022, November 10). Work From Anywhere! (Well, Not Really). *Wall Street Journal.* https://www.wsj.com/articles/work-from-anywhere-digital-nomad-well-not-really-11668018567.

Chávarro, J. M. (2023, February 27). Work-From-Home Regulations Are Coming. Companies Aren't Ready. *MIT Sloan Management Review.* https://sloanreview.mit.edu/article/work-from-home-regulations-are-coming-companies-arent-ready/.

Chen, T.-P. (2023, February 17). What CEOs Are Getting Wrong About the Future of Work – And How to Make It Right. *Wall Street Journal.* https://www.wsj.com/articles/what-ceos-are-getting-wrong-about-the-future-of-workand-how-to-make-it-right-8a84e279.

Herold, C. (2018). *Vivid Vision: A Remarkable Tool for Aligning Your Business Around a Shared Vision of the Future.* Lioncrest Publishing.

Hunsaker, T., & Knowles, J. (2022, March 21). Leading Change Means Changing How You Lead. *MIT Sloan Management Review.* https://sloanreview.mit.edu/article/leading-change-means-changing-how-you-lead/.

Kinni, T. (2023, January 30). A Goal Isn't a Mission. *strategy+business.* https://www.strategy-business.com/blog/A-goal-isnt-a-mission85432.

Pistrui, J., & Dimov, D. (2018, October 26). The Role of a Manager Has to Change in 5 Key Ways. *Harvard Business Review.* https://hbr.org/2018/10/the-role-of-a-manager-has-to-change-in-5-key-ways.

Saffo, P. (n.d.). *Paul Saffo: Futurist.* https://www.saffo.com/.

Index

Page numbers in *italics* and **bold** indicate Figures and Tables, respectively.

Printed in the United States
by Baker & Taylor Publisher Services